P9-ARN-567

2007

CALLED into HEALING

CALLED into HEALING

Reclaiming our Judeo-Christian
Legacy of Healing Touch

2nd revised edition

LINDA L. SMITH RN, MS, HNC, CHTP/I
Director, Healing Touch Spiritual Ministry Program

HTSM Press
Arvada, Colorado

DISCLAIMER

The material in this book is a guide to the practice of the laying-on of hands and to Healing Touch practice to facilitate self healing It is not a replacement for traditional health care, medical diagnosis, or medical treatment for illness Refer to a licensed medical practitioner for medical care

Called Into Healing: Reclaiming our Judeo-Christian Legacy of Healing Touch
2nd Revised Edition

A HTSM Press Book/June, 2006
All rights reserved.
Copyright © 2006 by Linda Smith
Cover design by Ben Wright
Layout and production by Pilgrims' Process, Inc.

****

No part of this book may be reproduced or transmitted in any form or by any means, electronic or mechanical, including photocopying, recording, or by any information storage and retrieval system, without permission in writing from the publisher.

****

Scripture quotations are from the New Revised Standard Version of the Bible, © 1989 by the Division of Christian Education of the National Council of the Churches of Christ in the USA. Used by permission. All rights reserved.

All quotations from the Psalms are taken from *Psalms for Praying,* by Nan Merrill © 1996 by Nan Merrill. Reprinted by permission of Continuum International.

Other permissions include the following. *From Prayer, Fear, and Our Powers,* © 1989 by Flora Slosson Wuellner. Used by permission of Upper Room Books. From *A New Look at Grace, A Spirituality of Wholeness,* © 1991 by Bill Huebsch. Used by permission of Twenty-Third Publications, P.O. Box 180, Mystic, CT. From *Meditations with Hildegard of Bingen,* © 1982 by Gabriele Uhlein. Used by permission of Bear & Co.

****

Library of Congress Cataloging-in-Publication Data: 99-091738

Smith, Linda L.
        Called into Healing, Reclaiming our Judeo-Christian Legacy of Healing Touch
        Includes index.

        1.Spirituality 2. Prayer

ISBN 0-9765972-3-3

Published by HTSM Press
P.O. Box 741239, Arvada, Colorado 80006

9 8 7 6 5 4 3 2 1

Printed in the United States

Dedication

I dedicate this revised second edition in memory of Janet Mentgen, who challenged me to follow my own heart and make a contribution to the world; and to all of my colleagues, peers, and students in the Healing Touch Spiritual Ministry program who courageously step out in faith and create healing ministries throughout the world. My hope is that we will all bring a harvest worthy of the Master.

Acknowlegements

Five years have passed since this book was first printed. Six thousand copies later, it is ready for an update. I could not have done the revisions without the able assistance of Pat Gewecke, the Healing Touch Spiritual Ministry Administrator who fielded my calls, and managed the business to give me enough time to write. And, to my able staff of teachers who weekly present this work somewhere across the United States and around the world, I acknowledge their dedication, persistence and courage to teach about Christian healing. They are Deb Reis, Claramae Weber, Jan Halbach, Judy Lausch, Barbara Girten, Rev. Dr. Constance Hammond, Pat Springer, Jeanne Clark, Margaret Leslie, Mary Frost, Gayle Mohr and Beth Jahncke. I also want to acknowledge the spiritual women and men in my life who support me, encourage me and bless me—Vicki Opfer, Jan Weger, Pamela Walker, Leslie Vornholt, Marilee Tolen, GailAnn Green, Ann Rojo, Jacque Cusick, Carol Komitor, Edee Webb, Eugenie Basu, Rev. John Wengrovius, Rev. Karla Kincannon, Rev. Louis Perrault, Mary Ellen Dunford, Jeffrey Lewis, John Daughtery, and of course, my parents, Laura and James Smith who truly believe that whatever their daughter does is good.

Table of Contents

Introduction

I first wrote this book as we turned the century mark and it has since gone through several printings. This is a testament, I believe, to the hunger of our spirits to remember our Christian calling to heal. I have learned a few things in the past five years and wanted to add a few thoughts before we print a revised edition. For all those loyal readers, I have not left out any of the juicy parts—only added some additional wisdom. Many readers loved how we put the scriptures and footnotes within a separate column in the text and so we will continue to honor this arrangement even if it makes for a more costly book.

We are now within the third millennium of Christianity. How shall we be remembered? Will future generations look at our contribution and know that we reclaimed Christ's mandate to heal the nations? That we remembered that as Christians we are to pray, lay-on hands and anoint all those who are sick in anyway—physically, emotionally and spiritually? For over 500 years, we have forgotten who we are and what we are called to by our very baptism. We have given the right to heal physically and emotionally to the medical community and settled for healing of spirit as the only acceptable involvement for Christian ministry. Yet that is not what Jesus and the early Christians practiced. For them, healing meant whole person healing. Healing was an expression of the deeper realities of faith, compassion, forgiveness, and caring for one another. Healing was not just for one's spirit—but also for their bodies and minds. For those early Christians, it was a way of life. Unfortunately, this way of being has been all but forgotten.

Many readers will be familiar with prayer and rituals like the laying-on of hands and anointing with oil in their own church traditions. Our scriptures tell us clearly that the early Christians healed one another with these practices. But those healing stories all happened a long time ago, and many believe they are but inspirational stories, not realities for our day. But if we look at recent times, we find many churches have begun to develop new expressions of those early forms of healing. They are rediscovering their Judeo-Christian roots as they form healing ministry teams, prayer ministries, parish nursing programs, and Stephen Ministries to meet the growing needs for healing in their own communities. Churches are taking up the responsibility to "watch over" the health needs of their flocks since healthcare in the United States is in such a crisis. The elderly, children and the poor are the most vulnerable as health insurance becomes less available to these fragile groups. As a result, this kind of church-sponsored "healing" is beginning to make a come-back even in our more traditional settings.

Medical knowledge is exploding at a rapid rate but so are the associated medical costs. Knowledge of how the body is integrated with our emotions, mind, soul, and spirit is becoming quite commonplace. The growing fascination with natural forms of healing has given rise to many forms of complementary healing. CAM (Complimentary and Alternative Medicine) is not such an oddity any more with some insurance companies paying for it. Even when it's not covered, people continue searching for it and paying out of pocket. At the same time, we are seeing an increased interest in deepening our

"He sat down, called the twelve, and said to them, 'Whoever wants to be first must be last of all and servant of all.'" Mark 9:35

spiritual lives. We are longing to care for our spiritual selves as well as our physical selves. We find people seeking out spiritual groups to join or looking for spiritual direction. This book aims to consciously bring the two realms together, to blend healing with a deepening of spiritual life. I said this over five years ago and am convinced more so now than ever that this is the true meaning of what it means to be a Christian servant in a hurting world.

Many people are beginning to feel *called* to some form of "spiritual healing" for one another. The Healing Touch Spiritual Ministry program is one of the many modern-day educational programs available in our world today. In the last eight years, over 8,000 students have taken courses in our program. Many have found it to be a path of spiritual healing that resonates within their spiritual selves and want to practice this healing art within the parameters of their own faith. They see the potential for this approach to healing within various ministry settings like churches and retreat centers and within pastoral care departments in hospitals, nursing homes, and hospices. They look to their ministers, trusted leaders, and teachers for direction in reclaiming healing within their faith. We are all *"called into healing"* as we awaken to those inner urges to reach out in compassionate service to one another. This book explores the intertwining of healing and spiritual yearning. It is an exploration of the spiritual call into healing service.

My Own Story with Healing

I have now been involved in this form of healing work for well over fifteen years and can say that it has dramatically changed my life forever. My faith has been the testing ground and, in the process, has become strengthened. Being a Christian healing practitioner has become a way of life and a way of service. Doing healing work has opened up new faith dimensions for me and changed forever my perception of ministry.

As a nurse, I have one of those eclectic backgrounds—critical care, nursing education and nursing administration. I enjoyed the creative challenge of bringing services to people in their homes as

"You did not choose me but I chose you. And I appointed you to go and bear fruit, fruit that will last, so that the Father will give you whatever you ask him in my name. I am giving you these commands so that you may love one another." John 15:16-17

the director of both home care agencies and hospices. I loved the challenge of looking for new ways to express a caring compassion for the sick and considered this the heart of nursing. In the early 90's I took my first course in Healing Touch which has a clinical approach to energetic healing. Much to my surprise, what happened in that class radically altered my life. I could no longer be the same kind of health care manager. I discovered that "healing" was the piece I had been missing only I didn't know at the time that it was going to radically change my direction in life.

I had entered nursing because I felt called to "work with my hands" in some way. Since nurses use their hands to touch people's lives I chose nursing to be my vehicle for this elusive call to "work with my hands." I can remember journaling for a long time on what this "call" meant and chose nursing areas where I could express that call in bedside nursing. I became a staff nurse working with the most fragile and critically ill.

As the years passed, I took opportunities to move into teaching and finally into administration so I could make a difference. I moved away from bedside nursing and all but forgot my call to use my hands in healing. That workshop in Healing Touch served to shake me out of my sleep and bring me back to a vision of hands-on healing. My heart was absolutely thrilled. Suddenly, I felt as if I had come home. As the director of a hospice, I brought this work to our hospice team. We found that Healing Touch is an excellent aid in pain management with hospice patients. I set about creating hospice teams that could integrate energy healing with traditional allopathic treatments. When we consistently used Healing Touch, we found that our patients required lesser amounts of narcotics to control their pain and it was a comfort both to patients and caregivers alike. My understanding of holism began to take on new meaning as I sought to teach others to pay attention to healing body, mind, soul, and spirit.

At this point in my nursing career my life was again turned upside-down. While attending the American Holistic Nurses Association's annual conference in 1992, I sat in the audience listening to the speaker describe the person selected that year as "holistic nurse of the year." It finally dawned on me that the speaker was describing me! I was humbled by receiving such a prestigious national award and at the same time felt totally undeserving of this honor. I still had much to learn about what it means to be a holistic nurse. This award has continued to this day to spur me on in my own holistic development and my promotion of wholeness in others.

Within the year, I left traditional health care to join Janet Mentgen, the founder of Healing Touch, in full-time teaching and promoting the work of Healing Touch. I brought to this new endeavor many years of administrative experience and 27 years experience as a Catholic sister in healthcare ministry. Although no longer active in this religious role, my work as a Healing Touch teacher and practitioner began to show me the potential of Healing Touch as a ministry within the Christian community.

While working with Janet, she constantly challenged me to find my own calling. It frightened me to think that Healing Touch was not it. Slowly, my vision of what I could uniquely offer to the world began to take shape. My many years in Christian ministry and service greatly influenced my contribution to healing work. I came to realize that the Healing Touch educational program could be used as a framework for launching a whole new approach to healing ministries within churches and spiritual settings. The curriculum teaches students about the body-mind-spirit connections, about self healing, about the need for cultivating the spirit, and about facilitating healing for others through various healing techniques using one's hands. And so I stepped beyond the Healing Touch curriculum to develop my own unique approach to healing—one scripturally based that included prayer and anointing. As I read the scriptures, I was convinced that what made the early Christians so successful was the fact that they integrated the laying-on of hands, prayer and anointing with healing oils. It is the scientists today who are pointing out that these are actually three forms of vibrational healing; but more on that later.

This work is really all about self healing—about coming into a sense of wholeness. Through my own process of self-healing, my life's work and purpose have become clearer. As I matured in the work, I explored the connections between this modern-day laying-on of hands and the spiritual healing described in the scriptures. Healing Touch was truly a catalyst for me, inspiring deeper investigation into the Judeo-Christian roots of healing and raising important questions. These questions formed the basis for writing this book and are just as valid today as when I first published them in 2000. For example,

What is the difference between "healing" and "curing"?

What do I really believe about spiritual healing and physical healing?

We say that all healing comes from a spiritual base, but how can this healing work be applied from a specific spiritual path, like Christianity?

How is this healing work the work of God?

What does it mean to be a healing presence for another person?

Am I truly a "healer," a vessel or instrument of God for others?

What are the historical roots of healing in Christianity?

How important is the role of prayer and meditation in the development of the healer and in the healing process itself?

What role does faith have in healing—both for the practitioner and the recipient?

What is the connection between intention of the heart and the flow of "healing"?

Exploring these issues has helped me not only write this book as a reflection of my own journey in healing but also to develop courses for a program in Christian healing called *Healing Touch Spiritual Ministry*. This approach to healing work is created for all those in ministry who wish to integrate prayer, hands-on healing and anointing within their Christian faith. It's a "hands-on" program teaching much like the early Christians must have done it—through apprentice work.

So, how has the work of Healing Touch Spiritual Ministry become a way of life for me? Besides giving me joy and filling my every waking moment, I have over these many years taught thousands and been moved by the light in my student's eyes as they too recognize their unique calling to healing ministry. Over the years, God's grace has changed me, and assisted me to become the person I am meant to be—whole and in balance—in body, mind, soul, and spirit. I see through new eyes, I feel with new hands, and I heal through a new heart. God's grace has helped me leave my old self behind and embrace my true self. I have not arrived, but I am certainly on the path of self healing.

The work of Healing Touch Spiritual Ministry has been a vehicle for this transformation. I am doing the work of my heart—the work I have been called to do in this life time. I love it, when others also recognize their unique callings to help others move towards healing. I have begun to see we all are on a spiritual path, moving towards home. We are here but for a brief moment in time and therefore I sense an urgency to do what I can for God's people.

What Is Healing Touch Spiritual Ministry?

Healing Touch Spiritual Ministry is an educational program that teaches hands-on healing, prayer and anointing with essential oils. Some would describe it as a sacred healing art that flows from our early Christian tradition. In the laying-on of hands, as we will see in later chapters, there is a flow of God's healing grace to the person who is receiving. Healing Touch Spiritual Ministry gives practitioners more healing techniques through which they can use their hands as God's instruments of healing.

The specific work of Healing Touch Spiritual Ministry grew out my experience of working with Janet Mentgen, who based her work of Healing Touch on "a philosophy of caring." We use our hands to care compassionately for another human being, with the aim of

"Energy system" refers to the "aura," which is composed of an energy "field" that surrounds the body, and energy "centers" which emanate from within the body.

restoring harmony and balance within the person's "energy system." This in turn enables the person to self heal. This healing work is offered to others through the practitioner's centered heart.

"Healing Touch is the art of caring that comes from the heart of the healer and reaches to the person who is receiving help."[1]
—Janet Mentgen

[1]Dorothea Hover-Kramer, Janet Mentgen and Sharon Scandrett-Hibdon, *Healing Touch, A Resource for Health Care Professionals*, p. 162.

The source of all healing is God—the Source, Creator, Spirit, Yahweh, Allah, Universal Energy, Higher Power, Ultimate Reality, Ground of Being—whatever name you give the Ultimate Source— the Oneness of all that is. It has amazed me over the years that this one line has struck such a cord with so many skeptics and critics. It is a world view shared by all the enduring religions of the world. God has many names which apparently is not acceptable to some well-meaning Christians. I make no apologies for recognizing the myriad of names for our Creator. Some of the names are more personal and others are less so. In Marcus Borg's words, God has more the quality of a "presence" than of a non-personal "energy" or "force."[2] I believe God is intimately involved in our lives and cares about our well being (the personal God). In St. Paul's words, God is the one in whom "we live and move and have our being." Acts 17:28. God is not just "out there," we are in God; we live in God, move in God have our being in God. As healing practitioners we are the instruments through which God's healing grace (energy) flows. God gave us to each other for a purpose. Connecting to the Divine, we learn the pivotal roles of centering and intentionality as we touch others in a healing way. Our work does not recommend or require a specific religious orientation or organized religious system. It can fit within all spiritual paths, although the focus of this book is to explore prayer, energy healing and anointing within the Judeo-Christian tradition. As practitioners, we welcome with a Christ spirit, all people regardless of their faith or lack of faith. My reaching out to others in compassion and love is not dependent upon it being returned. My extension of heart energy is simply because of my love of God and God's people—it is a response to the Christ call to love one another.

[2]Marcus Borg, *The Heart of Christianity, Rediscovering a Life of Faith*, p. 72.

Healing Touch Spiritual Ministry takes a holistic approach to health and healing, addressing the physical, emotional, mental, and spiritual dimensions of the human person. From this perspective, nurses find this work to be an expression of the art of compassionate nursing. For chaplains, the work is an extension of their spiritual duties to offer comfort and solace in times of pain and fear. For massage therapists, the work extends their ability to balance the body with loving touch. For others, this work takes them to deeper levels of self expression and inner healing. The ability to facilitate healing for someone else is inherent in anyone who desires to help another. All that is needed is a sincere intent to be of service as a healer. No matter what one's background might be, you can learn this work for your own healing as well as to help facilitate healing for another.

Healing Versus Curing—Is There A Difference?

Healing occurs on many levels. Curing is only one part of healing, yet we often confuse curing with healing. "To heal" comes from the Old English word, haelen, which means "to make whole." Our words for health and holiness are also derived from this same root word. Health is a state of wholeness, of balance and harmony in one's being. In wholeness, there is a fullness of peace, joy, and the fruits of the Spirit. Healing into wholeness is a transforming experience of one's whole being—body, mind, soul, and spirit—into a state of holiness—of oneness. It is an appreciation of mystery and an experience of the miraculous.

It may seem strange at first to refer to both our "soul" and our "spirit." What is the difference? The terms are often confused and many meanings overlap. According to the spiritual writer Richard Rohr, spirit tends toward mind, universals, absolutes, God; while soul tends toward psyche, experience, particulars, and "me." Soul seems to be the lost element and body tends to be the rejected element.[3] In St. Paul's letter to the Thessalonians, he speaks of the spirit, soul and body and the need for them to be kept sound (whole). Healing into wholeness is healing for body, soul, and spirit.

"May the God of peace himself sanctify you entirely; and may your spirit and soul and body be kept sound and blameless at the coming of our Lord Jesus Christ."

I Thessalonians 5:23

[3]Richard Rohr, *Everything Belongs, The Gift of Contemplative Prayer,* p. 119.

Healing is an ongoing process of transformation and growth throughout life. Holiness is intention, it is manifesting love; it is the essence of what it means to be totally in balance. When we are connected to our Source, to God, we are being and doing exactly what we are called to do. As Bruce Davis puts it, "holiness is not an option! It is our simple duty."[4]

[4]Bruce Davis, *Monastery Without Walls*, p. 166.

Our healing touch is aimed at more than the relief of physical symptoms, which is generally what is meant by curing. We do little to help a person on their path to wholeness and high-level wellness simply by eliminating the symptoms of disease. Healing Touch Spiritual Ministry is one way of enabling the transforming experience into wholeness. God's will for us is health and wholeness and holiness. We are not here to suffer, although suffering is a part of the human condition. Our path in life is one of transformation into wholeness. We grow into healing throughout our whole lives. Healing may lead to curing, but it is also possible to have healing without curing.

There are many meanings attributed to the word "cure," but usually we think of a reversal of events or a restoring to the original state. For some, "cure" means "miracle" or the "miraculous." Robert Keck in his book *Healing as a Sacred Path*, states that "miracle healings are quite natural because the divine is naturally within us."[5] Miracle healings are the manifestations of the possibilities that have been created within us naturally but which have been beyond our paradigm of understanding. Healing may lead to curing but it is also possible to be healed without having been cured. One may grow into a high state of wellness, wholeness, and holiness, while still living with the physical challenge of disease.

[5]Robert Keck, *Healing as a Sacred Path*, p. xiv.

Medical science in its search for "cures" has forgotten about healing. For science, either we are cured or we are not. Surely, we are led to believe if scientists just look hard enough, they will find the cure for cancer, heart disease, AIDS, and every other disease process. This has caused us to buy into the belief system that there are quick fixes and magic pills for everything. Many have become disil-

Even when we are cured—there is the false belief that we are somehow now rendered whole and healed and that may not be the case.

lusioned in their search for relief of suffering and have been lead to conclude that our health care system is somehow at fault.

There is nothing wrong with looking for relief of suffering, but when we put all our trust in the medical approach, expecting a reversal of events, we will often find ourselves disappointed. The unending search for the immediate cure denies faith and trust in the transforming process into wholeness. It denies the miraculous embedded deep within all of reality. It denies that we are whole beings—body, mind, spirit. It denies the power of God to act in the moment or in the many moments towards healing, and it denies that it is possible to be "healed" without being "cured."

Putting all possibilities before God, we can be open to the myriad ways God can bring healing into our lives. As we reach that place of wholeness—of transformation into holiness—our trust has carried us to oneness with God. "A 'miracle' occurs," as Keck says, "when we experience a dramatic breakthrough or awakening so different from our previous experience that we want to speak of it as something coming from the outside, something qualitatively different from what we have known before."[6]

[6]Robert Keck, *Healing as a Sacred Path,* p. 119.

God has given us to each other. We can be the means through which God delivers the mysterious miracle of healing (not necessarily curing). This is the message of this book. Through our awareness, our intentionality, and our knowledge, we can be instruments of God's grace for one another's healing into wholeness and into holiness on our individual paths of healing.

Our Healing Touch Can Be a Spiritual Ministry

Being called into healing usually signifies a call into service. At some level of our being, we recognize an urge to do good in the world that we can only acknowledge as coming from our soul's greatest desire. This call is, first of all, about our "being" and not about our "doing." It cannot be taught or imposed it is simply the expression of what one feels deeply at the soul level. There is an awareness of divine drawing or urging to be connected to one another.

"Like good stewards of the manifold grace of God, serve one another with whatever gift each of you has received."

I Peter 4:10

Our healing work, in my experience, is ministry at its highest level. It is about responding to that inner voice that calls one to be God's instrument, to act out of a compassionate heart with no attachment to the outcome. It is about being a vessel, a conduit, an instrument, a channel, and a courier through which God can act in another's life. It's about being in the "flow" of God's grace.

Healing Touch Spiritual Ministry brings the work to those who wish to use it within a spiritual setting such as church ministry. It can enhance the work of parish nursing, church healing ministries, pastoral care in hospitals and nursing homes, spiritual direction, retreats, hospice care, and home health care, to name but a few settings. It can be used within families wishing to bring wholeness back into their relationships.

Many ministers and laity alike have voiced to me the importance for them to have some kind of "credential" to do this work. Classes in the Spiritual Ministry program can lead to a certificate of completion showing that the recipient has completed a course of study. There are actually three programs offered within Healing Touch Spiritual Ministry—the basic program, an advanced program and a certification in aromatherapy for those who need to learn more about the healing powers of essential oils. See Appendix A for a complete description.

Walking the Christian Path

Healing practitioners who come from a Christian perspective recognize that touch was an integral part of Jesus' compassion for others. He reached out and healed those who were in pain, who were alienated, and whose suffering kept them from being themselves. Grace, which is God's power and energy, flowed through him, restoring and empowering those suffering to achieve wholeness.

"Grace,
    which comes from God,
    and is God,
comes through the powerful acts of
those around us,
    the acts of love,
    selflessness
    forgiveness
    and affection.
This grace,
    of which Jesus was full,
    this grace is the life of
God...
Do you realize what this means?
    This means that God's own
life,
    God's energy
    God's grace
        is within us.
And it means that we are empowered,
    (empowered!)
to energize others
    by loving them
    forgiving them
    accepting them
    and creating them."

[7]Bill Huebsch, *A New Look at Grace, A Spirituality of Wholeness*, p. 55-56.

"When Peter and John were approached by the lame man outside the temple, they had no money to give him. They could only extend their hands in the name of Christ." Acts 3:1-16.

Healing Touch Spiritual Ministry gives us more ways of expressing our love and compassion for one another. Besides knowing what to do with our hands, we understand from our hearts how we can help bring compassionate healing to another. It is a way of remembering our true natures as children of God and that we are meant to be good and whole. Our true selves are empowered through grace. As we read the scriptures, we begin to see the Gospel imperatives of not only justice, peace, and service—we also see the clear mandates to teach and HEAL.

When we give touch from the heart, God uses us as a conduit to pour compassionate graces where they are most needed. What is this "grace" we speak of? For most of us, the meaning of grace is a nebulous one. We know that grace is radically present in our lives yet it is difficult to grasp. Only in pausing to reflect on the "stuff" of life, do we recognize the grace that keeps us going. Totally unmerited, we are rich in this divine gift. When we discover God in our lives and in our sharing with one another, these are moments of grace. Healing is one of those moments of grace.

As Christians in healing ministry we have been sent out much the same as the disciples of the early church. Jesus didn't just send them out—he empowered them! Bill Huebsch shows us through poetry that God gave the disciples—and all of us—the grace to heal one another.[7] When we accept the empowerment of grace in our lives, we are accepting God's light and love into our hearts.

The early Christians exhibited this healing touch of Jesus to others in all aspects of their lives. Peter and John, as well as many of the other disciples, all healed just as Jesus had taught them. It was a way Jesus' followers were recognized: "see how they love one another." Somewhere in history, however, we lost sight of Jesus' imperative to us to "teach and to heal." We stopped behaving in a healing way towards each other and eventually lost it from our consciousness. Instead, mistrust occurred and only the clergy and royalty were allowed to touch with an intention to heal. Later, we relied upon physicians and those involved in providing health care to render healing (read "curing") in their touch. The Christian way of being with each other from the heart was lost, along with what it means to heal one another.

One Last Thought

You can use this book in a number of ways. It can be a resource to accompany the course, Introduction to Healing Ministry, the Christian Path. Many over the past few years have used it as a group study guide. It can also be used as a meditation guide to accompany your healing work. I have designed the pages so that in the inner column you will see references, scripture quotations, pertinent comments, and questions for your reflection and meditation.

This book seeks to explore healing as a way of life for the third millennium. In Part I, I examine what we know about the history of Christian healing. What are the roots from which Christian healing springs and how has healing faired over the centuries since Jesus modeled a healing ministry for us? How was Christian healing lost and how are we regaining our heritage today? In Part II, I explore a ministry that has come of age. The laying-on of hands is a foundational stone for modern hands-on healing or "energy" healing. The groundwork is laid for creating healing ministries in our churches and ministry settings. Part III is about becoming instruments of healing. The emphasis is on healing from the heart, which needs to become a way of life for those who aspire to be healers of others. Our intentions and our belief hold the keys to learning to cultivate a healing attitude of heart.

It is my hope that this book will become a stepping stone for your own continued search for Divine Grace breaking through in your life. Look for your call to wholeness and to "holiness" in healing work. And then, reflect on how God may be "calling you into healing" for others, calling you to be an instrument, a conduit, vessel, and courier through which God's divine grace flows.

"As a father has compassion
    for his children,
So the Lord has compassion
    for those who fear him."
Psalm 103

We are very close now
To understanding that we are
    empowered to be our
        most selves
            and that,
            when we accept that
            empowerment in faith,
then we accept Christ as well.
Then we become persons-for-others,
    persons sent to heal
    persons empowered for
        ministry in our everyday
        lives."

Bill Huebsch, *A New Look at Grace, A Spirituality of Wholeness*, p. 55-5.

Chapter 1

Digging For Our Roots

One southern Lutheran pastor remembers some of the old healing practices he grew up with. His father used to blow cigarette smoke into his ears for earaches, turpentine was widely used as a healing agent, and "pork fat" was generously used for deep wounds.

To understand our present day thirst for healing in body, mind, and spirit, we need to dig deeply for our Christian roots within our family and church traditions. Are there stories of healing in your family passed down from your great-grandparents and grandparents? Did your parents teach you how to heal yourself or others with healing practices? Or was healing one of those family secrets not mentioned in polite company? Perhaps you remember your mother or grandmother passing down healing recipes for colds, flu, or other maladies. Or, like my family, healing was something our family sought only from the doctor, hospital, or clinic. What did "healing" mean in your family? Most of us would have to admit that healing is absent from our family stories and traditions.

What about your church? Can you remember stories of healing within your church? Are there healing traditions, rituals, or practices? Does your church speak of healing prayer? Is "spiritual healing" even mentioned? Or, is healing thought of as something Jesus and the disciples did a long time ago, something beyond our reach today? Is healing only practiced by the minister and not the laity? Is healing feared in your church rather than welcomed?

Most people have few family or church-based experiences with healing. In our modern western world, healing has usually been left to our health care system and to medical practice and is focused on "curing" the body. Yet the American public is looking for more than a cure—it is looking for healing. Many people feel they are starved for healing in their lives and in their church and are looking to rather unconventional healing methods. Some are not even aware that there is healing deep within our Christian tradition.

History shows us that healing fell into disfavor and practically disappeared from Christianity nearly five hundred years ago. The Scripture stories were quite clear regarding the role of healing. They describe how the young Christian church became known as a healing church. In this chapter I want to explore those roots. To tell our story, let us look back into history and follow the thread of healing through our Judeo-Christian heritage. Our family and church traditions have been shaped by this history. To begin, let us look even further back to a time when healing was considered a natural part of life.

An Ancient Story

We begin the story of our healing traditions in those earliest of times when healing was tied to a "spiritual" dimension of life. The place of healing within any culture relates to its cosmology, that is, its beliefs about the nature of the universe. Their world views would reflect their own cosmic story. Beliefs about the Sacred, divine order and harmony, the source of health and the cause and meaning of illness, suffering, life and death, and the presence and cause of good and evil all derive from their cosmology. Burkhardt and Nagai-Jacobson tell us that healing has always been closely linked to these understandings of the sacred and spiritual forces.[1] From studies of these early societies, we know that humans gathered in small groups and individuals were identified with specific functions. For, perhaps a 100,000 years, the "healers" were the shamans or the medicine people who held this knowledge. Healing was for the body and the spirit within the body and always had a spiritual component. The shamans looked after the well being of the people. They were considered the wise ones and were respected by all.

The shamans fulfilled many roles: priest, priestess, healer, herbalist, mid-wife, doctor, and counselor. You went to the shaman not only when you were ill but also when something was troubling you. These men and women were in touch with the "great mysteries" of life and helped people interpret illness, as well as environmental changes like earthquakes, floods, and droughts, as something sent by the gods. These healers helped people understand disasters as well as the diseases that affected them. When they could find no meaning, the cause was interpreted as some darkness or force that often was referred to as "demons." Some of the medicine men and women had highly developed healing arts that included medicinals and surgery. Jeanne Acterburg describes how healers fell into several classes. The highest class of healers knew the invisible or magical realm and were the natural spiritual leaders. These shamans were at the top of the healing hierarchy and their skills were considered more advanced and important than either the herbalist or the bone-setter. This lower or simpler class knew the botanical prescriptions and the other treatments that were believed to influence the physical course of health. They were the keepers of the healing herbs for all kinds of maladies. Theirs was a creditable pharmacopoeia.[2]

Ancient peoples shared their knowledge of healing through their trade with each other. They also shared the stories and the myths that brought meaning to their lives. Mythology—the stories of how the universe began and how life came to be as it is—helped humankind to make sense of life's events. Various gods were ascribed power over life and death and illness. Most peoples believed in many

[1]Margaret Burkhardt and Mary Gail Nagai-Jacobson, *Spirituality, Living our Cennectedness*, p. 33.

[2]Jeanne Acterburg, *Woman As Healer*, p. 29.

gods and demons, but some believed that there was only one God who was the source of all that is good and bad. The ancient Hebrews held this belief.

Looking For Healing in the Hebrew Bible

The role of healing in the Hebrew Bible is quite profound but not always obvious. Aside from a few direct references to healing, the larger concepts of sin, salvation, and ultimate destiny also relate to healing. Tom Harpur, an Anglican priest and writer, calls attention to the common thread of human brokenness and how we can be restored to health. Our relationship with God was broken in the Garden of Eden, he says, and everything since has been affected by our turning away from the face of God. The story points to our need to be restored to wholeness—to health—to be healed and restored to oneness with God.[3]

[3]Tom Harpur, *The Uncommon Touch,* p. 52.

The stories of the early Hebrews existed for thousands of years as an oral tradition. These stories addressed the meaning of life, including how people were to behave. Gradually, this oral tradition was written down as sacred law and over time developed into what we now know as the Torah. It contains the five books of Moses and the books of the Prophets and the Holy Writings. All of these make up the Hebrew Scriptures or the Hebrew Bible. The Torah was written in Hebrew, typically without vowels. Understanding the meaning could be quite challenging, particularly since everything was viewed as a metaphor for hidden wisdom teachings. Unlocking the meaning of a passage was truly an accomplishment that was met with great rejoicing. The role of the sages was to memorize vast amounts of the law and the sacred teachings, a skill greatly relied upon by the people. In this way, they were able to live fairly ordered lives, knowing who they were as a people in relationship with God.[4]

[4]Rabbi David Cooper, *God Is a Verb, Kabbalah and the Practice of Mystical Judaism,* pp. 4-18.

In the Old Testament we can trace beliefs about the people's relationship with God and how healing figured in their lives. The God of Abraham and Moses led the people through the wilderness and protected them by day and night. Yahweh was the giver of all good things and the dispenser of sicknesses of all kinds. The proph-

"Learn then that I, I alone, am God, and there is no god besides me. It is I who bring both death and life, I who inflict wounds and heal them, and from my hand there is no rescue." Deut. 32:39

"If you listen carefully to the voice of the Lord your God and do what is right in his eyes, if you pay attention to his commands and keep all his decrees, I will not bring on you any of the diseases I brought on the Egyptians, for I am the Lord, who heals you." Exod. 15:26

"I in turn will do this to you: I will bring terror on you; consumption and fever that waste the eyes and cause life to pine away." Lev. 26: 16

"I will bring the sword against you, executing vengeance for the covenant...I will send pestilence among you, and you shall be delivered into enemy hands... But if, despite this, you disobey me, and continue hostile to me, I will continue hostile to you in fury; I in turn will punish you myself sevenfold for your sins." Lev. 26: 25-29

[5]Margaret Burkhardt and Mary Gail Nagai-Jacobson, *Spirituality, Living our Cennectedness*, p. 36.

ets warned the people to follow the law or grave things would befall them. Clearly, Yahweh was the bringer of both life and death and there was no escaping God's judgment. We find throughout the Scriptures a compassionate God who could also be a harsh God. Illnesses and even natural catastrophes such as earthquakes and floods were viewed as God's wrathful visitation upon his people; healing was God's unrelenting compassion and caring for his people.

The ancient Hebrews struck a bargain with God in the form of the Covenant. This bond tied them to Yahweh, the Source of all that is. Yahweh, in turn, agreed to care for the "chosen" ones. Obedience of the nation and physical health were linked, just as disobedience and disease were linked. The Covenant was made with the whole people, not just individuals. When King David sinned, his punishment was visited upon the whole people.

There are details in the Scriptures of all kinds of diseases that God would send his people when they did not live up to the Covenant. These include consumption, fever, pestilence, boils, scurvy, itch for which there is no cure, madness, blindness, distraction of mind, burning fever, and inflammation. Every sickness not specifically mentioned was promised in payment for disobeying the law. The Biblical notion of sickness meant a loss of rûah, the spirit of life that God breathes into a person, enabling the person to be in relationship with God.[5] Sickness often carried with it a breach in relationship with society.

Nowhere do the Scriptures describe attempts to influence God's hand in matters of life and death. If one "sinned," whatever punishment was meted out was deserved. "Sin" meant "missing the mark," being "off the path." A sinful life was punished with disease and misfortune. A righteous life, on the other hand, would be blessed by God with riches. This interpretation of the events of life was very straight forward as long as the "sin" could be identified. It faltered, however (as do all theologies), in explaining why bad things happened to apparently good people. The ancient Hebrews believed that surely some sin, perhaps even by one's parents, accounted for God's punishment.

The Book of Job addressed this issue with an allegorical story about a righteous man who by all appearances seemed to be in disfavor with God. Even his family and friends tried to convince him to see where he had "missed the mark." But Job was steadfast. He knew that he was God's faithful servant. In the end, he was justified by God. The story questions the assumption that goodness always wins God's blessing and punishment always is meted out for evil. This story had to be a comfort to those ancient Hebrews as they searched for the meaning of suffering in their lives, just as it is a comfort for all those reading it today.

The Psalms—Poetry of Healing

The theme of healing in the Old Testament becomes quite personal in the Psalms. Tom Harpur calls the Psalms the *"window through which we view the inner wrestling of the human soul."*[6] All struggles, hopes, fears, and longings of humanity are exposed to the presence of God in these prayers flowing from the heart of Jewish spiritual life. Tradition has it that the Psalms, seen as divinely inspired, are the most effective means in mirroring back the direct light of God. Since they believed that sickness was God's way of dealing with the individual, many of the Psalms call us to trust in the Holy One as a healer of mind, body, soul, and spirit. There seems to be a deep conviction on the part of the psalmists that God's natural inclination is towards healing of all creation. However, there are other psalms that appear to contradict this thought. These psalms call upon God to reign down terror on one's enemies, including diseases and other ills.

Rabbi Simkha Weintraub tells us about the Hasidic master Rabbi Nachman of Breslov who lived in the eighteenth century. This revered Master identified ten psalms as having special power to bring a true and complete healing of body and spirit. He called them the "Tikkun HaKlali" or "Complete Remedy" and said they embody the concentrated power of the entire Book of Psalms. Viewed together, the ten psalms reflect an unfolding of many emotions and reactions

"The Lord will afflict you with consumption, fever, inflammation, with fiery heat and drought, and with blight and mildew; they shall pursue you until you perish...the Lord will afflict you with the boils of Egypt, with ulcers, scurvy, and itch, of which you cannot be healed. The Lord will afflict you with madness, blindness, and confusion of mind... you shall be unable to find your way; and you shall be continually abused and robbed, without anyone to help...the Lord will strike you...with grievous boils of which you cannot be healed, from the sole of your foot to the crown of your head...All these curses shall come upon you, pursuing and overtaking you until you are destroyed, because you did not obey the Lord your God....Every other malady and affliction, even though not recorded in the book of this law, the Lord will inflict on you until you are destroyed." Deut. 28:22-61

[6]Tom Harpur, *The Uncommon Touch,* p. 53.

Psalms 41, 46, 62, 74, 116, 121, and 147

common to those dealing with illness. Mere recitation will have little value. Instead, you must identify with their contents in a deep and meaningful way, and seek to find yourself in every psalm. According to Rabbi Nachman, prayer is a dialogue between humans and their Creator and is absolutely key in the repair of the world. The ultimate goal in Jewish teaching is to bring the world to a state of *tikkun*. Rabbi Weintraub explains that this word implies repair, correction, wholeness, and perfection. *Tikkun* repairs the Covenant relationship and bridges the separation between the people and God.[7]

[7]Rabbi Simkha Y. Weintraub, *Healing of Soul, Healing of Body*, pp. 17-22.

The "Ten [healing] Psalms" are: 16, 32, 41, 42, 59, 77, 90, 105, 137, and 150.

"My son, do not scorn correction from Yahweh, do not resent his rebuke; for Yahweh reproves the man he loves as a father checks a well-loved son." Proverbs 32:11-12

Another book available to the ancient Hebrews was the Book of Proverbs, which is counted among the Holy Writings. It continues the theme found in the psalms, the Torah, and the writings of the Prophets. Here there are warnings that illness and misfortune are the results of sin. Over and over, we find this same theme: if we follow wisdom and the Law, we will be blessed with health and long life. These maxims were often committed to memory as words to live by.

For the Hebrews, life was seen metaphorically as a path to be walked. If they stepped off the path, they fell into sin. But what "influenced" them to step off the path in the first place? Were there greater forces out there working against God and ultimately against his people? Was there "evil" loose in the world? These were questions that their cosmology attempted to answer.

The Role of Satan and Evil Spirits

For the Hebrews, Satan originally was not evil or opposed to God. On the contrary, he was one of God's angels (messengers) of light sent to stand in one's path much like an adversary, until you saw your sinful ways and turned back to the righteous path. The Greek term *diabolos*, later translated as "devil," literally means "one who throws something across one's path." The Hebrew storytellers would often attribute misfortune to human sin. At other times, Satan, by God's order or permission, would block human plans and desires. Elaine Pagels, a respected Scripture scholar, describes the Hebrew term, *satan*, as an adversarial role.[8] If the path was wrong, then having Satan "throw a monkey wrench in the works" was not a

[8]Elaine Pagels, *The Origin of Satan*, pp. 39-40.

bad thing. In this sense, God might be sending the messenger Satan to protect a person from worse harm. The story of Job is a classic example of this adversarial role of Satan. In the tale, Satan challenges God to put his favorite servant, Job, to the test of loyalty. God authorized Satan to afflict Job, but to spare his life. Job passes the test, and in the end, Satan remains an angel, God's obedient servant.

Demons had no place in the Old Testament, but it is interesting to see that the Hebrew Scriptures are filled with angels. They are often referred to as the "shining ones" who serve as God's messengers. They brought good news as well as bad. For the Egyptians and Babylonians, the power of darkness was at the root of all misfortune. This was not so, however, for the Hebrews. Not until the time of the Exile, when the Jewish people were forced into captivity in Babylon, do we see spiritual powers being attributed to anything other than Yahweh. Until then, the only source of illness was believed to be Yahweh. During the exile, contact with Babylonians, Egyptians, and Persians began to affect Hebrew thought. They too, began to accept that the powers of darkness somehow played a part in misfortunes and illnesses.

Satan became "The Satan" and took on a personality antagonistic to God. Stories began to give him various names such as Beelzebuh, Semihazah, Azazel, Belial, and Prince of Darkness. There are many stories about the fall of this great angel, who took a horde of angels with him down to *sheol.* The Satan took on sinister qualities. No longer one of God's faithful servants, he was depicted as swollen with lust and arrogance and blamed for human's fall into sin. According to Hebrew cosmology, the forces of evil under the Prince of Darkness have continued to influence the people of the earth ever since. There is a great cosmic battle going on between the forces of good and the forces of evil. Even today, we have an expression that says "the devil made me do it!"

Where Were the Traditional Healers in Judaism?

"Any necromancers, sorcerers, witches, augurers, mediums or wizards were to be stoned to death." Lev. 20:27

"Is there no balm in Gilead? Is there no physician there? Why then has the health of my poor people not been restored?" Jer. 9:22

[9]Zach Thomas, *Healing Touch, The Church's Forgotten Language*, p. 11.

"In the 39th year of his reign Asa was diseased in his feet, and his disease became severe; yet even in his disease he did not seek the Lord, but sought help from physicians. Then Asa slept with his ancestors dying in the 41st year of his reign." II Chron. 16:12-13

Among other ancient societies, there were diviners, soothsayers, sorcerers, and those who believed in demons and other spiritual forces. Often these individuals tended the sick and assisted in childbirth. We read in Leviticus that the witches, augurers, mediums, and wizards were to be stoned, presumably because they called upon other forces besides Yahweh. Furthermore, those who practiced medical healing were thought to be trained in divination and magic, which were strictly forbidden. Even the skills of physicians were not held in high esteem. However, in the Book of Jeremiah, we hear the prophet lamenting the absence of physicians in Gilead. His cry was for his poor people, sinners that they were, whose health was in jeopardy. Zach Thomas, a Presbyterian minister, observes that "Judaism grew to be remarkably devoid of anyone designated as a healer."[9]

Since the Scriptures are quite clear that Yahweh is the only source of blessing and curse, there are few references in the Old Testament to the use of medicine or to the role of the physician. People thought it was better to pray for deliverance from their pain then to suffer at the hands of physicians. There is the story in II Chronicles about a King Asa who suffered from a debilitating disease. He sought the help of physicians and died; proof of the importance of putting faith in God, not earthly healers. His turning to physicians was interpreted as a "betrayal" and most likely involved pagan physicians.

The most positive reference to roles of the physician and medicine is in the Apocryphal book of Ecclesiasticus (Sirach). This passage describes the conditions under which God will heal. Notice in this passage that in order to be made well or "whole," there are four things required:

1) Pray first to the Lord for deliverance

2) Look within and see where you have missed the mark, then repent

3) Make an offering, the best you have

4) Finally, submit to the physician

This passage was probably written in the century after the Chronicles (about 190 B.C.), and represents a much later development in Judaic thought. Here the writer is saying that the person in need of healing is fulfilling the law by placing all his or her faith in God who is the ultimate healer. Then, the person looks within their heart, repenting of any wrong doing that may have brought on this curse or punishment. Important to all Hebrew ritual was making an offering or appeasement to God. This offering was supposed to be the very best of what the person had to offer and would show their sincerity in repentance. Finally, the sick person is advised to trust in the care and knowledge of the physician. The passage ends with words of wisdom that offer a "cheerful" thought: "If a man sins in the eyes of his Maker, may he fall under the care of the doctor."

This is the only passage in the Holy Writings that extols not only the role of the physician but also that of the pharmacist. Morton Kelsey, Episcopal priest and respected author, states that physicians and healers did attend the sick but were looked upon with great suspicion by the rabbis. The main rabbinical schools forbade the practice of medicine and healing since they were viewed as akin to sorcery and magic. In the Talmud, there are references that say those who participate in these roles will have no share in the world to come. The Talmud is like an encyclopedia of the meanings and intentions of the law. It assisted the rabbis in interpreting the holy Scriptures. Kelsey also points to a statement in the Talmud that Jesus was hanged on a tree on the Passover Eve because he practiced sorcery, which is a reference to Jesus healing the sick.[10]

Yahweh's Compassion

There are some healing stories in the Old Testament which show God's mercy and compassion on individuals. In the Book of Kings, both Elijah and Elisha heal a child and Elisha cleanses Namaan of leprosy. None of these incidents, however, include the idea that the presence of "sin" provoked illness. No reason is given for the illnesses, neither is there any judgment. There are other stories of healing after the proper sacrifices were made for sin, as

"Honor physicians for their services, for the Lord created them; for their gift of healing comes from the Most High, and they are rewarded by the King. The skill of physicians makes them distinguished, and in the presence of the great they are admired. The Lord created medicines out of the earth, and the sensible will not despise them. Was not water made sweet with a tree in order that its power might be known? And he gave skill to human beings that he might be glorified in his marvelous works. By them the physician heals and takes away pain; the pharmacist makes a mixture from them. God's works will never be finished; and from him health spreads over all the earth. My child, when you are ill, do not delay, but pray to the Lord, and he will heal you. Give up your faults and direct your hands rightly, and cleanse your heart from all sin. Offer a sweet-smelling sacrifice, and a memorial portion of choice flour, and pour oil on your offering, as much as you can afford. Then give the physician his place, for the Lord created him; do not let him leave you, for you need him. There may come a time when recovery lies in the hands of physicians, for they too pray to the Lord that he grant them success in diagnosis and in healing, for the sake of preserving life. He who sins against his Maker, will be defiant toward the physician."
Ecclesiasticus 38:1-15

[10]Morton Kelsy, *Healing & Christianity*, p. 31.

I Kings 17:17-23; 2 Kings 4:18-37; 2 Kings 5:1-14; Num. 16:47-50; 2 Samuel 24:10-25; Tobit 11:7-15; 2 Kings 20

"Moses made a serpent of bronze, and put it upon a pole; and whenever a serpent bit someone, that person would look at the serpent of bronze and live." Num. 21:9

We see the image of the caduceus in this story which is the healing symbol chosen by physicians.

Tobias 5:10; 6:7-9; 11:7-15

well as stories of how plagues were stopped when Moses and Aaron prayed and made atonement for the people. At one point, Moses is told to fashion a bronze serpent so that anyone bitten by the vipers in the desert would be healed. In a story in the Book of Samuel, King David builds an altar to the Lord and offers burnt offerings to appease God. The Lord answers his prayers by lifting a plague from the land.

In 2 Kings, Chapter 20, King Hezekiah becomes ill and is told by the prophet Isaiah that he would die. The King prays for his own recovery. Isaiah then gets a message from God that fifteen years will be added to the King's life. Almost as an afterthought, Isaiah makes a poultice of figs to apply to the King's boils. Medicine and prayer work together in this story for the King's recovery.

In yet another story, Tobias heals his father, Tobit, of his blindness through the help of the angel, Raphael. Raphael, whom Tobit does not recognize as an angel of God, tells Tobit to "take courage, the time is near for God to heal you." As the story continues, Raphael journeys with Tobit's son, Tobias, and teaches him about many things, including the healing properties of fish heart, liver, and gall. Burning incense made of the fish heart and liver will drive away demons and evil spirits that afflict people. Apparently, the smell can drive them all the way to Egypt! The fish's gall can be used to anoint a person's eyes where white films have appeared on them. Tobias following the angel's guidance, peels away the white film that covers his father's eyes, and he is able to once again see his son.

These are representative of the healing stories in the Hebrew Bible. On the whole, the healing stories were intended to show the supernatural powers of God. The theme of healing is relatively minor in comparison to themes like sin and salvation. Yet, the psalms, which were the prayers of the people, are filled with mention of the healing power of Yahweh. Although the healing stories may be few, belief in Yahweh's compassion and power to heal was strong.

The prophet Isaiah refers to the theme of healing in his references to the coming of the messiah—the one who will save the people. His writing encouraged many to hope for the day of Yahweh when all illness would be healed. "Be strong, do not fear," Isaiah tells us, "He will come with vengence, with terrible recompense. He will come and save you!" And how shall we recognize the messiah? The dead will rise, the deaf will hear, and the blind will see. God will come not only as a savior but as *a healer of God's people*.

Healing in the Rest of the World

What was going on outside the Hebrew nation with regard to healing? Among the Persians and Chaldeans, medical practice was quite sophisticated and included surgery, medical treatment, and prayer. All three were considered important in treating an individual in these societies. Some of their descriptions detail how diseases were to be treated and how surgery was to be performed. Egyptian writings even describe what the physician ought to charge the patient. The Egyptians and Babylonians believed the cause of sickness resulted from the ill will of demons loose in the world or from the actions of various gods or evil spirits.

The Greeks had several healing cults, the most famous being the schools of Asclepius and Hippocrates. Greek thought emphasized holistic healing of body and mind. Morton Kelsey observes that in the *Dialogues*, Plato stressed the necessity of getting at disease by treating the whole person. And in *Phaedrus*, Plato listed along with prophecy, art, and love as ways in which he saw the divine breaking through into the physical realm.[11] The Greeks also considered illness to be an affliction of the gods. It was simply your fate or an unlucky draw if you got sick. For healing, one could only turn to minor gods, such as Asclepius, whose temples were places of healing. In these temples, the sick would come and have their physical needs cared for by bathing, massaging, and the like. They were instructed to sleep within the temple and ask for a dream or vision that would give them insights about their own healing. The dream interpreters would then interpret the sick person's dreams, the meaning of their illnesses, and how they could heal. These temples were very popular.

Isaiah 26:19, 29:18, 61:1-11

"Then the eyes of the blind shall be opened, the ears of the deaf unsealed, then the lame shall leap like a deer and the tongues of the dumb sing for joy." Isaiah 35:5-6

[11]Morton Kelsey, *Healing and Christianity*, pp. 36-37.

The Greeks went to doctors to maintain their wellness but to the temples for healing.

Greeks who sought physical healing at Asclepian temples were expressing a longing for a god who cared about both their bodies and their souls. No wonder many of these temples were later transformed into Christian churches in the Greek world. The legend of Asclepius includes his two daughters Hygeia and Panacea who have long represented prevention and cure while his wife Epione was the patron saint for those in pain. Hygeia represented the principles of prevention, sanitation and nutrition and the general prescriptions for healthy living. Unfortunately, western medicine has identified with active intervention methods like surgery and drugs promoted by the Greek fathers of medicine.[12]

There were many schools that taught medicine. These ancient doctors possessed no legally recognized professional qualifications. They were in competition with the midwives, herbalists, and drug sellers. The school of Hippocrates was in the city of Cos and was known for its ethical ideals of compassionate discretion. Hippocrates' body of work, called his "Corpus," is evidently the work of a large number of medical writers. The Corpus contains practical manuals, lectures, and actual text books for medicine, pathology, surgery, and treatment. Although medical schools did not espouse one theory as to the cause of diseases, there was agreement on the naming of the known diseases.[13] Examples include diseases such as nephritis, hepatitis, pluritis, and arthritis—all names that most people today recognize.

Hippocrates gave instructions to those who tended the sick including directions regarding the spiritual well-being of the patient to "do no harm." Many of his prescriptions included hands-on therapies that we would today identify as "nursing" care. For instance, he recommended cold sponging for high temperatures and hot gargles for acute tonsillitis.[14]

It was the Greeks who developed the notion of the dichotomy of mind and body. The mind-soul was thought to be trapped in the

[12]Jeanne Acterburg, *Woman As Healer,* p. 30.

[13]Geoffrey Lloyd, *Hippocratic Writings*

grosser body, which was considered non-essential. This later developed into Gnosticism, in which healing of the body was viewed as unimportant.

The Hebrew's were not unlike the Greeks in one behavior—they all shunned those afflicted with disease. While the Greeks interpreted someone's illness as an affliction of the gods, the Hebrews called it punishment for sin sent by Yahweh.

As the ancient peoples traveled, traded, and intermingled, they influenced one another's cultures, beliefs, and healing practices. These influences from the Greeks, Egyptians, Babylonians, Chaldeans, Persians, and others, helped shape Hebrew healing and later became the foundation for Christian healing practices.

What about the Romans—did they fair any better? According to ancient Roman historians, there was little regard for medicine or its practitioners. Pliny writing in the first century AD, claimed that Rome had been without physicians for six hundred years. The male heads of families were expected to see to their sick family members. Roman women did have a degree of prestige and freedom however. They were allowed to practice in the professions. In the first centuries AD, many practiced a full range of therapeutics and midwifery. Most of the women who practiced the healing arts were aristocrats. By the time of Galen in the second century AD, more men were interested in medicine and the roles of women declined—taking care of the castoffs and those who could not afford to pay. Galen, the last of the fathers of medicine, wrote over five hundred books that remained unchallenged until the seventeenth century.[15]

Healing in the New Testament

Jesus as Healer

Jesus entered his ministry after his empowerment through baptism into the Spirit. He was totally submerged in the Spirit and

[14]Sister Mary Elizabeth O'Brien, *Spirituality in Nursing, Standing on Holy Ground*, p. 23.

[15]Jeanne Acterburg, *Woman As Healer*, p. 36.

afterwards began his preaching and teaching with what the Gospel writers described as "a new authority in his voice." The people were astonished because his teaching was not like that of the scribes. Jesus' authority was based on direct experience, on intuitive knowing, instead of an intellectual conceptualization. He was so powerful that his very presence was enough to stir the hearts of many. His words compelled his listeners to change their lives. Some left everything behind to follow him. He did more than teach—he healed physical and mental ills. This was the mark of a true prophet. Wherever he went, he was besieged by those who wanted to be healed. For Jesus, healing was a manifestation of God's great love and compassion for all of us. Had Jesus believed that illness and suffering were sent from God for our good, he would never have intervened in God's process. Thus, it is obvious that he did not subscribe to this belief—even if we are tempted to do so at times.

By the time the stories about Jesus were actually written down (by most accounts at least forty years after the crucifixion), they had been told countless times, probably with some embellishment and changing of facts. This point is accepted by the majority of New Testament scholars. According to Tom Harpur, however, the accounts in the Gospel of Mark of Jesus healing the sick and driving out the demonic forces are too primitive and too pervasive not to have their roots in actuality.[16] In addition, we know from John that many other stories could have been told as well, but were not written down.

[16]Tom Harpur, *For Christ's Sake*, p. 81.

"But there are also many other things that Jesus did; if every one of them were written down, I suppose that the world itself could not contain the books that would be written." John 21:25

"Go and tell John what you have seen and heard: the blind regain their sight, the lame walk, lepers are cleansed, the deaf hear, the dead are raised, the poor have the good news proclaimed to them." Luke 7:22

Early in Jesus' ministry, John's disciples came to him with the question, "Are you the one?" When Jesus answered, he did not say, "Yes, I'm the one you have set your hopes on." Rather, he pointed to the prophesy of Isaiah. All those listening recognized the importance of his words and their hearts burned within them. They were an oppressed people, subject to the Romans. By walking from town to town and healing, Jesus gave messages of hope to all who heard him. He was letting them know that these were the signs that the "Reign of God" had begun. God's people were being healed.

One fifth of the content of the Gospels is about Jesus' healing ministry. There are 41 distinct instances of physical and mental healings recorded in the four Gospels. Some of these are retold in several Gospels, so there are 72 accounts in all. Some of the accounts are about healing large numbers of people at one time; others describe individual healing or healing at a distance. Jesus taught his disciples to heal and empowered them to go out and carry out his ministry. Even from a brief look at the Scriptures, it is obvious that Jesus expected his disciples to continue his work.

It is striking to see that in all three of the synoptic Gospels the "call" to ministry for the Apostles and the disciples included healing. It was the mark whereby Jesus' followers would be known. Spiritual writers through the centuries have also connected the work of healing to a call from God. Many, however, defined that call so narrowly that few qualified in their eyes as "called by God." However, we now realize that we are all called into healing ourselves, and in various degrees, into healing our neighbor.

How Did Jesus Heal?

Jesus healed by the power of God. Connecting with God, he was able to release the fire and energy of God in the form of healing. He employed various healing methods, selecting whatever was most effective for the individual or the situation before him. He did not always heal the same way and therefore did not leave us a formula of how to go about it. He healed through his very presence, through love, word, touch, faith, and what Dr. Dale Matthews calls the ancient medicine of "saliva." There are healing properties in one's spit, he tells us, which was probably a well known fact to the people of that day. Jesus' most common means of healing though was by speaking words and touching the person with his hand. When he saw a need, he healed from a compassionate heart.[17]

Compassion means to know suffering together with another. Jesus so loved that he healed. When confronted with individuals who had been caught in "sin," his attitude was one of compassion as he healed and restored them to the community. Jesus looked into the

See Appendix B for a listing of the New Testament Healings.

"He sent them out to proclaim the kingdom of God and to heal." Luke 9:1-6

He told them to "cure the sick, raise the dead, cleanse the lepers, cast out demons." Matt. 10:5-10

"He called the twelve and began to send them out two by two and gave them authority over the unclean spirits...They cast out many demons, and anointed with oil many who were sick and cured them." Mark 6:7-13

[17]Dale Matthews, *The Faith Factor*, p. 241.

person's very soul, into their heart, and brought wholeness and healing.

Nowhere in the Gospels do we find Jesus asking anyone what they had done wrong before healing them. Instead, he responded with compassion and met their need. Rev. Lawrence Althouse observed that we do not see Jesus judging whether someone was worthy of healing. Personal worth was never a factor in Jesus' ministry. Jesus did not believe that God intended for a person to be ill in order to grow in faith, patience, or any other virtue. He did not subscribe to the belief that suffering is good for you. If he had, he wouldn't have healed people.[18]

The Healing Touch of Jesus

Jesus often touched others, and people likewise liked to touch Jesus. Ron Roth, a modern-day mystic and healer, explains that Jesus had reached such a state of perfect communion with God that merely being in his presence and being open to God's grace could heal a person.[19]

Nearly one half of all the recorded healings in the Gospels involve touching. Jesus held children, washed feet, touched blind eyes and deaf ears, crippled limbs, dead bodies. He touched men and he touched women. Most shocking of all, he touched the untouchables, the lepers. He even allowed notorious women to touch him and to anoint him.[20]

He was known for breaking all the rules and for putting human need above the law. As one might imagine, this angered the ones who upheld the rules. They accused him of healing by the power of Beelzebul, the Prince of Darkness. Obviously, this was as absurd to Jesus as it was to his followers. As we know, Jesus worked in God's light, so how could he heal from darkness?

The Gospels tell us that Jesus' opponents were most angered at his repeated healings on the Sabbath. He probably could have waited until the next day, but being totally present to the need before him, it mattered little to him what day it was.

[18]Lawrence W. Althouse, *Rediscovering The Gift of Healing*, p. 12.

[19]Ron Roth, *The Healing Path of Prayer, A Modern Mystic's Guide to Spiritual Power*, p. 29.

"All in the crowd were trying to touch him, for power came out from him and healed all of them." Luke 6:19

[20]Flora Litt gives an excellent chapter about how Jesus touched others in Graham, Litt, and Irwin's book, *Healing From the Heart*, Chapter 2, pp.25-40.

"If I cast out demons by Beelzebul, by whom do your own exorcists' cast them out? Therefore they will be your judges. But if it is by the Spirit of God that I cast out demons, then the kingdom of God has come to you." Matt. 12:27-28

Sacramental Healing

According to Morton Kelsey, Jesus' work was sacramental healing, the result of his conscious relationship with God. Through Jesus, the power of God touched the lives of people and they were made whole. God's grace entered and their lives changed as a result. This is the true meaning of sacrament, says Kelsey.[21] For the early Christians, their ordinary experiences like birth, death, and marriage became sacred events for celebrating. They created rituals for these sacred times, which later became known as sacraments. They used touch, prayer, water, and oil as the vehicles of God's divine grace.

[21]Morton Kelsey, *Healing and Christianity*, p. 67.

What is the biblical understanding of "sacrament?" Carolyn Myss describes them as "sacred ceremonies that imprint the individual with specific qualities of 'grace or Divine energy.'"[22] It is those moments when divine grace breaks into our lives and empowers us in our Christian faith. From those earliest of days, Christians recognized Baptism and the Eucharist as events of divine grace. In the years to come, many rituals were identified as "signs pertaining to things Divine, or visible forms of an invisible grace." The Greek-speaking Christians called these ritual religious experiences *mysteria,* or "mysteries." It was the Latin writers who began using the term *sacramentum,* or "sign," to describe the same thing. Any ritual that celebrated the divine saving action was a mystery or sacrament.[23] This included feast days like Easter and Pentecost, blessed ashes, and ritual washing of feet. Centuries later, there were as many as thirty sacraments celebrated in some areas. Eventually, the church in the thirteenth century settled on seven sacred events as sacred rituals (sacraments). These were celebrated in Latin, a language that by this time was even poorly understood by the clergy and beyond the common person's understanding. The Reformation of the 1500s, challenged much of Catholic sacramentality. Most Protestants in the reformed tradition kept only two sacraments, baptism and communion because they are clearly mentioned in Scripture.[24]

[22]Carolyn Myss, *Anatomy of the Spirit, The Seven Stages of Power and Healing,* p. 70.

[23]Paul J. Achtemeier, editor, *Harper's Bible Dictionary*

The sacraments continued as special events in everyone's life that merited celebration by the whole community. It was at these

[24]Greg Dues, *Catholic Customs and Traditions*, p. 150.

"Now there was a woman who had been suffering from hemorrhages for twelve years; and though she had spent all she had on physicians, no one could cure her. She came up behind him and touched the fringe of his clothes, and immediately her hemorrhage stopped. Then Jesus asked, "Who touched me?" When all denied it, Peter said, "Master, the crowds surround you and press in on you." But Jesus said "Someone touched me; for I noticed that power had gone out from me." When the woman saw that she could not remain hidden, she came trembling; and falling down before him she declared in the presence of all the people why she had touched him, and how she had been immediately healed. He said to her, "Daughter, your faith has made you well; go in peace." Luke 8:43-48

times that God healed both individuals and the community through the most ordinary means—touch, prayer, water, and oil.

Some Healing Stories

The Woman with a Hemorrhage

There are a number of healings described in the Gospels where Jesus does not touch the person at all. My favorite healing story is about a woman who touched his garments. We don't know her name but we know intimate details about her life particularly that she suffered from a hemorrhage for many years. She was convinced that if she could merely touch Jesus' clothes as he passed by, she would be made whole. When she did touch him, she "knew" that the bleeding had indeed stopped. Knowing the background to this story will help us understand her courage.

In Jewish society, the Law laid out appropriate behavior. A menstruating woman was considered "unclean" and therefore had to stay indoors during her bleeding time. This was not a punishment for uncleanness but was meant to be a time of introspection and self review. In reality such a menstruating woman could not go to the market place or even step outside her door. Family members were supposed to take care of any outside activities for her. This would have been an enormous inconvenience for the family since the woman in the story was bleeding for twelve years. If this woman were to risk going out into public places, it meant she was breaking the law, an act which called for stoning. Her kinsfolk and neighbors would be breaking the law if they did not pick up a stone to throw at her.

Now, Jesus was aware that something had happened when she touched him. According to Tom Harpur, the Greek text states:

"that having realized within himself that energy (power) had flowed out of him, Jesus turned around and asked those immediately following, 'Who touched me?'" [25] Luke 8:46

The disciples could hardly believe that Jesus would ask such a thing since the crowd was pressing all around him. We can imagine the disciples' exasperation when Jesus wanted to know who "touched him." The woman, knowing that she had been found out, acknowledged that she was the one. Jesus spoke to her saying

"Daughter your faith has made you whole. Go into peace and be whole from your plague." Luke 8:48

Jesus was aware when energy or power went out from him—even when his back was turned. Ron Roth says that Jesus was in such perfect communion with God that by simply being in his presence, one could be healed.[26] In the Healing Touch Spiritual Ministry program we would refer to this as the "electromagnetic energy" of the Spirit of God operating in Jesus. When the woman touched him, this energy passed directly through his clothes to her. Jesus served as the conduit through whom God's healing energy was able to move unimpeded.

Healing the Blind

Sometimes Jesus made use of spittle (saliva mixed with dirt), which as already noted, was believed to have healing or sacred power not only by healers of that time but also by many aboriginal peoples today. On one occasion, he mixed it with dirt to form a paste and rubbed it into the eyes of a blind man. He seemed to understand when these external measures were necessary. Presumably, he did not need to touch at all. In one particular case, Mark records that the healing occurred in stages rather than instantaneously. Upon administering the spittle and the laying-on of hands, Jesus asked the blind man if he could see anything yet. He replied, "I can see people that look like walking trees." At that point, Jesus laid his hands on his eyes a second time and then had him look up. This time, his sight was restored and he could see everything quite clearly. In comparing this case with the case of the blind man Bartimaeus, we see that Jesus used none of these ways to heal him. When Bartimaeus asked for his sight to be restored, Jesus replied:

[25]Tom Harpur, *The Uncommon Touch,* p. 56.

[26]Ron Roth, *The Healing Path of Prayer, A Modern Mystic's Guide to Spiritual Power,* p. 197.

"Some people brought a blind man to him and begged him to touch him. He took the blind man by the hand and led him out of the village; and when he had put saliva on his eyes and laid his hands on him, he asked him, "Can you see anything?" And the man looked up and said, "I can see people, but they look like trees walking." Then Jesus laid his hands on his eyes again; and he looked intently and his sight was restored, and he saw everything clearly. Then he sent him away to his home, saying, "Do not even go into the village." Mark 8:22-26

"Call him here.' And they called the blind man, saying to him: "Take heart; get up, he is calling you." So throwing off his cloak, he sprang up and came to Jesus. Then Jesus said to him, "What do you want me to do for you?" The blind man said to him, "My teacher, let me see again." Jesus said to him, "Go, your faith has made you well." Immediately he regained his sight and followed him on the way." Mark 10:49-52

"A leper came to him begging him, and kneeling he said to him, "If you choose, you can make me clean." Moved with pity, Jesus stretched out his hand and touched him, and said to him, "I do choose. Be made clean!" Immediately the leprosy left him, and he was made clean. After sternly warning him he sent him away at once, saying to him, "See that you say nothing to anyone, but go show yourself to the priest, and offer for your cleansing what Moses commanded, as a testimony to them." But he went out and began to proclaim it freely, and to spread the word, so that Jesus could no longer go into a town openly, but stayed out in the country, and people came to him from every quarter." Mark 1:40-45

"'Go on your way; your faith has made you whole.' And immediately he saw, and he followed Jesus along the road." Mark 10:52

In Bartimaeus' case, Jesus didn't feel the need to use the laying-on of hands. Bartimaeus was ready and the healing took place.

Healing the Lepers

In the story that Mark tells, a single leper came begging to Jesus. He knelt before him and gave Jesus a choice. "If you choose, you can make me clean." Mark goes on to say that Jesus was moved with compassion and he did the compassionate thing and touched him, saying—

"I do choose. Be made clean!" Mark 1:41

Several things are important here. At that time, any skin disorder, even psoriasis and eczema, qualified as leprosy. Lepers were constrained by the law to stay apart from the rest of society. They were to wear torn clothing, not tie their hair back and they were to cover their upper lip with their hand and cry "unclean" to all those around them. This enabled others to get out of their way and sparked many a rock-throwing at the helpless lepers. Society was most cruel towards this affliction since it was the common belief that leprosy was somehow "catching" even with the most casual of contact.

In choosing to have pity on this poor person, Jesus broke the taboos. He touched an untouchable. This alone would have caused grave scandal. The story goes on that Jesus sent him to the priest to make the required offering for his cleansing and asked him to keep quiet about this whole event. The man was probably so delirious about the lifting of this curse that he told everyone. This actually had an unexpectedly positive effect on Jesus' ministry. He was no longer able to walk freely in the town, so, he stayed outside, probably on a hillside, and people came from every quarter to see him and hear his words. Here in the open air his teachings could be heard by larger crowds than in the town. By touching the leper, Jesus modeled again that healing does not have to stay within social constraints.

Healing at a Distance

There was a Roman centurion who was kind to the Jewish people and even built a synagogue for them. When his favorite servant became gravely ill, he sought the aid of Jesus, whom he had heard was a Jewish healer. He did not call upon Jesus himself, either because he was a busy man or because it was not the socially acceptable thing to do so, or because he was aware that, as a pagan, he could not presume to call upon this famous healer himself. In any case, he sent some of the Jewish elders to speak on his behalf, asking for healing for this special servant. Jesus' immediate response was to go right then to cure his servant. The centurion astounded him with yet another message, this time from his closest friends. There was no need to come to his house since he was unworthy of Jesus' presence. He had great faith that Jesus was a man of authority and could just say the word and his servant would be restored to health. Jesus was utterly amazed and commented to all those around him that he had not found such faith in Israel.

There are a number of things going on in this story. First it is a story about a powerful man's love for his servant and how he would even ask for help from the people he ruled. This centurion knew about power for he used it wisely in doing his job. He did it so well that the people he ruled actually loved him. Jesus recognized this man's integrity, his leadership, and his understanding of how power (energy) works, and granted his request. Jesus showed us that distance of time and space is not a barrier unless we make it so. God's healing grace is not linear. Healing at a distance is what we have come to know as intercessory prayer.

Expelling Demons

We observe that Jesus took every opportunity to expel demons, which he felt were the cause of both mental and physical illnesses. The prevailing Judaic belief at that time was still that God punished sin with affliction and that it was God who was therefore the source of illness. However, many (including Jesus) also believed in unclean spirits roaming the world, wrecking havoc with God's people. Jesus

There are two versions of healing the centurion's servant. In Matt. 8:5-13, the centurion comes to Jesus himself; in Luke 7:2-10, the centurion first sends Jewish elders to speak for him, then later he sends friends to tell the master not to come to his house but only say the words.

"Just then there was in their synagogue a man with an unclean spirit, and he cried out, "What have you to do with us, Jesus of Nazareth? Have you come to destroy us? I know who you are, the Holy One of God." But Jesus rebuked him, saying "Be silent, and come out of him!" And the unclean spirit, convulsing him and crying with a loud voice, came out of him." Mark 1:23-27

"For he had cured many, so that all who had diseases pressed upon him to touch him. Whenever the unclean spirits saw him, they fell down before him and shouted, "You are the Son of God!" But he sternly ordered them not to make him known." Mark 3: 10-12

[27]Morton Kelsey, *Healing & Christianity*, p. 75.

"And ought not this woman, a daughter of Abraham whom Satan bound for eighteen long years, be set free from this bondage on the Sabbath day?" When he said this, all his opponents were put to shame; and the entire crowd was rejoicing at all the wonderful things that he was doing." Luke 13: 16-17

"The one who believes in me will also do the works that I do and in fact, will do greater works than these, because I am going to the Father." John 14:12

went around rebuking these unclean spirits and freeing the captives who were possessed. He even did these actions on the Sabbath, proving again that his compassion was greater than the law. To Jesus, God was not the source of illness and took no joy in seeing human beings suffer.

Morton Kelsey says that Jesus believed the primary cause of sickness was an evil force loose in the world that was hostile to God.[27] Relieving suffering was restoring the individual to wholeness and to God. Once, Jesus told a group that he had come not for the well but for those who were sick. He literally "hung out" with the sinful, proving that holiness was not a prerequisite for healing. He kept company with prostitutes, thieves, tax collectors, and those considered by our society to be the "lowest of life." He never asked whether someone had repented of their sins before he healed them. Only afterwards, when they had been restored, did he ask them to sin no more. For Jesus, illnesses of every kind kept human beings from their fullest human potential and healing restored them to God's grace.

Healing in the Early Church

Jesus gathered followers—first the twelve, then the seventy—and he taught them daily about God, about life, and about how to relieve suffering. We can imagine what it must have been like to be daily with the Master who made their hearts burn within. They went from village to village, traveling by foot. This gave them many opportunities to engage Jesus in discussions that challenged and stretched their faith. All of the Gospel writers tell us that many more stories could be told about how Jesus healed. His disciples were with him day and night except for the times when Jesus would go off alone to be with God in prayer. When Jesus felt the disciples were ready, he sent them out with clear instructions on what to heal and how to do it. Just imagine what those debriefings must have been like as his followers returned to tell their stories. Jesus was giving them actual hands-on experience to reinforce his teachings. When he was no longer with them they would be strong enough to carry on the healing work.

There is no indication in the Scriptures that Jesus only did healings to catch people's attention or that healing was only something for his first disciples to carry out. He modeled a ministry of healing touch and commissioned his followers to go and do likewise. He told them they would do even greater works. Sadly, we have not understood these words of Jesus nor have we understood that Christian healing is part of being a follower of Jesus.

The Women Disciples

We tend to forget that there were women among the disciples whom all the Gospel writers list by name. They make special mention of these women who provided out of their own pockets for Jesus and the other disciples. Nowhere in the Gospel does it say Jesus went without food or shelter. He was able to carry on his work thanks, in part, to the efforts of these faithful women disciples who did not run away. Jesus did not discriminate between the roles of men and women. Both appear to be equally important in the Kingdom.

The texts clearly say the women "followed him," that is, were his disciples throughout his ministry. Following and serving are both expressions that describe the life of the disciple. Discipleship involves a change in one's living situation—those who traveled with Jesus, abandoned home, family, property and security. Ingred Maisch points out that the consequence of this radical abandonment and letting-go within the community of disciples was the *equality of all.*[28] Service then was practiced by all disciples—male and female and included proclamation of the word, healing the sick and the offer of divine peace. Women were acknowledged to have been given the spirit of prophecy by Luke and were valued in the mission work of the church. Paul mentions by name, Mary, Tryphena, Tryphosa, Perses, Apphia and many others who labored for the Lord. What is most interesting is that many of the "gospels" eliminated by the church extolled the roles of women and the divine feminine. Acterburg's research shows that women healers of the period reflected the early

"There were also women looking on from a distance; among them were Mary Magdalene, and Mary the mother of James the younger and of Joses, and Salome. These used to follow him and provided for him when he was in Galilee; and there were many other women who had come up with him to Jerusalem." Mark 15:40-41

"The twelve were with him, as well as some women who had been cured of evil spirits and infirmities: Mary, called Magdalene, from whom seven demons had gone out, and Joanna, the wife of Herod's steward Chuza, and Susanna, and many others, who provided for them out of their resources." Luke 8:1-3

"Many women were also there, looking on from a distance; they had followed Jesus from Galilee and had provided for him. Among them were Mary Magdalene, and Mary the mother of James and Joseph, and the mother of the sons of Zebedee." Matt. 27: 55-56

[28]Ingrid Maisch, *Mary Magdalene, The Image of a Woman Through the Centuries*, p. 9.

"In the last days it will be, God declares, that I will pour out my Spirit upon all flesh, and your sons and your daughters shall prophesy." Acts 2:17.

Romans 16:6, 12.
Philemon vs. 2

religious teachings of the church—that Christian love was manifested in caring for the physical and spiritual needs of everyone.[29]

Christian Community Healing

Prior to Pentecost, the disciples performed healing miracles even though they did not understand Jesus' words about his coming death and resurrection. Once they came to know and believe in Jesus, they were able to access the power and love of God. They were changed personally. When the pouring out of the Spirit came at Pentecost, it was an event of great power and fire. All four Gospels relate that the coming of the Spirit was like the sound of wind—actually, the sound of an immense amount of energy. The Spirit descended in the form of flames (powerful energy) and then it transformed all those present. Immediately, they went out to preach to those they had been afraid of just the day before. We are told that "awe came upon every one"—they were powerfully transformed by this experience and strengthened to carry out Jesus' mission.

As the little community of followers increased, the Christian leaders in turn empowered others to act with compassion to those who were suffering in any way. They had learned that the source of all healing is God, and they were to be instruments through which God would then manifest wholeness and healing.

In his letter to the early Church, James stated that Christian healing is not a special gift only for a few. Rather, it is a gift freely given to the whole community, which means it is entirely within our capabilities. For centuries the church interpreted the meaning of James's writing as "the act of saving a person from spiritual death." Kelsey, however, states that modern studies on the original Greek text reveal that the words in Greek mean healed, cured, and saved from illness or death.[30]

We have lost the meaning of Christian healing through the centuries, but now Christian churches of many denominations have begun to return to anointing and the laying-on of hands exhorted by James to the early Church. The same Spirit who empowered Jesus

[29]Jeanne Acterburg, *Woman As Healer,* p. 39.

"Awe came upon everyone, because many wonders and signs were being done by the apostles...day by day the Lord added to their number those who were being saved." Acts 2:43,47

"If anyone among you is ill, let him call in the elders of the church and they must anoint him with oil in the name of the Lord and pray over him. The prayer of faith will save the sick man and the Lord will raise him up again; and if he has committed any sins, he will be forgiven. So confess your sins to one another, and pray for one another, and this will cure you." James 5:14-16

[30]Morton Kelsey, *Healing & Christianity,* p. 92.

in his healing ministry was now acting and working through the ministry of Peter, Stephen, Paul, Mary Magdalene, and the entire Christian community. The apostles and disciples were healing just as Jesus did, according to the Book of Acts. The source of healing energy, both for Jesus and the Apostles, was unequivocally God. Jesus was filled with God's Spirit, and the early Christians who were healing in his name were likewise filled with the very same Spirit.

Dr. Kenneth Bakken and Kathleen Hofeller describe the Church as a strong and vital healing community during those first hundred years. Healing was a natural and integral part of the work and the lives of Christians, which was a sign to them that the kingdom of God was surely at hand. It is no wonder that thousands flocked to this new religious group. They came not just for personal healing but because their hearts burned within them as they came in contact with the followers of Christ.[31]

Jesus' word and ministry were about healing bodies and spirits, about wholeness, forgiveness, new life, and touching others from a compassionate heart. Jesus healed with compassion, as did the early Christians. As healers, they were the conduits of healing for the Spirit of God. They served as deacons and deaconesses in committed service. We do not see these healers stopping to question whether or not to relieve someone's illness when that action would restore the individual to God's love. Their occasional failure to heal did not stop their reaching out nor did it stop their faith in healing. They visited and nursed the sick just as the Master had modeled for them. They were especially zealous in seeking out cases of need and often brought the sick into their homes. These settings according to Mary Elizabeth O'Brien, were "precursors to modern hospitals," and were called "diakonias" associated with the diaconate work of nursing. These diakonias were called "Christrooms" suggesting a direct association with Jesus teaching: "I was a stranger and you took me in."[32]

Thich Nhat Hanh, a Buddhist priest writing about Buddhism and Christianity, observes that whenever we see someone who is loving, compassionate, mindful, caring, and understanding, we know

[31]Kenneth Bakken and Kathleen Hofeller, *The Journey Toward Wholeness*, p.14.

What other stories from Acts stir your heart toward compassion for others?

[32]Mary Elizabeth O'Brien, *Spirituality in Nursing, Standing on Holy Ground*, p. 26.

"And whoever gives even a cup of cold water to one of these little ones in the name of a disciple—truly I tell you, none of these will lose their reward." Matt. 10:42.

that the Holy Spirit is there. Those first Christians were intoxicated with the fire of the Spirit. They were "Christed" individuals for others, and that Spirit of God has continued to dwell in the hearts of men and women through the darkest of nights down through the ages.[33]

[33]Thich Nhat Hanh, *Living Buddha, Living Christ,* p. 24.

Chapter 2

Healing Falls Into Disfavor—and Is Lost

We turn now to the story as it unfolds in history—a story of how we lost our way, how healing fell into disfavor and healing rituals vanished from Christianity altogether. It is a story about the misuse of power and the effects of fear. And, it is a story of bright shining moments when individuals faithful to the Gospel message reached out in healing to their fellow man and woman.

Healing was a way of life for the early Christians. So how was it lost from our rituals and from our very consciousness? This chapter explores some of the events that helped shape our Christian heritage of healing. From those earliest days up to the present time, Christianity has been profoundly affected by historical events, the prevailing world view, and trends in science and philosophy. Through all of this, the Holy Spirit has continued to guide God's people in their search for wholeness, holiness, health, and healing.

The Early Foundations and the Struggle for Power

The first three centuries saw the establishment of a Christian healing community. These first Christians not only expected healing, they experienced it as part of their ordinary life. Healing was evidence of a creative spiritual power. Eager to heal, they even sought out the sick to care for them and heal them, just as they sought out the lost and morally broken to bring them to new life. Since it is God who gives health and restores life, they believed, like their Jewish forebears, that we should turn first to God, the Creator, for healing. Mental illness, which was thought to be caused by spirit possession, was so frequently brought to these Christian healers that exorcisms became a regular part of the church's ritual life. They also believed that medicine had been created by God and should be used. They established the first hospices to care for the homeless and the dying. Often, these hospices were even built on the ruins of earlier healing temples.

How did early Christians experience healing in their lives?

The threat of persecution and death for the Christian men and women healers increased as they became famous. Theodosia, Nicerato, Theckla, Cosmos, and Damien, who were all known for their Christian healing powers, were martyred. Their healing powers lived on through miracles that were reported at their shrines.[1]

In what ways did they celebrate healing in their communities?

There were others who devoted their lives to care of the sick poor. Perhaps earliest mentioned is Phoebe, a deaconess whom St. Paul mentioned in his letter to the Romans. We know that she was a woman of some social status and that she spent many hours caring for the sick in their homes. There were others like St. Paula, who founded the first hospice for pilgrims in Bethlehem. She also built hospices along the roads to cities. She personally nursed the sick for many years. St. Marcella founded a community of women whose primary concern was the care of the sick. St. Helena, the mother of

[1]Jeanne Achterberg, *Woman As Healer*, p. 39.

I commend to you our sister Phoebe, a deacon of the church at Cenchreae, so that you may welcome her in the Lord as is fitting for the saints, and help her in whatever she may require from you, for she has been a benefactor of many and of myself as well. Romans 16:1-2

[2] Sister Mary Elizabeth O'Brien, *Spirituality in Nursing, Standing on Holy Ground*, p. 26.

Constantine the Emperor, devoted her life to care of the sick poor after her conversion to Christianity. All of these valiant women followed Jesus' exhortation to give "a cup of cold water" in His name. Healing the sick seemed to be their passionate call to serve humanity.[2]

We begin to see within those first 200 years of the Christian experience differences of opinion develop about the role of healing among Christians. Some saw healing as natural Christian behavior, while others thought that it was only to be used to prove to heretics that Jesus was God. Even in those early years, a need for "conformity" in thought and action was taking root. Decision-making for the whole community was set down in a patriarchal fashion that mirrored their patriarchal society.

In the year 313 C.E. an event occurred that shaped the future of the developing Christian church. Emperor Constantine granted religious freedom to the Christians and essentially made Christianity the state religion. Suddenly, it was not safe to be a non-Christian because of the threat of persecution. As a result, the church was flooded with nominal Christians. These new Christians were not very interested in participating in Christian community, which was generally a healing community. As time went by, healing became more and more formally associated with the developing liturgy of the church and moved away from individual practice in ordinary Christian life. The baptismal rite, Eucharist, and blessed healing oil were already considered agents of healing and were used in the church's rituals. Christians began looking only to the sacraments for healing in body and spirit. They developed special church services in which the laying-on of hands and anointing with oil could be used. In some cases, Christian healers would instruct the sick to return every week to these services for prayers and anointing until they were healed.[3]

It was also Constantine who decided to eliminate any copies of "gospels" he personally did not approve. Many of the gospels that espoused what we might consider a more feminine approach to theology were deemed heretical and efforts were made to obliterate

How did the influx of half-hearted Christians affect the role of healing in Christianity?

[3] Avery Brooke, *Healing in the Landscape of Prayer*, p. 17.

any trace. That is why so few copies survived hidden away in the dry desert in earthenware jars.

Greek Philosophy Influences Christian Thought

By the time of St. Augustine of Hippo, an extremely influential bishop in the fourth and fifth centuries, there were fewer accounts of miraculous healings from the various Christian communities. Initially, Augustine expressed doubt in his writings that much healing still occurred. He changed his mind later, however, when a young man and his twin sister were both healed of epilepsy. This healing impressed Augustine deeply enough for him to investigate the occurrences of healing in his churches. Eventually he was led to retract his earlier writings, but since they had already influenced his followers, few people ever saw his *Retractions (Revisions)*.[4]

Augustine's early writings have formed much of the basis of church doctrine to this very day. He taught that God sent affliction not so much as punishment—as the Jewish people believed—but rather to purify the souls of men and women. Physical suffering was accepted as necessary to the attainment of spiritual perfection. This is substantiated in many New Testament writings. Augustine's beliefs were greatly shaped by Greek philosophy, particularly by the works of Plotinus. Greek thought had became extremely popular in the western world and offered a plausible understanding of body and spirit. Plotinus believed that humans are on a path toward "perfection," which will be reached when our souls achieve independence from our bodies. God could be known through the intellect, and the most important part of human beings was their soul. Interestingly, Plotinus also taught that the body was contained within the soul. The soul gave life to the body but was never united with it. This philosophy still permeates church thought to this very day.[5]

Another Greek influence on early church thought was the philosophy of Gnosticism, referred to in the previous chapter. Followers of Gnosticism held that the body was irrelevant to the all-important soul. The soul was trapped in the grosser body. The soul lives on while the body goes into the earth. For the Gnostics, the role of

St. Augustine, *The Confessions*

"It was fitting that God, for whom and through whom all things exist, in bringing many children to glory, should make the pioneer of their salvation perfect through sufferings." Hebrews 2:10

[4]Morton Kelsey, *Healing & Christianity*, p. 146.

"And if children, then heirs, heirs of God and joint heirs with Christ—if in fact, we suffer with him so that we may also be glorified with him." Romans 8:17

"By your endurance you will gain your souls." Luke 21:19

(see entire passage Luke 21:12-19)

[5]Kenneth Bakken and Kathleen Hofeller, *Journey Toward Wholeness, A Christ-Centered Approach to Health & Healing*, p. 16.

Can you identify any aspect of this Greek philosophy in your church's teachings?

healing was unnecessary. This Gnostic point of view devalued the body and had a disastrous effect on healing ministry in the church. Gnostic ascetic practices inflicted extreme punishment on the body, denying, as Morton Kelsey says, "the idea of incarnation and the ministry, death, and resurrection of Jesus."[6]

Preserving the Scriptures

A key event in early church history was the church's desire to preserve the Christian Scriptures. Many Christian communities had gospels in addition to the more popular ones attributed to Mark, Matthew, Luke, and John. Many people believed that these "non-canonical" writings also carried the revealed truth about Jesus. Some of them were quite fanciful legends, while others shed additional light on the healing stories of Jesus. Recent scholarship can now produce either whole manuscripts or fragments of at least twenty gospels due to the Nag Hammadi texts discovered in Egypt in 1945.[7]

The Scriptures were originally written in Greek on papyrus, which deteriorates after only about 50-75 years, so the "Good News" had to be constantly recopied for the next generation. Many of the original manuscripts were already in fragments or missing valuable pages by the time church scholars began to collect, select, and translate what would become the New Testament. St. Jerome, a respected biblical scholar of that day, was chosen to lead a team of scholars to translate all the accepted scriptures into the Latin Vulgate, which was the scholars' common language. No original manuscripts from the hands of the authors of the gospels existed by the time these translations occurred. Unfortunately, Jerome was not a Greek scholar, and all of the Gospels were originally written in Greek. He translated both the words "heal" and "cure" as salvo in Latin. Salvo refers to the salvation of the soul. This narrow interpretation reversed the earlier belief that God sent health and healing power, not illness. As Kelsey points out, Jerome "helped turn the church's attention away from healing, focusing it on what healing represented symbolically."[8]

[6]Morton Kelsey, *Healing & Christianity*, p. 109-110.

[7]Robert J. Miller, ed., *The Complete Gospels*, p. 4.

St. Jerome lived c.348-c.420

How has this effect continued to shape church belief about saving? Healing? Curing?

[8]Morton Kelsey, *Healing & Christianity*, p. 152.

The Beginning of Pilgrimages

Over the next few hundred years, healing played a smaller and smaller role in church life. By the seventh century, western civilization was deteriorating. Barbarian invasions plundered cities, and scattered, tortured, and murdered the people. St. Gregory the Great, leader of the Christian world, as well as most Christians of that era, regarded sickness as a discipline sent from God. Life was so miserable for the majority of people that one could only hope for a better life in heaven. Gregory taught that miracles had to be a sign of the "end times." However, he believed saints could heal and he encouraged people to remember these holy ones as "friends at court" in heaven so they might intercede for them. This teaching actually laid the foundation for pilgrimages to the burial sites, the "shrines" of the saints. Holy people were venerated since they were in heaven and could reach across the veil of this existence to assist others.

After 800 C.E. healing became pretty much the prerogative of the clergy through the dispensing of sacraments. Zach Thomas describes their hierarchical view of the world. They placed at the top, God, heaven, spirit, and man. On the bottom, one could expect to find the devil, hell, the body, and women.[9] Though women were natural healers by virtue of their roles as mother, nurturer, and midwife, they faired badly at the hands of church beliefs. Viewed as the cause of "sin" because of the literal interpretation of the Genesis account of the Garden of Eden, their healing roles shrank and they were greatly feared and oppressed. Regardless of social class, women spent most of their time tending pregnant women and nursing sick children. Jeanne Acterberg tells us that most people had access to the wise women healers whose herbs and rites were believed to be quite powerful. These healers were usually sought out in secret and only in a crisis. They worked with powerful plants and learned their trade through the oral tradition and apprenticeship.[10]

It was men who assigned healing duties to the clergy who, by this time, were all male. This was their way of bringing "order" into their chaotic world. They passed the power of healing from higher

[9]Zach Thomas, *Healing Touch, The Church's Forgotten Language,* p. 30.

The nobility had their healers in the way of physicians, but what about the poor? Who cared for the poor when they were ill?

[10]Jeanne Acterberg, *Woman As Healer,* p. 42.

levels to lower levels. The bishops and popes even conferred divine rights to kings by anointing and laying-on hands. Since the church exercised complete rights over human souls, it was thought more appropriate to put concerns for the body in the hands of physicians (men) whose guilds were emerging at the time.

Healing in the Middle Ages—The Turbulent Times

The church's understanding of healing began to be interpreted as something God meant only for Jesus and his disciples. In the Middle Ages, we see a return to Old Testament understanding of sickness, sin, and punishment. People reasoned that sickness had to be God's wrath at our human sins. God was seen as an exacting God, ready to condemn at the first infraction. With this belief system, care of the soul was much more important than care of the body. The body, after all, eventually dies and decays into the earth—where everyone believed the devil lived.

People also forgot, or it was intentionally erased from history, that some of Jesus' disciples were women and served as both priests and bishops during those first centuries. Those roles began disappearing as the prevailing societal views turned against women. Many found an outlet in Christian service. One of the best known early women healers was Fabiola, a wealthy patrician who dedicated her life to healing the sick. Jeanne Acterberg tells us that she was a lifelong friend of St. Jerome. Jerome greatly liked Fabiola and spoke highly of her and her work. But Jerome also had a low opinion of women in general. He is quoted as having said that, "woman is the gate of the devil, the path of wickedness, the sting of the serpent."[11] Oppression of women began to mount and their roles in the church shrank. Their contributions to society were wiped away and they were treated as little more than chattel by the Middle Ages.

[11]Jeanne Acterberg, *Woman As Healer,* p. 39.

Monastic Orders Became Islands of Healing

Monasticism of the fourth, fifth and sixth centuries developed out of a desire to live deeply spiritual lives away from the active world. However, caring for the sick who came to the doors of these monasteries could not be ignored. Eventually, caring for the sick became a chief focus and duty of many of these monasteries. One famous abbess in particular, was Brigid who founded a monastery at Kildare in Ireland sometime in the fifth century. Here the sick, especially the lepers were treated with charity and compassion. Brigid became known as the "patroness of healing."[12]

Two of the most famous medieval Christian hospitals outside monastic walls were the Hotel-Dieu of Lyon (542 AD) and Hotel-Dieu of Paris (650 AD). These "Houses of God" served as facilities for care of the sick, almshouses and orphanages as well as hostels for pilgrims. They were run by religious women who devoted their lives to charity.

During the Crusades, thousands of crusaders returned home injured and weak. Orders of men rose up to care for those wounded in battle. The Knights Hospitallers of St. John of Jerusalem, the Teutonic Knights and the Knights of St. Lazarus were three groups whose members were knights, priests and brothers. The Knights of St. John had a characteristic dress—a black robe with a white linen cross.

The faithful went on pilgrimage to the holy places during this period for many reasons: personal healing of body, mind, and spirit, to fulfill vows, to seek answers. Resting places, the hospices, were a part of the abbeys and mother churches of Europe and the Middle East.[13] There the monks and nuns, out of compassion, practiced the healing arts, which included surgery, laying-on of hands, the use of healing herbs, and other holistic treatments for the wayfarers traveling on pilgrimage. In an effort to separate physical healing from spiritual healing, the church council of Clermont in 1130 declared that monks could not study medicine and churchmen were prohibited from performing surgery. They were told to be healers of souls only.[14] This prohibition marked the beginning of the transformation of so-called monastic medicine into a scientific discipline that was from then on taught at the newly formed universities. This was the birth of scholastic medicine and eventually the demythologizing and the secularization of science. To further impress upon people their

[12]Sister Mary Elizabeth O'Brien, *Spirituality in Nursing, Standing on Holy Ground*, pp. 28-30.

[13]Morton Kelsey, *Healing & Christianity*, p. 165.

[14]Mary Palmquist and John Kulas, translators, *Holistic Healing by Hildegard of Bingen*, p. xv.

need for spiritual health above physical health, a doctor who dared to visit a sick person before the priest would be excommunicated. This punishment was tantamount to ostracism from the community and few dared to challenge it.

Hildegard of Bingen—Medieval Holistic Healer

Several years ago, I visited the German abbey of Hildegard of Bingen, the twelfth century abbess who has been "rediscovered" in our century as a woman of great healing power. I found an active abbey of her nuns still in existence as well as the original abbey ruins at Disbodenburg where Hildegard, the tenth child of a noble family, was given by her parents to the church as their tithe. Here among the ruins was a huge hospice where wayfarers stayed while traveling on pilgrimage. This hospice, typical of those throughout Europe, was many stories high and could accommodate hundreds of pilgrims at a time.

St. Hildegard, the beloved patron saint of Germany, was a mystic, visionary, herbalist, scientist, natural physician, composer, author, artist, and consultant to kings and popes. She was called the "Sybil of the Rhine." Heinrich Schipperges called her "the most outstanding representative of the spirit of medieval medicine."[15] To the common people, she was known far and wide as a healer. The sick who came to the abbey would be examined by Hildegard, who would then prescribe the proper diet, herbs, etc. The nuns would carry out her orders, and the sick person would stay until well enough to leave. Hildegard took very seriously the Benedictine Rule concerning the care of the sick:

> *"The primary duty of monks is to take care of the sick. The sick are, indeed, to be served as Christ himself...The abbot should exercise the greatest care that they not be neglected." Chapter 36 of the The Rule*[16]

So serious was this obligation for her that she even permitted men who were sick to come into the cloister to receive medical attention.

Wighard Strehlow and Gottfried Hertzka's, *Hildegard of Bingen's Medicine* is an easy introduction to Hildegard's medicine of healing plants, gemstones and crystals.

[15]Heinrich Schipperges, *Hildegard of Bingen, Healing and the Nature of the Cosmos*, p. 65.

[16]Quoted in *Holistic Healing* by Hildegard of Bingen, translated by Mary Palmquist and John Kulas, p. xiv.

Her two medical books were written around 1159 and called *Physica* and *Liber Composite Medicinae.* These described anatomy and physiology and the symptoms and care of illness and disease. The title of the second book was inaccurately translated for hundreds of years as *Cause et Cure* but is more properly translated in English as *Holistic Medicine.* In her writings, Hildegard took as her model Christ the physician (*medicus*) and Savior of the world (*salvator mundi*)—the dual role of Christ the healer and priest, the physician of both body and soul. Her prescriptions, medications, and treatments are in general in integral part of monastic medicine or just plain common sense. Medicines she believed were to help remove noxious humors from the body and restore it to a proper balance. In this she followed Galen's teachings which were the prevailing medical teaching up until the seventeenth century.

Palmquiest and Kulas who have translated the work comment on the growing interest in Hildegard's teachings in *Holistic Healing* which is second only to that of her visionary writings. A couple of years ago when I was in Belgium, I ran across an herb display and discovered that they were offering courses on Hildegard's medicine which was well attended by people across Europe. She truly has been "rediscovered" for our modern age and many of her recommendations regarding health and wholeness are quite solid in today's holistic approach to wellness.

Barbara Lachman, An American who has studied Hildegard's writings for over twenty years, identified the mystic's early awareness of the body-mind connection when she writes that "Hildegard reminds us that the body can be afflicted with sickness and torments only the spirit can heal."[17] She treated the whole person and was not content only with a relief of physical symptoms. Her skill as a healer and her knowledge about the medicinal use of plants, diet and attitude were remarkably well known in her life time. In fact, most Benedictine monasteries and abbeys would send representatives to her to learn her healing ways. Where did Hildegard learn these healing arts? She writes that she produced all of her works through her heavenly or spiritual vision. She did not rely on medical experience

[17]Barbara Lachman, *The Journal of Hildegard of Bingen*, p. x.

or upon traditional learning. In today's language, she "heard voices" and "channeled" all of her teachings. Her influence on health and medicine though lay hidden for centuries, carefully preserved by her nuns. Considering the beginning of the "burning times," this was probably prudent.

Through the whole period of the Middle Ages, wars were a constant interruption to the healing activities in the religious houses. Many of the abbeys fell into disuse or were destroyed by war. Hildegard founded only two abbeys. The first at Rupertsberg was destroyed in the Thirty Years War in the sixteenth century. Her second abbey, a daughter house, was located in Eibingen on the Rhine above Rüdesheim. It was destroyed by Napoleon but rebuilt in the early 1900's. It continues to this day as an active order of contemplative nuns after 900 years.

The Meaning of the Sacrament of Anointing Shifts

Sin and illness were now firmly linked in people's consciousness and God's healing compassion, revealed in Jesus Christ, seemed very distant. Liturgies and rituals aimed at healing the whole person were disappearing from Christian life.

How was healing nullified by the Council of Trent?

Anointing with oil was no longer used for healing but instead for expiating one's sins, committed through the five senses. Restrictions were placed not only on anointing but also on visiting, exorcising, and laying hands on the sick. In 1551, the Council of Trent declared that anointing (unction) was to be used only for the dying at the extreme (final) moment. With this ruling, healing essentially ceased to exist as an official rite of the Catholic church (although it has returned in recent times). This healing balm, which had been used regularly by the early Christian church, was now to be withheld until the moment of death, presumably to give the recipient a spiritual advantage. Anointing thus prepared one for the next life, which one hoped would be better than this one.[18]

[18]Zach Thomas, *Healing Touch, The Church's Forgotten Language*, p. 31.

Today we have to deal with "ethnic cleansing," which is nothing more than the determined extermination of people who think or look different. The times are not all that different.

Healing Plunges into Darkness

Not everyone could get to the abbeys where healing was practiced by the nuns and monks. When the common people became ill, they relied predominantly on the wise women who practiced folk healing. This included knowledge of child birthing, use of herbs, and other folk remedies. Women, however, were not allowed to train as physicians at the universities or join the physician guilds. They were thought inferior and any healing that occurred at their hands was therefore suspect. These women healers were eventually branded as witches having the "evil eye" and were persecuted throughout Europe. Midwives in particular suffered greatly because of their knowledge of cycles and birth and thus were thought to deal with the devil. Even herbs were thought to be a concoction from the devil. Since it was commonly believed that women were inherently inferior to men, and because of Eve's role in the Garden of Eden, their healing practices were judged to be the work of demons. Thus, there were both theoretical and scientific arguments against women practicing the healing arts. Indeed, women were blamed for all of humankind's failures.[19]

[19]Bakken & Hofeller, *The Journey Toward Wholeness, A Christ-Centered Approach to Health and Healing*, p. 30.

As healing disappeared, it was replaced by a touch that was more about politics than healing. The Inquisition and the Crusades put millions to death in the name of Christianity. Originally invoked in 1231, the Inquisition was to be a special court to curb the spread of heresy. These papal tribunals took different forms in different countries over the next few centuries, investigating and stamping out heresies ranging from witchcraft to Judaism. Judaism was considered a heresy by the Inquisition. Women healers suffered terribly in those days. Even torture was sanctioned to extract the truth from suspects. The fires in Europe raged for hundreds of years and it is said that in some villages, not a single woman was left alive. Hundreds of children were also burned as having intercourse with the devil. The church not only permitted these persecutions, but promoted them.

Pope Innocent VIII issued a key document called *Malleus maleficarum (The Hammer of Witches)* which became a step-by-step how-to manual for dealing with witches and was translated into all the languages of Europe. Crimes against women included aiding the sick, birthing babies, and caring for the dying. The wise women were accused of healing without having studied and were charged with "laying on cures!" Possession of oils and ointments as well as botanical knowledge was grounds for accusing a woman of being a witch.[20]

[20]Jeanne Achterberg, *Woman As Healer,* p. 85.

King James, who commissioned the first English translation of the Bible (The King James Version), was extremely fearful of witches. In this translation of the Bible, the word "witch" appeared in Exodus 22:18: "Thou shalt not suffer a witch to live." (In the New Revised Standard Version, it appears as "You shall not permit a female sorcerer to live.") This scriptural quote gave further justification for murdering thousands of women. Hysteria seemed to rule Europe for centuries and did not come to an end, according to Jeanne Achterberg, until the power base of governments shifted. Why such vehemence against women? Achterberg again surmises that women were a threat to power—both that of state and church.[21] Women offered remedies or used magic in times of stress and thus possessed an awesome power. Healing—even in the simplest possession of the recipe for chicken soup, is power of a very basic nature. The last recorded witch was burned in England in 1684; in America, 1692; and in Germany, 1775. It is estimated that literally millions perished in the name of Christianity with the worse atrocities happening in Germany. No wonder Hildegard's nuns hid her writings.

[21]Jeanne Achterberg, *Woman As Healer,* pp. 95-98.

In the 1300s, during this witch hysteria, Europe was further devastated by the Black Death—bubonic plague. Women were blamed for the ravages of disease as well as the changes of weather that plunged Europe into icy winters and resulted in widespread famine. It is estimated that the earth's population dropped between a third and a half because of these scourges. The theological explanation was that God had sent the plague as punishment for humanity's sins. As it happened, women survived the plague at a rate of seven times greater than men. People believed that women were surely using magic to ensure their recovery or to cause the death of men and therefore were dealt with as a witch. In addition to plague, there were the wars. The Hundred Years' War between France and England began about the same time as the Black Death. Other European countries also had battles and wars that left the countryside in ruin. The cost of maintaining armies was enormous and exacted a terrible toll on the people.

The People Continue to Believe in Miracles

Perhaps because healing was no longer an official rite of the church, an interesting phenomenon occurred. People believed in miracles wrought by the saints. They frequently went on pilgrimages to shrines, venerated relics of the saints, and wore amulets for healing. Their faith and hope was that God still cared and still had compassion on their suffering. They had little else to rely on since their religious rituals no longer included healing.[22] When I visited some of these shrines in Europe, I was amazed to find numerous glass enclosed cabinets in churches containing the skulls of the saints. Some were wrapped in silk or fine cloth. Also, there were many reliquaries containing bits of saintly bones, which were displayed for the veneration of the faithful.

All through the Middles Ages, despite the official church's stand on healing, great saints stood out as healers of the sick and the poor. Hildegard of Bingen, Clare of Assisi, Francis of Assisi, Francis Xavier, Philip Neri, Catherine of Siena, Catherine of Genoa, Vincent de Paul, Louise de Marillac, Teresa Lisieux, and many other holy men and women were beacons of light in these darkest of times. The women saints in particular ran the risk of being deemed a heretic and a witch because of their healing abilities.

[22]Avery Brooke, *Healing in the Landscape of Prayer,* p. 24.

Theology of the Importance of the Soul Becomes Solidified

If God is known primarily through intellectual activity rather than experience, where is there room for the gifts of the Spirit?

In the thirteenth century, in the midst of inquisitions, crusades, and wars, a Dominican monastic scholar in England left a lasting influence on church thought. St. Thomas Aquinas emphasized in his great *Summa Theologica (Summary of Theology)* that the soul is more important than the body. His twenty-six volumes of theological synthesis is heavily influenced by the Greek philosopher, Aristotle. Aquinas' work reinterprets Christianity in light of the cosmology of his era. He argued that one could know God solely through the intellect and rational thought. His views provoked a great deal of controversy between the fundamentalists of his day and the secularists. In the last year of his life, Aquinas was mute as a result of a vision and could only say, "All I have written is straw."

Cosmology is a philosophical study of the universe and all that is in it.

The purpose of the early Christian healing miracles, according to Aquinas, was solely to prove Jesus' teachings and to demonstrate his divinity. It was fitting for Jesus to heal, but not necessarily for us to do so. He did make an exception for the saints, whom he believed healed not necessarily out of compassion for our suffering but rather to foster knowledge of salvation. For Aquinas, the gifts of the spirit, including healing, were quite unnecessary in order to experience God. His teachings helped to solidify church doctrine on miracles, healing, the roles of women and men in the church, and the significance of sacraments.

Aquinas also dealt with the nature and purpose of the angels, which stand between God and humanity. For people in the Middle Ages, angels and spirits were commonplace. Although Aquinas believed that the angels were created by God, he thought some fell from heaven through the great sin of pride. There were good angels who did not succumb and there were bad angels who did. These good and evil angels influenced human behavior, according to Aquinas. There is a delightful discussion of Thomas Aquinas' thought on angels in a dialogue between theologian Matt Fox and scientist Rupert Sheldrake, who discuss the physics of angels.[23]

[23]Matthew Fox and Rupert Sheldrake, *The Physics of Angels, Exploring the Realm Where Science and Spirit Meet.*

The Great Reform

By the time of the Reformation in the 1500s, many healing shrines had become highly profitable for the church, and superstition had replaced faith for many. Luther and Calvin, who were among the early reformers, had witnessed many abuses that detracted from genuine faith and authentic spirituality. They eventually rejected healing along with other practices that had become corrupt, such as the selling of indulgences, blessed oils, and relics. Indulgences granted by the church were supposed to save one from purgatory or expedite the transition to heaven. Furthermore, Luther and Calvin did not support the gifts of the Spirit but instead taught that we should rely on "ordinary prayer" in caring for the sick. Faith, prayer, love, and the sacraments of baptism and Eucharist were considered far more important than miracles and healing.[24]

[24]Bakken and Hofeller, *The Journey Toward Wholeness, A Christ-Centered Approach to Health and Healing*, pp. 23-24.

The Protestant reformers believed that healing was practiced by Jesus so that ministers could later do "greater works than these" by teaching, converting, and saving people's souls. Luther wrote that Jesus healed simply to get our attention and to prove his identity to non-believers. This was known as the doctrine of dispensationalism. Since we no longer need such proof, healings were thought completely unnecessary. In his later days, Luther changed his mind about healing and even wrote a prayer service on healing. Unfortunately, his earlier opinion had already influenced his followers. The pendulum had swung totally away from healing, and not even the change of heart of one of Christianity's great reformers could stem the tide.

Calvin went one step further with his doctrine of divine providence. Everything in life is ordained by God, so why would you want to intervene in God's providence? One was "ordained by God" to suffer in this life. This theology is reminiscent of Old Testament thought. Some healing did occur among the Protestant churches, but it was met with open criticism.[25]

[25]Earle E. Cairns, *Christianity Through the Centuries, A History of the Christian Church.*

Healing Undercover

In the 1700s there was a tremendous upheaval in all of the European societies, with religion as a source of conflict. Healing, meanwhile, continued very quietly among some Protestant groups. George Fox, the founder of the Society of Friends (Quakers), wrote a *Book of Miracles,* but the manuscript was destroyed by his own followers. Fearing for their lives, they tried to erase any hint of the supernatural that could be interpreted as demonic by those outside their belief system. According to Avery Brooke, Fox's manuscript was partially reconstructed from other sources in the late 1940s.[26]

John Wesley, Anglican priest and founder of Methodism, emphasized Christian discipleship empowered by grace. He felt healing needed to include prayer. His journals describe numerous miracles of God's healing through his prayer. In one interesting account, he relates how his horse had gone lame while he was on a preaching mission. Quite naturally, he placed his hands on the horse and prayed. The horse was then able to continue carrying him on his mission. Given his understanding of healing through prayer, it seems strange that he experimented with a "machine" to heal. While living in London, he was so moved by the amount of suffering all around him that he used a new invention, a direct-current voltage generator (a battery) to heal people. He recorded many occasions where he "electrified people" and claimed to have helped thousands.[27]

Charles Yregoyen writes that Wesley was so keenly interested in the physical well-being of the poor that he organized "Visitors of the Sick." He felt that women in particular were well suited for this work, following in the path of the early church deaconesses. In 1747, he published *Primitive Physick; or an Easy and Natural Method of Curing Most Diseases.* This book was written for those who had no access to medical care. For a brief time, Wesley even dispensed medicine from his chapels in several English cities. Wesley had a special compassion for those who needed healing.[28]

[26] Avery Brooke, *Healing in the Landscape of Prayer,* p. 27.

[27] Morton Kelsey, *Healing and Christianity,* p. 184.

[28] Charles Yregoyen, Jr., John Wesley, *Holiness of Heart and Life.*

The Scientific Era and the Continued Search for Healing

With the advent of the Scientific Revolution, healing of the body and healing of the spirit were completely separated. This revolution had its roots in the work of philosophers like Rene Descartes (1596-1650), John Locke 1632-1704), and David Hume (1711-1776), whose writings promoted a new method of seeking knowledge and truth through the pursuit of empirical data and the rational, scientific method. New theories were introduced in mathematics, physics, philosophy, and theology. The goal was to be as scientifically accurate as possible.[29]

Descartes proposed the mechanistic principle that the human body is like a machine and could only be studied by analysis of its parts. Cartesian duality separated body and spirit. "I think, therefore, I am," was Descartes famous affirmation. The body belonged to science; the spirit belonged to the church. Nonetheless, scientists felt body, mind, and spirit somehow interacted, although they did not know how. Later, in the early twentieth century, the "mind" was assigned to the new science of psychiatry. By separating body (and mind) from spirit and soul, invasive procedures like biopsies could be done to the body without fear of damaging the soul. Since God and experiences of God could not be scientifically proven, religion was left out of any role in science and medicine.

These scientific principles were later applied to historical biblical criticism. Many critics analyzed the New Testament with the same methods that were being used to study the literature of ancient Greece and Rome. One result was that they "discovered" that the miracles in the Gospels were invented to inspire the faithful.

With the emphasis on science and scientific measurement, there was little use for healing touch. By Victorian times, touching was considered base, animal behavior—or, even worse, sexual behavior. As such, it was judged sinful. Better to leave what touching was necessary to the physicians.

[29]Dale Matthews, *The Faith Factor, Proof of the Healing Power of Prayer*, pp. 17-18.

How does this thinking still influence our religious beliefs and our understanding of life?

A Medical Model Is Created

This separation of body and spirit can lead to fear and mistrust. How is our present health care system still struggling under this duality?

The belief of the separation of the body from the spirit greatly influenced the modern practice of medicine and surgery, creating the "medical model." The physical body became the domain of physicians; the soul was the domain of the church. The wisdom of treating the body, mind, and spirit as an integrated whole was obscured by an insatiable appetite for scientific proof. Compassion and intuition, expressions of caring in the healing arts, were subtracted from science and medicine in this Cartesian duality. Curing became the goal, and caring was considered unnecessary for the cure.[30] Robert Keck notes that this reductionistic propensity to separate spirituality and physicality was so entrenched that it has led to the total disempowerment of our innate inner healer.[31]

[30]Jeanne Achterberg, *Woman As Healer,* pp. 100-101.

[31]Rebert Keck, *Healing as a Sacred Path,* p. 211.

The body was thought of as a machine that could be "fixed." The most sophisticated machine of the day was the clock. Using this analogy, just as a broken clock could be fixed the body could also be fixed. The physician could introduce chemicals to mimic what the body was supposed to do, or could cut out the broken part to see if the body could do without it, or (in recent times) could even replace the part.

Physicians also began the study of the mind in earnest. Zach Thomas found that Freud used to touch the forehead or hand of his patient's to encourage recall of memories. But in order to make his work as "scientific" as possible, he advised that no touching take place in Freudian analysis.[32]

[32]Zach Thomas, *Healing Touch, The Church's Forgotten Language,* p. 33.

Healing Regains Popularity

In the nineteenth century Roman Catholics again began to go on pilgrimages to healing shrines, the most famous of which is Lourdes. For Protestants, houses of healing were created by Christian healers. Avery Brooke tells one story about a German Lutheran pastor, Johann Blumhardt, who prayed over a parishioner who was mentally ill. When she recovered, the church authorities were quite alarmed and forbade his healing. After some argument, Blumhardt continued, and the sick flocked to his church. He eventually opened a house of healing in Bad Boll, which became quite famous in Europe as a place of healing. The area of Bad Boll contains hot mineral springs where people have gone for healing for thousands of years.[33]

Many religious orders (mostly female) began to spring up in the 17th, 18th and 19th centuries to care for the sick and dying as part of their mission and charism. Their members could be found nursing in the slums and battlefields, and caring for the most destitute of society. Many women saw a life of service in Catholic religious orders, lay groups like the Beguines, or the Protestant deaconesses as a viable way to live the Christian mandate.

The Beguines were founded sometime during the thirteenth century and continued for hundreds of years. Their lay movement was a constant source of irritation to clergy since they lived a common ascetic life in community like religious nuns but were not under vow.[34] Their members were single, married and widowed women who earned their living by working. They were constantly under the threat of the Inquisition for their unusual life style. There is a Beguine conclave preserved to this day in Amsterdam.

The Kaiserwerth deaconesses were founded around 1836 by a young Lutheran minister, Theodor Fliedner, to nurse the sick poor. In this period prior to Florence Nightingale, nurses who weren't nuns were generally prostitutes, alcoholics, and unseemly women. The deaconesses took vows for five years but were expected to renew these for a life time of service.[35]

It was challenging as well as dangerous to answer a call to God's service to others. Thousands of European nuns left their families and their countries to become pioneers spreading the Gospel to the New World. They came at first to minister to their own people who were seeking a new life and religious freedom. Later, they traveled with the wagon trains west to minister to the indigenous peoples.

Since America was founded on the principles of religious freedom, many sects fled Europe for the New World in order to

[33]Avery Brooke, Healing in the Landscape of Prayer, p. 28.

Compassion for the suffering became a way of life for many. Do you know of individuals or groups that today continue to offer this kind of compassionate service?

[34]Erwin Fahlbusch, editor, *The Encyclopedia of Christianity, Vol. 1, A-D.*

[35]Sister Mary Elizabeth O'Brien, *Spirituality in Nursing, Standing on Holy Ground*, pp. 43-44.

practice their beliefs. Liberty was carried in the thoughts and hearts of men and women as they sought to worship God in their own ways. Many stories describe the establishment of Christianity in America. Some of these are wonderful stories about healing. For example, Ethan Allen was healed of tuberculosis after a Methodist class leader prayed for him. As a result, he began a full-time ministry of healing for the poor. He was later influenced by the Holiness revival within the Methodist church, which taught that holiness could be reached instantaneously through the baptism of the Spirit. This "holiness movement" flowed into the Pentecostal and evangelical denominations which stressed healing, signs, wonders, and other gifts of the Spirit. These beliefs are quite active today.

The Pentecostal-charismatic movement of the twentieth century is a rich mosaic of groups who generally are in agreement on basic biblical truths. Although they may differ on key aspects of theology, they express a religion of the heart that includes healing. In fact, these groups have helped preserve hands-on healing through the ages.[36]

Florence Nightingale's Call to Nurse the Sick

For many years, Florence Nightingale struggled with what God might be calling her to do with her life. Her diary shows many references to God calling or speaking to her. In 1848, she made a ten day retreat under the guidance of an Italian nun, Madre Santa Colomba who became one of Florence's great spiritual friends. Under her direction, Florence discerned her call from God to surrender her will to God. Shortly after her thirtieth birthday, she wrote:

"Today I am 30—the age Christ began his Mission. Now no more childish things, no more vain things, no more love, no more marriage. Now Lord, let me only think of Thy will, what Thou willest me to do. O, Lord, Thy will, Thy will."[37]

For Florence, this call was to serve God's people through nursing. Hearing about the great work the Kaiserwerth deaconesses and the Daughters of Charity in Paris were doing, Florence decided to

[36]Earle E. Cairns, *Christianity Through the Centuries, A History of the Christian Church*, p. 490.

[37]"Suggestions for Thought," by Florence Nightingale, *Selections and Commentaries*, edited by Michael D. Calabria and Janet A. Macrae, p. xxvii.

spend time with both these groups to learn nursing. Pastor Fliedner himself showed Florence around his Protestant Institute which
served 100 patients and had 116 deaconesses. Before she left, Pastor Fliedner prevailed upon Miss Nightingale to write an informa-
tional piece on the institute. She agreed providing she would be
anonymous as the author. And so Florence wrote her first published
pamphlet entitled *"The Institution of Kaiserwerth on the Rhine for the
Practical Training of Deaconesses under the Direction of the Rev. Pastor
Fliedner, Embracing the Support and Care of a Hospital, Infant and In-
dustrial Schools, and a Female Penitentiary."* In this treatise, she traced
the roots of nursing to the "very first times of Christianity…for the
employment of women's powers directly in the service of God."
"Deaconess" or nurse had existed along with "deacon" in the early
church. The importance of deaconesses was widely accepted by all
divisions of Christians, she stated, and they accordingly existed, "free
from vows or cloistered cells." Clearly, Florence was establishing her
rationale for women's professional roles for the "unmarried women
and widows."[38]

She largely taught herself, however, the art of nursing through
her observation and experience. She took every opportunity to care
personally for the ill both in the public hospitals and among the
poor in the villages near her home. In her *Notes on Nursing* (1860)
she writes that healing is a lawful process, regulated by nature. It is
a manifestation of God. She advised her nurses to "discover the laws
of healing such as the need for proper nourishment, ventilation,
cleanliness, and quiet…" "Nature alone cures," she advised, "and
what nursing has to do…is to put the patient in the best condition,
for nature to act upon him." Barbara Dossey writes that her "primary motivation for nursing was spiritual, linked to training and effective administration."[39] Her gift to us of modern nursing theory and
practice flowed from her "call to action." "My meat is to do the will
of Him that sent me and to finish His work," she wrote. Nursing then
was God's call to compassionate healing of the sufferings of others.

Nightingale's nurses, along with the Irish Sisters of Mercy, were
sent by the English government in 1854 to care for the wounded sol-

[38]Barbara M. Dossey, *Florence Nightingale, Mystic, Visionary, Healer,* p. 69.

[39]Barbara M. Dossey, "Florence
Nightingale, A 19th-Century Mystic"
in *Journal of Holistic Nursing,* 16, no.
2, pp. 111-164.

ders during the Crimean War. The English people were so grateful for the work she did, that they established the Nightingale Fund to start the first non-sectarian nursing school at St. Thomas's Hospital in London. Through her untiring efforts, Florence and her nurses were able to drop the mortality rate from 42% to 2.2% in only six months. This alone would gain for her a place in human history.

Intellectual Backlash among Mainline Churches

The healing movement of the nineteenth century never took hold among mainline churches. By the early twentieth century, no major Christian church had a theology of prayer for the healing intervention of God through the gifts of the Spirit. The mainline Christian churches emphasized sin and salvation with hardly any mention of physical or spiritual healing.

If this is true, why would we continue to look for healing today?

As the years passed, the healing fervor of the nineteenth century was forgotten both by theologians and historians, much like the history of healing in the early church. Modern theologians like Bonhoeffer, Bultmann, and Barth all believed that the gospel accounts of healing were imaginative stories to strengthen the faith of the early Christian community. This approach further alienated mainline churches from the Pentecostal churches that practiced charismatic healing and the gifts of the Spirit.

Some of the women leaders in this movement include: Mary Baker Eddy, Ellen Gould White, Maria B. Woodworth-Etter, Aimee Semple McPherson and Mary Caroline (Myrtle) Fillmore.

It is interesting to note that women healers figured prominently in many of the unorthodox religious groups in America at this time. It was the women who were returning healing to the church. Christian Scientists, Seventh-Day Adventists, Mormons, Jehovah's Witnesses, Unity, and Pentecostals all had a strong interest in religious healing, and women were some of their strongest leaders.

The Revival of Healing Ministry in America

After the ravishes of two world wars, many American healers became famous all over the world for their healing and preaching abilities. Millions perished in these wars which led to soul searching and deep reflection in both Europe and America. The human spirit needed healing. People were spiritually hungry for healing of body, mind, and spirit. Pilgrimages were almost impossible after the destruction of Europe, but people gathered by the thousands to hear some of these great revivalists. Whether the healers were authentic or not, healing was again becoming popular with the masses.

Leadership for this twentieth-century healing revival passed to the Pentecostalists, many of whom had little in the way of seminary training. However, the thirst for spiritual healing is so great, that growth in these churches has continued to this day at a phenomenal rate. Pentecostal churches are today the fastest growing segment of Christianity. One gift of the Holy Spirit that came to be emphasized in Pentecostalism was "speaking in tongues." Combining the gifts of the Spirit with a healing ministry has enabled this branch of Christianity to gain national attention and increase in numbers, while more traditional churches are losing membership.[40]

Four revivalists were particularly famous for their healing abilities: William Branham, Oral Roberts, Agnes Sanford, and Kathryn Kuhlman. Branham (1909-65) was a "Holy Ghost" Baptist minister who gained fame when he healed a U.S. Congressman who had been crippled from birth. Oral Roberts (1918-) had a highly successful television ministry, founded Oral Roberts University, and established the City of Faith Medical and Research Center. He later fell into disfavor with the American public when he stated "God would call him home" if listeners did not send him millions of dollars for his medical center. Tom Harpur calls him an "embarrassment to many who call themselves Christians." His medical and research center closed for lack of patients and money.[41]

Probably the hands-on healer who has had the most influence through her writing is Agnes Sanford (1897-1980s). Brought up in China by Presbyterian missionary parents, she later married an Episcopal priest and began a healing ministry within her church in the 1940s. Her book, *The Healing Light*, records her experiences with hands-on healing. She tells about her call to this healing ministry in her autobiography, *Sealed Orders*. Both of these books are still in print, and *The Healing Light* has become an all time classic on the

William Branham, Oral Roberts, Agnes Sanford, Kathryn Kuhlman, Olga and Ambrose Worrall, and Edgar Cayce were sought after as famous healers.

[40]Avery Brooke, *Healing in the Landscape of Prayer*, p. 34.

[41]Tom Harpur, *The Uncommon Touch*, p. 30.

Agnes Sanford, *The Healing Light*.

Agnes Sanford, *Sealed Orders*.

Francis MacNutt, *Healing.*

laying on of hands. She and her husband later founded the School of Pastoral Care, offering resident conferences for clergy and their wives. One of her students, Francis MacNutt, became a popular Catholic charismatic healer as well, and established a program called Christian Healing Ministries that is active today.

Morton Kelsey, *Healing and Christianity.*

I have often quoted Morton Kelsey in telling the story of Christian healing. Rev. Kelsey, an Episcopal priest, knew Agnes Sanford. In fact, she was a member of his church where she often spoke about healing. Kelsey participated with Sanford in the church's healing ministry which included a psychological clinic as well as four healing services. In Kelsey's opinion, Sanford was a genuine healer who lived from the heart.

Kathryn Kuhlman (1907-1976) started out as an evangelist and later concentrated on a healing ministry. She would speak to thousands of people at her gatherings in Los Angeles. Her preaching soon grew into what became known as the "charismatic movement" crossing all denominations. This movement revived the practice of the laying-on of hands and spread to many churches of all denominations.

The Second Vatican Council (1962-1965), opened the windows of the Catholic Church. One of its actions was to restore the sacrament of anointing (healing of the sick) to its original meaning. No longer was it to be used just at the time of death. Rather, it was to be available for healing when the person was ill or anticipating surgery.

Other healing movements have developed in the twentieth century that are not specifically Pentecostal or charismatic. One of these is the Order of St. Luke, founded in the 1930's by two Episcopalians, Ethel Tullock Banks and John Gaynor Banks. This international ecumenical organization is made up of laity and clergy interested in Christian healing. It emphasizes the need for lay people and clergy to practice a discipline of prayer and a healing ministry.

Not all of the twentieth century healers have been authentic. With the advent of mass communication and mass entertainment, there have been charlatans ready to take advantage of the public. These false "faith healers" have played upon the uneducated, the sick, and the hopeless by selling all kinds of blessed "baubles" and prayers for money. Hollywood made a movie about these imposters called *Leap of Faith*, starring Steve Martin and Debra Winger. Even though there are faith healers who are imposters, there is still tremendous evidence that many others are true channels of God's healing energy and that many people are healed in body and spirit.

Healing in Modern Times

We live in a world that is adamant about the separation of church and state. We can understand the origins of this concept from the history we have examined. When the physician guilds were forming in the Middle Ages, they were careful to work only with the physical body and not delve into the spirit. That would have resulted in charges of heresy, punishable by torture and death. People went to the physicians when they were ill or when all their own remedies ceased to work. They certainly did not go to maintain wellness.

The human being was divided into various parts: the body belonged to the practice of medicine and later to science; the soul belonged to the church. As we have seen, many people never completely bought into this belief system, for they continued their practices of going on pilgrimages to seek healing, wearing amulets, and utilizing wise women healers. So, people throughout the ages have continued to seek other forms of healing not espoused either by their churches or their doctors.

Today there is an explosion of interest in healing and holism. Though medicine and science have made great strides in the last century, they have not been able to significantly increase our general state of health at an affordable price. In some ways, our general health has actually declined because of pollution and contamination of our food supplies and our environment. Many people are now turning to non-traditional ways of thinking about their health and well-being. Reasons for this include frustration with the healthcare system, greater education of the population, media attention, and greater spiritual awakening to a sense of wholeness.

It is as if we have emerged from a long darkness into the light as we rediscover our ability to heal from within as well as to be instruments of God's healing for others. Science and spirituality are closer now than they have ever been. We are amazed with our new-found discovery that spirit and body cannot be separated—that we are whole, and any healing must address the whole.

Theologians and spiritual writers are inquiring why healing is emerging at this time in our history. How does healing figure into our understanding of creation and our purpose in life? Physicists and scientists are making similar observations and asking how spirituality and science are interconnected. Is this the new frontier of scientific inquiry? Why now? We are all rediscovering that:

> *What affects the spirit, affects the body and the mind;*
> *What affects the body also affects the mind and the spirit;*
> *What affects the mind, has affects on the body and spirit as well.*

Where East Meets West

Bill Moyers, *Healing and the Mind.*

In 1993 Bill Moyers presented a groundbreaking PBS series on *Healing and the Mind* with a follow-up book that became a best seller. He interviewed healers from the East and from the West, seeking some understanding as to why so many Americans were seeking healing outside of "traditional" health care. From his lengthy investigation, he concluded that in the next millennium we will need a combination of Eastern and Western healing. What was so striking in his interviews with these healers was their similar understanding of the role of energy in their diverse approaches to healing.

The American public and the American Medical Association (AMA) in particular were shocked at a 1994 study published in the New England Journal of Medicine on alternative choices for healing. It reported that 34% of the American public sought "alternative" or "complementary" forms of health care, paying out of pocket for these services, and for the most part, not telling their allopathic physicians about it.[42] We have seen this behavior throughout history. People innately know what they need to maintain balance in their lives. As spiritual beings, we continue to search for wholeness in life and wholeness in our bodies and spirits.

Multiple forms of healing have sprung up around the country, many relying on the 5,000 year old knowledge from the East in their pursuit of health, holism, and healing. The AMA is not the only group to have received a wake-up call with this report. Many Christian churches are wary of anything Eastern and some are alarmed and fearful. However, when we examine many of the new forms of healing that have developed, there really isn't anything new—it is all quite ancient. There are striking similarities between healing practices from the East and Christian healing which includes the laying-on of hands, prayer and anointing.

There is much to learn from other cultures and other spiritual paths, but in the end, Christians, will weigh this knowledge with what Jesus taught. Those from the East are not the only ones to have knowledge about "energy", "energy fields," and "energy centers." We can look to the scriptures themselves, to Christian mysticism, to our understanding of the gifts of the Holy Spirit, and to the saints and holy ones who have gone before us. Here we find a rich source of knowledge with striking similarities to that of the East. This will be expanded on in later chapters.

We are beginning to address the hard questions in our churches: "How have we in the past two thousand years, been wise stewards of Jesus' healing ministry? Has that empowerment to heal been passed down from generation to generation? Are we today extending our hands in healing for one another?" When I look at our churches for evidence of healing ministries, I do take heart. Although the major churches have been reticent to embrace forms of complementary healing, many are taking a new look at healing. Individual churches within all denominations are seeing the health and wellness of their members as part of their ministry. This is particularly true as their

[42]David Eisenberg, et al. "Unconventional Medicine in the United States," *New England Journal of Medicine.*

We are now seeing churches offering courses in prayer ministry, hands-on healing such as Healing Touch, Therapeutic Touch, and Reiki, and even offering courses in stress management and parenting. Some churches are developing parish nurse programs. While the majority of these are volunteer programs, some churches are hiring nurses to "watch over" the health needs of their ailing members.

What do our Christian scriptures tell us about healing and Christian responsibility towards healing?

What is your denomination's belief about Christian healing? The gifts of the Spirit?

members are aging and have many problems that need healing in body, mind and spirit. Compassion for the suffering of others is again the driving force that enables these churches to reexamine the healing ministry of Jesus.

Final Thoughts

The Holy Spirit's healing action is alive and well in our churches, and we see the evidence springing up as Christians rediscover the healing mandate in the scriptures.

I have been in many Roman Catholic, Anglican, Episcopalian, United Church of Christ, United Methodist, Presbyterian, Lutheran, and Unity churches that have begun healing and anointing services. Many Pentecostal, Gospel, and Christian Disciple churches have led the way for this revival of healing.

Through this brief review of history, we have seen how people have always searched for health, wholeness, and healing, and, in the process, have yearned for holiness. We go to the far corners of the earth seeking these things for ourselves and our loved ones. We are eager to learn about the latest remedy, be it an herb, a treatment, a prayer, or being touched by a healer. In the end, however, all healing is self-healing. When we open our hearts to receive God's love and grace, our energy fields likewise open and healing occurs.

As practitioners, when we open to divine grace, surrender our need to control the outcome, the Spirit slips in and brings healing and holism. As instruments of God, as couriers of divine grace, we can facilitate this healing for others.

What power will be unleashed when enough of us remember the healing ministry of Jesus and take it back into our churches. Science and spirituality are coming back together. We are remembering our wholeness as human beings. And as this happens, we find Christianity is on the brink of rediscovering its biblical mandate to teach, preach, and *heal.*

CHAPTER 3

Science Investigates
the Laying-on of Hands

Richard Gerber's book, *Vibrational Medicine*, and Zach Thomas's book, *Healing Touch, The Church's Forgotten Language*, give historical contexts for the use of touch in healing.

Healing Touch Spiritual Ministry has its foundation in the laying-on of hands found in the Christian scriptures and in our Christian traditions. The use of the laying-on of hands to heal human illness actually goes back thousands of years before Christianity. Its origin is lost in antiquity, but knowledge of its benefits can be found in virtually all cultures. Evidence of the healing use of touch can be found in Egyptian papyrus dating as far back as 1552 B.C.E. The Greeks used laying-on of hands for healing in their Asclepiad temples. The writings of Aristophanes tell the story of the use of laying-on of hands in Athens to restore a blind man's sight and return fertility to a barren woman.

In the sacred scriptures we see many stories of healing through touch. Whether in the Old Testament or the New Testament, the stories challenge our faith and understanding. Our logical brains want to ask "how can healing in body, mind, soul, and spirit occur simply through touching?" We know that Jesus sometimes spoke words of healing, or touched the person before him, or did both. In Mark's final verses, Jesus said that one of the ways we will recognize his followers is that

"They will lay their hands on the sick, and they will recover." Mark 16:18.

Paul was healed of blindness when Ananias laid hands on him. The beggar at the temple gate was healed when Peter took him by the right hand and raised him up. James exhorted the community not only to pray for the sick but to anoint (touch) them with oil. The Christian community continued this tradition of touch through healing rites well into the second century, as we see in the writings of St. Irenaeus (150 C.E.) He reported that he and others "still heal the sick by laying hands on them and they are made whole."

The laying-on of hands in the early church was not just for healing. Barbara Shlemon Ryan and her co-authors, Dennis and Matt Linn, describe how touching imparted the power of the Holy Spirit to new members of the Christian community.[1] Rituals for ordaining deacons or elders also called for laying-on of hands. Paul's letter to Timothy exhorted him not to forget the gift that was given him when hands were laid upon him and warns him not to ordain others too hastily. In this letter, he conveyed the seriousness of the laying-on of hands, which was quite powerful and therefore to be done only under the direction of the Holy Spirit.

Healing with Touch

Throughout the ages, touch has been used to convey many things: love, compassion, and healing. At one time, royalty were sought for their touch. People believed healing could occur by virtue of their privileged birth. Those in power were also believed to possess a healing touch. Tom Harpur goes so far as to call "touch"

"And so Ananias went and entered the house. He laid his hands on Saul and said, 'Brother Saul, the Lord Jesus, who appeared to you on your way here has sent me so that you may regain your sight and be filled with the Holy Spirit.' And immediately something like scales fell from his eyes, and his sight was restored." Acts 9:17-18

[1]Barbara Shlemon Ryan, Dennis Linn and Matthew Linn, *To Heal As Jesus Healed*, p. 53.

"Do not neglect the gift that is in you, which was given to you in prophecy with the laying on of hands by the council of elders." Tim. 4:14

"Do not ordain anyone hastily." Tim. 5:22

a therapeutic activity. Touch serves to soothe, energize, or encourage us. He further declares that anyone can learn through focusing how to be a healer for others.[2] Jesus and his disciples touched out of a sense of compassion and healing occurred. Our focus in Healing Touch Spiritual Ministry is the compassionate therapeutic healing that occurs when we touch another with intent to heal.

What actually happens when we touch another with intent to heal? Can science help us understand what is happening when we touch in a healing way?

How we touch another and whether or not it leads to healing has long been a topic of discussion. It is well known that "not touching infants" in orphanages has had disastrous effects. The lack of human contact leads to a condition called mirasmus where the children waste away and die. Babies need holding, touching, rocking, and soothing. Human touch is as necessary as food and water.[3]

Even ordinary touch can have healing and sustaining effects upon us. Stanley Jones and Elaine Yarbrough did a study in 1985 in which they were able to identify a number of meaningful ways we communicate through touch: support, appreciation, inclusion, sexual interest, affection, playfulness, compliance, attention getting, feeling, and ritual hellos and good-byes.[4] They found that touch not only facilitates verbal communication, it also brings those communicating into closer relationship. You cannot touch and be uninvolved with the other person.

Zach Thomas, who is both minister and massage therapist, writes that just as touch can build relationships, it can also dissolve relationships. Touch can be used to abuse or misuse another.[5] We have learned that touch may not always be safe. The media frequently informs us of clergy molesting children, of trusted counselors, psychologists, and doctors taking advantage of patients, of sexual harassment in the workplace by both men and women, and of health care workers molesting the frail and defenseless. This is touch gone awry, not a healing touch. This has resulted in a sobering state of affairs for people who desire and feel called to extend compassionate

[2]Tom Harpur, *The Uncommon Touch, An Investigation of Spiritual Healing*, p. 139.

[3]Morton Kelsey, *Healing and Christianity*, p. 314.

[4]Stanley E. Jones and A. Elaine Yarbrough, "A Naturalistic Study of the Meanings of Touch," *Communications Monographs 52* (March, 1985) pp. 20, 51.

[5]Zach Thomas, *Healing Touch, The Church's Forgotten Language*, p. 42.

and therapeutic healing through touch. A healing touch is not used to control another nor to express fear, anger, or resentment.

Dr. Clyde W. Ford, a chiropractor, has written several books on the effects of touch upon the body and how touch aids the healing of body, mind, soul, and spirit. He has found that we hold persistent emotional and psychological scars of abuse within our bodies. Dr. Ford, whose work requires hands-on therapy, developed a "Safe Touch" protocol to use with people who have suffered sexual abuse. I believe his protocol is helpful for all clients regardless the type of abuse that has been suffered. It includes:

1. *Respect the physical boundaries of the person at all times.*
2. *Get permission to touch.*
3. *Remember that any area of the body can hold emotional issues.*
4. *Avoid directly touching sensitive areas.*
5. *Be aware of feelings that rise up in you as you work with another person.*[6]

[6]Clyde W. Ford, *Compassionate Touch, The Role of Human Touch in Healing and Recovery,* p. 147-149.

How we, as healers, approach a person makes all the difference. Our touch can be a determining factor in the outcome of healing.

Scientific Explorations into Touch

Scientific explanations can help us understand what is happening when we touch another with intent to heal. We can first ask, "What exactly is touched in healing work?" The answer is, the whole person: the body and the energetic field. This "field" extends anywhere from a few inches to several feet out from the body in all directions. The belief that the human body actually possesses a vibrating energetic field that surrounds and interpenetrates the body is quite ancient and is found in all cultures. In the West, our artists have depicted fields around saints and holy ones as halos. Those who have the ability to see the field say they see glowing light and sometimes colors around the body. Some people are born with this ability to see; sometimes this sight will develop with practice and spiritual discipline. Each culture may call the energetic field by different names but all have gained some glimpses of its importance.

Scientists, particularly over the past century, have sought to produce credible evidence of not only the existence of energetic fields but also their role in our health and well being.

One of the early attempts to explain what happens when someone touches with an intention to help or heal was the work of Dr. Franz Anton Mesmer in the late 1700s. It is important to remember that research in the eighteenth century was making a great effort to be scientific. Mesmer, both a physician and a scientist, noticed that magnets could sometimes affect physical as well as mental cures. During treatments, the patient would experience muscle spasms when magnets were used. From this he postulated that a sort of ethereal fluid had flowed from his own body to create subtle healing effects in the patient. The magnet was just the conductor, he thought. The real healing was coming from within the healer. He knew that this energetic force was magnetic in nature but that it was different from magnetism produced by minerals or by iron, thus he called it "animal magnetism." Later this magnetic force was called "fluidum." This fluidum filled the universe, and he thought it was the *connecting medium* between people and other living things.[7]

Mesmer tried to understand this "electromagnetic force" around living objects and how objects both affect and are affected by each other. "Fluidum" was essential, he said, for the body to function. Disharmony in the body's magnetic field allowed illness and disease to develop. In further research he discovered that the human body itself generated fluidum or magnetic energy and that it also flowed from the hands of healers. Recharging and rebalancing would restore the body to homeostasis (balance). Mesmer believed that techniques such as the laying-on of hands, practiced for centuries, could influence the course of one's health. His technique of laying-on of hands was known as "magnetic passes" and became quite popular for a time in Europe. This method resembled the same laying-on of hands used by Jesus and other religious figures. Modern methods include therapeutic touch, healing touch, Reiki and Healing Touch Spiritual Ministry.

[7]James Eden, MD, *Energetic Healing, The Merging of Ancient and Modern Medical Practices*, is an excellent resource to explore the scientific basis of the laying-on of hands healing.

Mesmer discovered that placing magnets over areas of the body afflicted with disease could affect a cure. Modern-day magnet therapy is a resurgence of this older form of healing. No researcher can yet explain why it works. Scientists in the forefront of bio-electromagnetic research have no technical rationale—yet.

In Mesmer's quest to be objective in his scientific studies, he claimed that healing could be effected without faith or belief in the outcome. He believed that a patient's faith in the healing or faith in God or even in him as the doctor would cloud his investigations. "Belief" was outside the realm of science and outside his ability to measure. There is still much discussion on this topic today, especially where the placebo effect is concerned.

Mesmer's colleagues were not impressed with his theories. They thought his magnetic passes were quackery and questioned the validity of his experiments, which they believed involved hypnosis. Since then, the term "mesmerism" has been associated with hypnosis. Mesmer was brought before a scientific panel-which included our own Benjamin Franklin—and his work was discredited. Modern studies, however, have begun to substantiate much of what Mesmer postulated. For instance, we now know that the heart's electromagnetic field can be measured several feet away from the body. The frequencies within the electromagnetic field change as our thoughts and emotions change. The Institute of HeartMath researchers have found that sincere "heartfelt" experiences bring about increased coherence in the heart's electromagnetic field. These coherent frequencies of the heart have healing power.[8] Doc Lew Childre reports from HeartMath that when one consciously tunes into "higher frequencies" (for example, shifting out of anger to forgiveness), blood pressure can be lowered and T-cell counts increased.

Today, we can point to Mesmer's work and credit him with perhaps the first plausible theoretical framework for the existence of subtle energy fields. Disharmony in the body's "magnetic field," as Mesmer termed it, can lead to illness and researchers like those at the Institute of HeartMath are producing credible evidence to support this belief.

James Oschman reports in his book, *Energy Medicine, The Scientific Basis,* that medical research is demonstrating that devices that produce pulsing magnetic fields of particular frequencies can stimulate the healing of a variety of tissues—bone, nerve, skin, capillary and

[8]G. Stroink, "Principles of Cardio-magnetism," in *Advances in Biomagnetism,* S.J. Williamson, et al., editors.

"Coherence" is an aligning of the frequencies of the heart which generates an increase in power (strength).

Doc Lew Childre, *Freeze Frame* and *Cut-Thru* are two books that describe this process.

[9]James Oschman, *Energy Medicine, The Scientific Basis*, p. xiv.

[10]James Eden, MD, *Energetic Healing, The Merging of Ancient and Modern Medical Practices*, p. 64-66.

[11]Richard Gerber, MD, *Vibrational Medicine*, writes at length about the experiments of Burr and the collaborating work of Kirlian. pp. 51-53.

[12]James Oschman, *Energy Medicine, The Scientific Basis*, p. 20.

[13]H.S. Burr and F.S.G. Northrop. Evidence for the existence of an electrodynamic field in the living organisms. *Proceedings of the National Academy of Sciences of the United States of America, Vol. 24, (1939),* pp. 284-288.

ligaments.[9] We have seen this with electrical stimulation and other devices that produce a magnetic field. It is too bad that pioneers such as Mesmer could not live to see this day!

In the early part of the twentieth century, Mesmer's theories were revisited by Wilhelm Reich, a psychiatrist and colleague of Freud. Reich introduced the concept of *orgone* or universal energy field. He thought that disturbances in the flow of this energy field or orgone resulted in physical and psychological disease. His treatment methods combined psychotherapeutic techniques based on Freudian analysis with physical techniques (touching through pressure) to release blockages of the orgone flow throughout the body.[10] He believed that he could heal mental illness by releasing energy blocks with these methods. Although Freud abandoned any touching of the patient in order to be scientific, Reich continued to use touch in his psychotherapeutic process. Like Mesmer, Reich's peers were not impressed with his research.

In the period between 1932 and 1956, Harold Burr, a researcher at Yale University, did some interesting studies of electrical fields surrounding sprouting seeds. His studies suggest that the development of an organism is determined by a "template pattern" that is in the energy field of the species. When he studied diseases in the human body, he found that many, including cancer, caused significant changes in the subtle energy field. Where disease was present, there were changes in the microvoltage levels in the tissues. Burr was one of the first to show that subtle energetic changes are linked with organ and tissue diseases. His theory was that if the disturbed energy field could be detected and restored to normal—the pathology could be prevented. Thus he was convinced through his research that the progression of disease can be reversed by restoring the energy field to normal.[11, 12, 13]

During this period when Burr was researching energy fields, most scientists were certain that energy fields and "life forces" were utter nonsense. Patients of energy practitioners were obviously duped by deception, illusion, trickery, fakery, quackery, hallucinations or the placebo effect. Healing with energy fields was considered fantasy and foolishness. Burr was way ahead of his time and laid the ground work for the scientific breakthroughs of our day.

Also in the 1940s, the Russian scientist Semyon Kirlian developed what is now called Kirlian photography, which pictures the energy field surrounding living organisms. This electrographic photography shows us the aura around living substances. It appears as a glow up to several inches or feet beyond the organism. Like Burr, Kirlian found that diseases like cancer caused significant changes in the electromagnetic fields of living organisms. These "corona discharge" images confirmed disease-associated energy-field changes. However, the weight of evidence today is still too weak and our science too inaccurate for physicians to use electrographic photography as a predictor of disease. Gerber suggests that the key that will allow researchers to view the subtle bioenergetic fields of human beings may be close at hand. With MRI scanners, we are already using energetic principles to image the inside of the body.[14]

In the late 1960s, Dr. Bernard Grad at McGill University in Montreal was quite intrigued with the therapeutic power of spiritual healers and psychic healers.

In one of his studies he worked with mice in an effort to control for the "placebo effect." Some of the mice were simply held by a spiritual healer versus a control group that were not treated (held by the healer). His data showed a significant increase in wound healing for the treated mice versus the untreated. What we don't know about this study was how the "control group" of mice were handled by their caretakers. It could be argued that the increased wound healing was simply a mind-body effect resulting from the mice being carefully handled by caring attendants.[15]

Grad did another interesting study where water held by a spiritual healer was then used for plant seeds. Only Grad knew which seeds had been given water held by the spiritual healer. The control seeds received non-held water. Again, there was significant growth for the seeds given water held by the spiritual healer in comparison

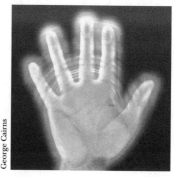

George Cairns

The term "Corona discharge" comes from the discharges observed around circular objects. It resembles the spark pattern seen in the outer corona around the sun. Depending on the film used and the electrical field generator, beautiful colors and spark patterns are observed in "aura pictures."

[14]Richard Gerber, MD, *Vibrational Medicine*, p. 53.

[15]Bernard Grad, "The Biological Effects of the 'Laying On Of Hands' on Animals and Plants: Implications for Biology," in *Parapsychology: It's Relation to Physics, Biology and Psychiatry*, ed. by G. Schmeidler.

with the control seeds. He then took this experiment a step further by making some of the seeds "sick" by soaking them in salt water to retard their growth. He then had the spiritual healer hold a sealed jar of salt water which was then used for germinating the seeds. Grad found that the seeds placed in the healer-treated saline water sprouted more often than those in the regular saline group. Grad also had depressed patients hold containers of water. The seeds that received water from the containers held by these sad patients showed a retarded rate of growth.[16]

There have been other studies, such as those done by Sister Justa Smith, that show the influence of spiritual healers. She measured the effects of the energies from healers' hands on test tubes of the enzyme trypsin. In one study, she asked both the healer and non-healers to hold test tubes of enzymes. Only the tubes held by the healer were found to have accelerated enzyme reaction rates over time. In another study, she exposed the enzyme trypsin to ultra-violet light, which damages the enzyme. Test tubes of these enzymes were then held by a spiritual healer. The results showed the enzymes regained their normal structure and became reactivated. In her studies, it appears that the healers caused changes that enhanced the activity of the enzymes.

In the 1980s, Dr. Valerie Hunt, a biophysiologist at UCLA, recorded the frequencies of low millivoltage signals from the human body during deep muscle massage sessions. During these sessions, several clairvoyants, including Rev. Rosalyn Bruyere, observed and recorded the auric colors of the person performing the massage and the person receiving. These colors were later correlated with frequency wave patterns monitored by Dr. Hunt. This study is the first to provide scientific electronic evidence of frequency, amplitude, and time components of the auric field along with the visual observations of a person who sees changes in the aura. The colors observed in the auric field correlated to specific frequency profiles of the instrumentation. Hunt's study also indicated that the human energy field changes with emotional states, with interpersonal relationships, and with other stimuli to the field. Although her research

[16]Bernard Grad, "Some Biological Effects of Laying on of Hands and Their Implications," in *Dimensions in Wholistic Healing: New Frontiers in the Treatment of the Whole Person*, ed. by Otto and Knight.

[17]Justa Smith, "The Influence on Enzyme Growth by the "Laying On of Hands," in *The Dimensions of Healing: A Symposium*.

Valerie Hunt, *Infinite Mind* describes her many experiments using Rev. Bruyere as the psychic observer.

lends support to the existence of the energy field, no one has duplicated this research to date.[18]

Also in the 1980's, Dr. John Zimmerman, at the University of Colorado School of Medicine, conducted studies that contributed to our understanding of the magnetic nature of healing energy. By using a device called the SQUID (superconducting quantum interference device), he found that there is a highly significant increase in the magnetic field emitted from the hands of healers. The magnetic field strength of healers' hands was hundreds of times stronger than background noise but was considerably weaker than "normal" magnetic fields.[19] SQIIDS are now being used in medical research laboratories around the world to map the biomagnetic fields produced by physiological processes inside the human body.[20]

Oschman sites a study conducted in Japan that confirmed an extraordinary large biomagnetic field emanating from the hands of practitioners of a variety of healing and martial arts techniques, including QiGong, yoga, meditation, Zen, etc. These fields were measured with a simple magnetometer and were far stronger than field emanation from either the heart or the brain. According to Oschman, the evidence shows that practitioners can emit powerful biomagnetic fields in the same frequency range that biomedical researchers have identified for jump starting healing of soft and hard tissue injuries.[21]

Some exciting research on the fringe of science is that of Harry Oldfield—inventor, scientists, thinker and healer. He has been conducting research for the past twenty years in London, looking into the human aura and energy fields seeking to prove their existence through science. One of his inventions is the PIP—polycontrast interference photography. These are amazing colored images of the human energy field captured by the computer. The PIP can give information about imbalances in the energy field. It can also give "echos" of past traumas or illnesses. PIP not only shows disease which is already present, it also shows us areas of the body where disease might manifest itself at a future date. Another invention of Oldfield's

[18]Valerie Hunt, "Scientific Validation of Human EM Fields," video tape, 1988.

[19]John Zimmerman, New Technologies Detect Effects of Healing Hands. *Brain/Mind Bulletin, 10, no. 16,* (Sept. 30, 1985).

[20]James L. Oshman, *Energy Medicine, The Scientific Basis,* p. 31.

[21]James L. Oshman, *Energy Medicine, The Scientific Basis,* pp.79-80.

[22]Jane and Grant Solomon, *Harry Oldfield's Invisible Universe*, p. 24.

is the EMS—electro-scanning method. It is a hand-held scanner that gives quantitative measurements of the energy field using sound and radio frequencies.[22]

Other research studies over the last 100 years collaborate what we intuitively or experientially know: that there is a human subtle energy system or human aura and that healing can occur when someone touches with the intention to heal. Researchers James and Nora Oschman believe that energy therapy and modern science are beginning to converge. Science is proving what spiritual healers have experienced. We know that, with practice, healers can sense distorted energy fields as a result of diseased or damaged tissue, and healing can be facilitated when healers use their hands to bring about a "balanced" and "coherent" field.[23] Science is now slowly providing the data for us to understand this healing phenomenon. The modern trend in research is toward explaining and validating the experiences of practitioners and recipients of energetic therapies including the religious type of "laying-on of hands." The role of spirit is not to be discounted, Oschman states.[24]

[23]James L. Oschman and Nora Oschman, "Researching Mechanisms of Energetic Therapies," *Healing Touch Newsletter, 8, no 3,* (1998).

[24]James L. Oshman, *Energy Medicine, The Scientific Basis,* p. 22

Spiritual Healing

The entire universe is made up of energy. Every time we interact with another person there is an exchange of energy. We have the expression that when we see someone in need, "our hearts go out to them." We "give away" our energy, which is only natural when we see someone in need. We allow our energy to be "attracted" to the other person, as to a magnet. We give out of our personal vitality and energy reserves. However, when the reserves are used up, we may feel depleted, tired, and weak, and our own health may be impaired. Literally, we become empty or "burned-out."

There is a better way of extending healing to those in need. In spiritual healing the practitioner attunes through meditation to the "forces of the Divine" and becomes the conduit of this higher energy for someone else's healing. It is not a transference of the healer's own energy; in fact, it is revitalizing for both the practitioner and the recipient. In a sense, the healer acts as a guide to direct higher energies to the recipient. This energetic "boost" assists in resolving present disease processes and helps the individual return to a state of balance.[25] Healing Touch Spiritual Ministry is one of several kinds of spiritual healing modalities. Others include Healing Touch, Therapeutic Touch, Reiki, Polarity, Cranial-Sacral, and many others.

I teach many classes in Healing Touch Spiritual Ministry and have witnessed the exuberance of new students for the work. I often advise the students to remember it is not their energy they are giving away. If they feel exhausted at the end of a treatment, something is not right. If we are to persevere in this work, we must learn not only self care, but also the art of "spiritual healing." Since higher energy is moving through us for the highest good of the client, the practitioners should feel better, not exhausted.

Healing through the laying-on of hands affects the etheric field, which extends two to four inches away from the body. Dr. Richard Gerber explains that this field is a "holographic energetic template." It is an exact duplicate of the physical body. When this etheric field is healthy and orderly, the body, in turn, reflects a state of health. When it is distorted and disrupted by any number of causes, the physical body will generally begin to manifest some kind of illness. The etheric field controls the flow of life energies into the body.[26] Energy therapists believe from their experience as healers that patterns of illness occur at the energetic level long before they are manifested in the physical body just as science is now proving. They can "sense" or "feel" or "see" pattern changes in the field. The laying-on of hands and other forms of energetic healing are useful in restructuring this etheric field toward a more healthy pattern. In spiritual healing, there is not only a direct energy transfer through the hands, but higher energies are also facilitated for the recipient's use. This method of healing works through all layers of the energy field as well as with the physical body.

[25]Georgina Regan and Debbie Shapiro, *The Healer's Hand Book, A Step-by-step Guide to Developing Your Latent Healing Abilities*, p. 9.

[26]Richard Gerber, MD, *Vibrational Medicine*, p. 51.

What Science Has to Offer

To gain a scientific understanding of what is happening when someone lays their hands on another with an *intention* to heal, we need to turn to physics.

Looking back, we see that the Newtonian world view from the seventeenth century became the paradigm for modern scientific thinking. Life was viewed from a perspective of mechanistic or mathematical precision. Nature was ordered and ruled by the changeless laws of God's creation. For those early scientists, God was like a mathematician.

Not until the 1800s do we see a new theory, developed by Michael Faraday and James Maxwell, called the Unified Field Theory. They viewed the universe quite differently from Newton's mechanical model. In their theory, the universe was filled with electromagnetic fields that were constantly creating and changing forces as they interacted with each other. Faraday and Maxwell's unified theory of electromagnetism enabled scientists to think mathematically about magnetism, electricity, and light. This laid the groundwork for Albert Einstein's special theory of relativity. Einstein believed that fields were nonmaterial in nature and existed as an aspect of matter. His theory considered energy and matter as one and the same and not as separate aspects of reality. Mass, space, and time were no longer separate quantities. Einstein later added a fourth-dimensional factor, which he called the space-time continuum. Time is curved by the very existence of matter in space. This concept is very important in understanding psychic phenomena or energetic (spiritual) healing. Newtonian concepts do not address this phenomenon.[27]

Einstein and German physicist Max Planck later hypothesized that matter has a dual nature—it is both waves and particles. As this quantum theory has been refined and developed, modern physicists have concluded that energetic or wave forms of matter are not similar to sound waves or the waves in water. Rather they are waves of probability or chance. The entire universe is a dynamic web of

[27]James Eden, MD, *Energetic Healing, The Merging of Ancient and Modern Medical Practices,* pp. 50-51.

Diarmuid O'Murchu, *Quantum Theology, Spiritual Implications of the New Physics,* and Larry Dossey, MD, *Recovering The Soul, A Scientific and Spiritual Search,* both examine in greater detail the explorations of science into spiritual phenomenon.

energy fields that continually flow, change, and interact. These fields are never static or disconnected.

The "Hundredth Monkey"

Rupert Sheldrake, who is both a biochemist and philosopher, developed the concept of morphogenetic fields. He observed that cells exhibit the knowledge that they are to differentiate and also know what they are suppose to be. What kind of blueprint are they following? How do they know what they are supposed to be and when? Unlike the scientists of the seventeenth century, Sheldrake believes that nature is not governed by mathematical laws but instead by habits that have grown up within nature. The more often an event occurs in nature, the deeper the habit becomes, until the event behaves as if it is governed by eternal laws. A collective memory develops over time. Sheldrake hypothesizes that this memory depends on a process he calls "morphic resonance," which is the influence of "like upon like" through space and time. If we apply this hypothesis to human behavior, it should be easier for people to learn what other people have already learned. The causative field for the whole species has been changed, ever so slightly. For example, the more people who learn to "surf the net," the easier it should become for the rest of us to learn. Many have referred to this as the "hundredth monkey" principle.[28]

This hypothesis of the "hundredth monkey" was tested by a group of researchers in England. Wayne Irwin tells us about their simple experiment using crossword puzzles. If morphic resonance is correct, then it should be easier to do yesterday's crossword puzzle today since many people have already solved it. The researchers showed statistically that it was easier to solve the puzzle the day after than the day the puzzle was printed.[29]

Understanding morphic resonance by no means denies the presence of a creative intelligence—a supermind or the mind of God. Physicists are gradually becoming aware there is purposefulness and intention even in seemingly random occurrences. There is order and degrees of order in everything, including human beings.

[28]Matthew Fox and Rupert Sheldrake, *Natural Grace, Dialogues on Creation, Darkness, and The Soul in Spirituality and Science*, p. 165.

[29]Rochelle Graham, Flora Litt and Wayne Irwin, *Healing From The Heart, A Guide to Christian Healing for Individuals and Groups*, p. 72.

A Holographic Look at Being

Physicist David Bohm, who early in his career worked with Einstein, is concerned about wholeness as the primary reality. He states that everything in the universe is connected; the universe itself is a hologram. ("Holo" means whole, "graphic" means write). Human beings are part of a seamless whole with the universe. In this sense, we are all "holons." It was philosopher-scientist Arthur Koestler who first described a holon as a whole made of its own parts, yet itself is a part of a larger whole. Everything then is part of a continuum. As living creatures, we can never be entirely independent. We are holons within a larger holon (society), dependent upon our environment. The whole universe appears as a dynamic web of inseparable energy patterns and thus can be looked upon as a dynamic inseparable whole.

All that unfolds before us is an external fragment of an underlying unbroken wholeness. With this understanding, Bohm realized that it is impossible to treat any part of the body without affecting the whole. We are not separated parts of a whole. We are a Whole. Our primary reality, he states, is the unbroken wholeness, which he calls the "implicate order." This has tremendous implications for our work in healing the whole person (body, mind, soul, and spirit) and begins to help us explain how healing can occur at a distance.

Dr. Karl Pribram, a neurosurgeon and researcher at Stanford University, applied the concept of the hologram to his study of the brain. He discovered that the human senses of sight, hearing, taste, and smell are distributed throughout the entire brain. Within the hologram every aspect of the whole is written in every part. Each part, can in turn, reproduce the whole. The brain uses holographic processes that interconnect and communicate information instantaneously. But logically, if you lose part of the brain through a stroke or other damage, you can't regain all of your faculties again.[30] During the years I worked as an intensive care nurse, I can testify that this last statement is not always true. I saw severely brain damaged individuals regain nearly all function. Such outcomes, which do

David Bohm, *The Implicate Order.*

Dr. Dennis Gabor constructed the first hologram in the early 1970s. It is created by a complicated process involving lens-less photography in which a wave field of light scattered by an object is recorded on a plate as an interference pattern. When this hologram is placed in a laser beam, the original wave pattern is regenerated into a three- dimensional image. Any piece of the hologram will reconstruct the entire image.

Karl Pribram, *The Language of the Brain.*

[30]Michael Talbot, *The Holographic Universe*, p. 31.

occur with some frequency, can not be medically explained. The human brain is a marvel that defies absolutes.

Dr. James Eden, who is a physician and a healer, believes that Pribram's observations can be applied to energy fields as well. His book implies that all energy fields, all thought forms, and all intelligence patterns exist irrespective of a space-time framework, and that no energy is required for the transmission of these qualities of reality. They exist potentially in every conceivable aspect of the cosmos.[31]

Fr. Tom Hand, SJ, makes an interesting application of the hologram in looking at the soul. We each have a soul, and, as Hand states, the whole soul is holographically present in all parts of the body. (Remember, each part of the hologram contains the whole; therefore, the soul can be found throughout the whole person.) Just as we are part of God (a holon within God), God is holographically present in every one of us. God is the animating principle of the whole cosmos, the "anima mundi," the soul of the world. That means that the whole "form field" of God is present in every creature. Thus, all of creation is but a reflection of the whole—of God. When we accept the unity of life, then we can say with St. Paul that "in God, we live and move and have our being." The holographic presence of God within us is a reality. The whole infinite Source—God—is contained in each one of us. And out of that infinite Source flows infinite Movement—Spirit.[32]

Even if we cannot fully explain scientifically what is happening when one performs the laying-on of hands or energetic healing, healers know it works. Marilyn Schlitz, director of research at the Institute of Noetic Sciences, reflects what many already feel. It is only a matter of time she says, before physicists and researchers from many different fields will be able to understand not only how body/mind/spirit are connected, but also what is happening when someone touches another with an intent to heal. The most profound implication is that we are all interconnected at a level that boggles most of our minds. If I touch another with the intention to heal, I can influence that person's energy and physiology. This requires that

[31]James Eden, MD, *Energetic Healing, The Merging of Ancient and Modern Medical Practices*, p. 55.

Fr. Hand was a missionary in Japan for nearly 30 years. While there, he studied Zen meditation and now works to further East-West dialogue between Buddhism and Christianity.

[32]Chwen Jiuan A. Lee (Sister Agnes) and Fr. Tom Hand, SJ, *A Taste of Water, Christianity Through Taoist-Buddhist Eyes.*

[33]Marilyn Schlitz, "Intentionality in Healing: Mapping the Integration of Body, Mind and Spirit," *Alternative Therapies*, Nov. 1995

[34]Dolores Krieger, *The Therapeutic Touch: How to Use Your Hands to Help or to Heal*, pp. 4-8.

Oscar Estebany was the same healer used in the studies conducted by Bernard Grad and Sister Justa Smith.

[35]Dolores Krieger, RN, PhD, *Accepting Your Power to Heal, The Personal Practice of Therapeutic Touch*, p. 12.

I be more thoughtful and responsible for my actions. How we connect to our Source, to God, is a critical factor in all of healing.[33]

Nurses Rediscover Healing Through Touch

The studies done in the 1960s and 1970s by Grad, Smith, and others were promising. One nurse who was attracted to these findings was Dolores Krieger, PhD, who was on the faculty at the New York University School of Nursing. Since researchers had validated the energetic nature of the laying-on of hands, Krieger wondered whether anyone could learn it or was it a special gift only a few people possessed. To test the hypothesis that anyone could be taught to be a facilitator or channeler of healing for another, she studied a famous spiritual healer, Oscar Estebany, a recent Hungarian immigrant to Canada. Collaborating with her was a famous clairvoyant, Dora Kunz.[34]

After study and practice, Krieger found that she could impart this "subtle energy" to others. Her students gradually became proficient in doing the laying-on of hands as well. Also, the more Krieger worked with the process, the more effective she became as a healer. Together, she and Kunz named this modern-day laying-on of hands, *Therapeutic Touch*. At first, Krieger taught this new healing technique as a Master's level nursing course at New York University. Six of her first students did their doctorate theses on the subject. Since then, Therapeutic Touch has become one of the most researched and well documented nursing techniques of all times.

In her writings, Krieger states that although the source of all healing comes from the "universal energy field," it is the practitioner's energy that "acts as a human support system" during the healing intervention. The healer must be able to sensitively draw upon the "universal energies" and not impart his or her own energy.[35]

Calling Therapeutic Touch "The Imprimatur of Nursing," Krieger, in an article in 1975, identified touch as integral to basic nursing skills. It is impossible to do nursing without touching. In the article, she reports that she had heard from hundreds of nurses all over the world telling her of incidents where the spontaneous use of touch during acts of nursing intervention brought about therapeutic results so unusual that they came as a surprise. When nurses touch with awareness and intention, the touch is different from ordinary touching. This touch is healing.[36] More recently, Sister Mary Elizabeth O'Brien, nursing professor at Catholic University, stated that "Loving empathetic, compassionate touch is perhaps the most vital dimension of a nursing theology of caring." In other words, touching is within the very fabric of being a nurse.[37]

As a researcher, Dr. Krieger looked for a scientific understanding of this hands-on healing. Not finding anything at that time in Western literature, she turned to the East for an understanding of this healing phenomenon. What she found was 5,000 year-old knowledge about subtle energy flow, auras, and energy centers. She used this knowledge as a theoretical backdrop for understanding what happens when one touches another with an intent to heal. Krieger later conducted studies on the oxygen-carrying capacity of hemoglobin in blood to see if Therapeutic Touch would affect this sensitive indicator of health. She decided to study the hemoglobin in patients who had received hands-on healing by Mr. Estebany, the renowned healer. When compared to a control group, those treated showed a significant elevation in hemoglobin. The control group did not. Many have discounted her research, citing there were not enough controls for the placebo effects. However, the significance of her work for us is that hands-on healing can be taught to anyone rather than being limited to a few gifted healers.

It is helpful to put Krieger's work into the perspective of the times. During the 1970s the nursing profession emphasized high-tech nursing and looked to science for justification of nursing interventions. Nursing was trying to prove its worth among other health care professions. The pendulum had swung away from the "art" of nursing to emphasize the "science" of nursing. Krieger's nursing technique of Therapeutic Touch, however, was based on her observations of the spiritual healer, Oscar Estebany, who attributed his healing to the power of Jesus Christ. Her rationale and explana-

[36]Dolores Krieger, RN, PhD, "Therapeutic Touch: The Imprimatur of Nursing," *American Journal of Nursing, 75:5*, pp. 784-7.

[37]Sister Mary Elizabeth O'Brien, *Spirituality in Nursing, Standing on Holy Ground*, p. 16.

The reader is directed to recent writings of the following authors who explore healing as the movement of energy.

Doc Lew Childre, *Freeze Frame*, and *Cut-Thru*.

Paul Pearsall, PhD, *The Heart's Code, Tapping the Wisdom and Power of Our Heart Energy*.

Mehmet Oz, MD, *Healing From the Heart, A Leading Heart Surgeon Explores the Power of Complementary Medicine*

Carlos Warter, MD, *Who Do You Think You Are? The Healing Power of Your Sacred Self*.

Dale Matthews, MD, *The Faith Factor, Proof of the Healing Power of Prayer*.

[38]Robert Keck, *Healing As a Sacred Path*, pp. 168, 171.

[39]Rochelle Graham, Flora Litt, and Wayne Irwin, *Healing From The Heart, A Guide to Christian Healing for Individuals and Groups*, p. 21.

tion of this laying-on of hands had to be in words that the scientific community could accept. Krieger believed that the ability to heal was an expression of a deep inner desire by the individual to help or heal another—to be of service. This was a foundational concept that formed the underpinning to how Therapeutic Touch worked. In the end, she concluded that healing flows from compassion and is an expression of love at the highest level. For her, compassion and intentionality were the prerequisites for becoming a healer. This is not scientific language. It is "heart" language and it is an expression of the art of nursing.

This is a key point about Therapeutic Touch that I would like to explore further. Many researchers, including those at the Institute of HeartMath, are conducting studies about the effects of this "heart" language. One of the missions of HeartMath is to prove what people already know intuitively—that love or true care is the forgotten factor in health. Many recent authors are writing from their own experiences about the power of our heart energy: Dr. Paul Pearsall, Dr. Mehmet Oz, Dr. Carlos Warter, and Dr. Dale Mathews, to name a few.

Dr. Robert Keck, a psychologist, writes that love can be an incredibly powerful healing force and its scope, its capabilities and its mystery far exceeds what our left-brain can comprehend. We would be foolish, he says, to underestimate the healing power of human connectedness fueled by the energy of love. He equates the power of love with miracle. He further identifies that "profound healing can occur through the power of love manifested through intimacy, trust, compassion, touching, forgiveness and altruistic service."[38] Graham, Litt, and Irwin's book, *Healing From the Heart*, summarizes what many of us are coming to understand about healing. That is,

"the heart as the inner point of human personality is open directly to God…"

and

"What flows from the heart is love, an emotion as necessary for health as water."[39]

As we learn through our experiences about the Source of healing and how to draw upon that Source, we cannot help but be changed in heart. For it is the heart that receives that divine Source in the form of unconditional love and compassion for others. Dolores Krieger, as well as many others have tapped into this awareness and have found ways to express that love and compassion. For Krieger, it became Therapeutic Touch.

The Work of Therapeutic Touch Goes On

One of the most impressive research projects on Therapeutic Touch was conducted by Daniel Wirth, a lawyer. He studied the healing rates of non-contact Therapeutic Touch on full-thickness dermal wounds. He found the subjects who received non-contact Therapeutic Touch healed faster than those who received no treatment.[40] None of the subjects knew the nature of the study and therefore could not be prejudiced one way or another. This research is considered a landmark study.

Therapeutic Touch is one of the most researched nursing techniques. Dr. Janet Quinn RN, PhD, one of Dr. Krieger's first graduate students, has become an outstanding spokesperson for this work.[41] Based at the Center for Human Caring in Colorado, she has successfully defended this work before the University of Colorado Board of Regents and convinced them that more money is needed to study this phenomenon. Quinn created a video series for the National League of Nursing on Therapeutic Touch, which is taught in nursing schools and institutions around the world.

The most helpful resource that I have found for Therapeutic Touch is Dr. Janet Macrae's book, *Therapeutic Touch, A Practical Guide.* Macrae, like Dr. Janet Quinn, was one of Krieger's first students and is now assistant professor of nursing at New York University and the author of several books. Her book on Therapeutic Touch is an excellent guide for the professional and lay person alike in learning this powerful healing technique. Macrae's work is simple yet direct, and she attributes the source of healing to the Universal Energy Field and not to the practitioner.

[40]Daniel P. Wirth, MS, JD, "The Effect of Non-Contact Therapeutic Touch on the Healing Rate of Full Thickness Dermal Wounds," *Cooperative Connection, XIII, no. 3 (Summer 1992).*

[41]Dr. Janet Quinn, *Therapeutic Touch,* produced by The National League for Nursing, (video).

I have met Dr. Quinn and have been impressed with how she brings Christian values to her work. As she describes her story, Therapeutic Touch has helped to bring her back to her Christian roots.

Dr. Janet Macrae, *Therapeutic Touch, A Practical Guide*

Dolores Krieger, *Therapeutic Touch Inner Workbook.*

Healing Touch Research

Healing Touch is actually the "new kid" on the block. Research projects began in earnest only about ten years ago. As nurses across many practice settings began learning this approach to healing, they naturally wondered why and how it worked. The many studies that have been completed demonstrate that there is support for considering Healing Touch for providing integrative care and that patients evaluate it highly. For instance, a study on women receiving radiation treatment for gynecological and breast cancer showed significant changes in improved quality of life and greater reduction in fatigue. They also showed pronounced improvements in their levels of depression, anxiety and anger compared to the control group.[42]

One patient satisfaction survey conducted for Cancer Patients Experiencing Healing Touch showed that those who received Healing Touch experienced 98% improved relaxation, 75% improved sense of control, 87% positive change in energy, 63% improved interpersonal relationships, 92% improved sense of well-being, 85% decreased pain and 77% decreased side effects of cancer treatments.[43]

Another study looked at whether massage and Healing Touch would affect pain, nausea, fatigue and anxiety for chemotherapy patients in comparison to caring presence alone or standard cancer treatment alone. Both Healing Touch and massage reduced B/P and heart rate and level of pain in comparison to healing presence alone. They reduced mood disturbance during the intervals between treatments but there was little effect on anxiety and tension and none on nausea.[44] Other studies conducted in hospice and palliative care show an increased relaxation, increased relief of pain, spiritual benefit, increased calmness and improved breathing.[45]

The popular magazine *Spirituality & Health* has run a number of articles over the past few years featuring the Scripps Center for Integrative Medicine in La Jolla, CA, Mimi Guarneri, MD, CHTP and Raunie King, RN CHTP/I use Healing Touch in the cardiac intensive care unit. Dr. Guarneri states that their high-tech heart scanner

[42]Cook, C.A.L., Guerrerio, J.F., Slater, V.E. (2004). "Healing Touch and quality of Life in women Receiving Radiation Treatment for Cancer: A Randomized Controlled Trial," *Alternative Therapies in Health and Medicine, 10(3)*, p. 24-41.

[43] *"A Patient Satisfaction Survey for Cancer Patients Experiencing Haling Touch at the Cancer Wellness Center."* Conducted by Judy Brannon.

[44]Post-White, J., Kinney, M.E. Savik, K., Gau, J.B., Wilcox, C. and Lerner, I (2003) "Therapeutic massage and Healing Touch improve symptoms in Cancer" *Integrative Cancer Therapies, 2(4)*, pp. 332-344.

[45] *"Use of Healing Touch Energy Therapy in Improving the Quality of Life Among the Dying."* Conducted by Neil Gilbert, Michele Goldberg, Jessica Ziembroski, Robert Bossarte.

helps earn enough money to support the time-intensive healing programs like Healing Touch and acupuncture that typically don't pay for themselves in modern hospital settings.[46] She is definitely a different kind of physician who sees the connection between mind, spirit and body.

Nurses are recognizing the potential of hands-on healing within their nursing care and finding satisfaction in relieving distress when science fails to have all the answers. The nurse as healer stands as God's instrument and as a vehicle of God's words and compassionate, caring touch. The nurse conveys that the other person really matters. Sister Mary Elizabeth O'Brien states it succinctly when she says, "In the sacred interaction between nurse and patient, the spiritual healing dimension of holistic health care is exemplified and refined."[47] Through presence, listening and touch, nurses are reawakening to the art of nursing. Healing is occurring not only for the patient, but for the nurse as well.

[46]"High-Tech & Healing Touch" *Spirituality & Health*. March/April 2004. By Stephen Kiesling.

[47]Sister Mary Elizabeth O'Brien, *Spirituality in Nursing, Standing on Holy Ground,* p. 9.

Chapter 4

The Role of Belief and Prayer in Healing

Many hold the belief that whether one believes in something or not will affect the outcome. Most Christians will attest that as youngsters we were taught to pray for the outcome of the school football game or for beautiful weather for the church picnic. We believed that if enough of us prayed for these events, God would hear us and our requests would come true. Our collective prayer was more powerful than individually praying. We also learned to pray for someone's recovery from illness or trauma, knowing that God, as the source of all goodness and compassion, would hear our pleas. We expected God to dutifully answer these prayers. And when the outcome we wanted did not happen, we were disappointed in God's apparent deaf ear or even absence.

Our faith was seen as important if God was to "hear our prayers." We believed that through our prayers and (also our good works), we would "earn" God's love—as evidenced by the outcomes we desired. Many of our modern-day faith-healers would have us think that if we only have enough faith, God will heal us, and if we are not healed, it is because we lack sufficient faith. Our lack of healing is, therefore, our fault. In effect, these "healers" blame the people and heap guilt upon their shoulders. These "healers" conclude that a lack of healing is not their fault but instead lies squarely with the one seeking the healing. This belief system calls upon God to reward our faith with the action we want. This is not only faulty theology, it is also harmful and unethical behavior.

Faith has a powerful impact on our lives. Without belief in something greater than ourselves, we are set adrift in our world without an anchor. Our beliefs contain our deepest understanding of life, death, and the hereafter, of creation, relationships, and purpose. Our beliefs form the foundation of our spiritual selves, connecting us to heaven and earth.

When we are facilitating healing for others, our belief in a good outcome, whatever that may be, does affect the healing work and bears our further investigation. God's unconditional love is always available to us when we are open to receiving. Belief on the part of the one receiving healing, on the other hand, is not always necessary. The recipient can be skeptical or not even believe in the healing power of God and still receive God's healing grace through the interventions of others. Furthermore, healing can even take place at a distance, through healing prayer.

There is no doubt that one's faith can be a powerful part of the healing when receiving the laying-on of hands, but we have seen time and time again that it is not required. Comatose patients can benefit from a healing touch as well as newborn infants, the frail, elderly, animals, and plants. Presumably, they are not consciously aware of being prayed for. One's faith, then, is not necessarily a pre-

What is "enough" faith? What is the biblical understanding of having "great" faith or having "little" faith?

Reflect for a few moments on your own faith. Is it relevant in your life? Do you call upon God to do your bidding? Are you ever disappointed?

requisite for receiving healing, but when it is present, it can add to the outcome.

If we believe that our prayers and healing can have positive outcomes, then it is only logical to ask if they can also work to the detriment of the one receiving. Can we "hex" or "curse" with our prayers and intentions? Is there a dark side to this work? Holding all these thought-provoking questions in mind, let us take a closer look at the role of faith and belief in healing work.

The "Faith Factor"

Over the last few decades, Dr. Herbert Benson, and Dr. Dale Matthews have been at the forefront of research on the role of faith in healing. Dr. Matthews, writing as a Christian doctor, states "Our religious traditions teach us to expect great things from God, which sets in motion the health-boosting effect of positive expectancy—hope."[1] Medicine has often derisively referred to this as the *placebo effect*, the phenomenon in which patients get better simply because they believe they will.

Dr. Benson coined the term "faith factor." He defines this as a combination of "remembered wellness" (the placebo effect) and eliciting the relaxation response. Remembered wellness is activated by one's own set of beliefs about health and wellness. Everyone, he says, can "remember" the calm and confidence associated with health and happiness. This is not just an emotion we are experiencing. This memory is also physical. As for research, this factor makes predicting or reproducing the same effects in someone else very difficult. Benson identifies three components of this remembered wellness:

1. *Belief and expectancy on the part of the patient*

2. *Belief and expectancy on the part of the caregiver*

3. *Belief and expectancies generated by a relationship between the patient and the caregiver.*[2]

[1] Dr. Dale Matthews, MD, *The Faith Factor, Proof of the Healing Power of Prayer*, p. 51.

[2] Dr. Herbert Benson, MD, *Timeless Healing, the Power and Biology of Belief*, p. 32.

Benson found that when patients believed in what their doctor prescribed, they got better. But if their confidence was undermined, the treatments began to show little effect. He quotes a nineteenth-century French physician, Armand Trousseau, who said, "You should treat as many patients as possible with the new drugs while they still have the power to heal."

The relaxation response refers to the body's decreasing metabolism which allows the body to not have to work so hard. Breathing becomes slower and deeper, and muscles relax. This is similar to the state of sleep. Eliciting the relaxation response can help us "disconnect" from our worries of the day, thus calming our bodies and minds more quickly. Benson notes that when he teaches patients to initiate the relaxation response, they often choose prayer as their eliciting focus. He found this to be true for all people—Jewish, Christian, Buddhist, or Hindu. When our beliefs are added to the relaxation response, the effect is even more dramatic, quieting worries and fears. Benson's research shows what many of us already believed: one's spiritual and religious beliefs play a significant role in the depth of relaxation. In fact, that is why he came to call the combination of remembered wellness and the relaxation response, the "faith factor." Prayer, he says, has a transforming power to produce a peaceful state.

All Things Are Possible to the One Who Believes

A story in the Scriptures tells of a father who brings his child, who is suffering from a "demon," first to the disciples, then to Jesus. The father believes that a demon is responsible for throwing the child into a fit, resulting in great harm to the child. He asked Jesus' disciples to cure him and they could not. The man then pleads with Jesus, asking, *if he is able*, to have compassion on their suffering. We can almost hear Jesus' exasperation when he chides the man about his lack of belief. "All things are possible for the one who believes," he says. And then we hear the depth of this man's agony for his child as he cries out,

"Teacher, I brought you my son; he has a spirit that makes him unable to speak; and whenever it seizes him, it dashes him down; and he foams and grinds his teeth and becomes rigid; and I asked your disciples to cast it out, but they could not do so." ...

"Bring him to me...How long has this been happening to him?" And he said, "From childhood... but if you are able to do anything, have pity on us and help us." Jesus said to him, "If you are able!—All things can be done for the one who believes." Immediately the father of the child cried out, "I believe; help my unbelief!" Jesus... rebuked the unclean spirit...took him by the hand and lifted him up, and he was able to stand. When he had entered the house, his disciples asked him privately, "Why could we not cast it out?" He said to them, "This kind can come out only through prayer." Mark 9:17-29

"Have faith in God. Truly I tell you, if you say to this mountain, 'Be taken up and thrown into the sea,' and if you do not doubt in your heart, but believe that what you say will come to pass, it will be done for you. So I tell you whatever you ask for in prayer, believe that you have received it, and it will be yours. Whenever you stand praying, forgive, if you have anything against anyone so that your Father in heaven may also forgive you your trespasses." Mark 11:22-26

"I believe, help my unbelief!" Mark 9:24. We hear his silent plea: help my prayer to be full of faith for I am not strong enough! Help me, for I don't know how to pray! Help me, for I have no where else to turn.

And then we see Jesus reaching out and surrounding this man with the power of his Spirit, imparting to him the kind of faith that comes from the depth of prayer and forgiveness. It is this kind of healing that he taught his disciples so that they would continue his ministry when he would no longer be with them. It is this kind of healing that comes from a place of deep prayer and connection to God.

The same story is told in Matthew 17:14-21 but with a slightly different twist. Here, Jesus, instead of scolding the father, speaks to all those present—including us—and says,

"You faithless and perverse generation, how much longer must I be with you?" Matt 17:17. We can hear what isn't said: You haven't caught on yet, you aren't understanding with your hearts. Wake up!!

When the disciples later ask him why they were not able to cast out the demon, Jesus flatly tells them, "because of your little faith." Like a knife, Jesus cut to the heart of the matter. "Little" faith is not referring to quantity but about quality. One's faith is more about trusting in God's love and power than about believing that a certain result will be achieved. Our faith must be more than mere words—more than understanding with our minds. It must be felt at the heart, at the core of our spirit. Faith is soul work.

Throughout the Scriptures, we hear Jesus speaking about the power of belief that is experienced in the heart. In John's Gospel, he told the disciples they would do greater works than he. To believe this called for tremendous faith on their part. They were, after all, only fishermen, tax collectors, zealots, carpenters, and housewives. But when the need presented itself after Pentecost, they were able to put their faith into action, and they too became instruments of healing for others. They had learned that faith, indeed, can move mountains if you do not doubt in your heart but believe that your prayers have already been answered.

In many of the healing stories, Jesus speaks about the role of faith and belief to the person requesting healing. To the woman with the hemorrhage, he said, "Daughter, your faith has made you well" (Mark 5:24); to the blind man, "Go your way; your faith has made you whole" (Luke 18:42); to the Canaanite woman who asked for healing for her daughter, he said, "Woman, great is your faith! Let it be done for you as you wish" (Matt. 15:28); in speaking about the centurion, Jesus remarked to his followers, *"Truly I tell you, in no one in Israel have I found such faith!"* (Matt. 8:10). And when the four men lowered their friend down through the roof, Jesus saw their faith, forgave the man his sins, and then healed him. (Mark 2:5). For Jesus, faith, prayer, and forgiveness are but one action that leads to healing and wholeness. We can heal ourselves as well as others when we learn how to pray, when we learn to tap into that well of healing that we know as the healing energy—the healing Light of God.

Faith is not a factor in many of the other healings that Jesus performed. In fact, as Tilda Norberg and Robert Webber point out, some people whom Jesus healed were not people of faith but just happened to be in the right place at the right time.[3] For instance, there is the man healed in the synagogue (Mark 1:23-26), the man beside the pool (John 5:2-9), and the man born blind (John 9). So it is not accurate to think that faith and healing are necessarily always connected. We can only conclude that faith is reliance upon God and trust in Jesus as the healer, and that this understanding of faith is important to our healing prayer.

[3]Tilda Norberg and Robert D. Webber, *Stretch Out Your Hand, Exploring Healing Prayer*, p. 43.

Why is faith important for some and not for others?

Unbelief

Why are some people healed and not others? Does it have anything to do with one's lack of belief or with God not listening? We know from the Scriptures that God hears and answers all prayers. When we ask God for healing, some kind of healing takes place, although it may not be in the form we expect. Why some people are healed physically and others are not can never be fully explained or understood. But we know that it is not because of our belief or unbelief. It has nothing to do with our goodness or lack of goodness. We also know, however, that an individual can block healing through willfulness. When we intentionally deny forgiveness to another, or hold on to resentment, anger or rage, we close off entrance for God's grace and energy in our lives.

One of the most amazing stories in the Gospel is when Jesus took his disciples and went home to Nazareth, where his friends and neighbors knew him. When Jesus returned, it was with some notoriety, for he had been out making quite a name for himself in the surrounding territory. When he began to teach on the Sabbath in the very synagogue he grew up in, the people took offense. "Who is this upstart?" they must have wondered. "It's only the carpenter. We know his parents and his brothers and sisters." They could not fathom how he managed to get such knowledge. Jesus was probably disappointed at the level of their unbelief. The Gospel of Mark goes on to say he could do no deed of power there except for a few healings. Healing in other words, was the *least* of what he could do. Even in the midst of their unbelief—their resentment and anger—Jesus was able to manifest some rays of God's healing energy for a few individuals.

Let's look at their rejection and lack of faith a little closer. What prevented these friends and kin from accepting Jesus' words and his healing ministry? What blocked their minds and ultimately their hearts? As long as he stayed in the role of carpenter, he had a place in their society. But preaching throughout the countryside, healing the sick, and acting like an educated rabbi was more than these townspeople could bear. They were used to everyone having their place and acting within a set role. It was scandalous for one of their own to cause such a spectacle. Again, Luke tells the story differently (Luke 4:16-30). In his version of these events, Jesus' words so enraged the town's people, so indicted their hearts that they led him out of town, intending to throw him off the cliff. We are reminded that a prophet is often without honor in his own land.

"He came to his home town and his disciples followed him. On the Sabbath he began to teach in the synagogue, and many who heard him were astounded. They said, 'Where did this man get all this? What is this wisdom that has been given to him? What deeds of power are being done by his hands! Is this not the carpenter, the son of Mary and brother of James and Joses and Judas and Simon, and are not his sisters here with us?' And they took offense at him....And he could do no deed of power there, except that he laid his hands on a few sick people and cured them. And he was amazed at their unbelief." Mark 6:1-3, 5

Negative Thought Patterns

This story about the people of Nazareth can be seen from yet another viewpoint. Could it be that their hearts were so encased in negative thought patterns about themselves as men and women and negative thought patterns about others that this young teacher actually presented too much Light for them to cope with? The Jewish people were under Roman occupation. Even though they thought of themselves as the chosen people, they were a conquered people who were put down and treated as little more than slaves. Years and years of this kind of treatment does affect the psyche of the people and what they feel about themselves and others.

Are there negative thought patterns of energy in your life, preventing you from fully claiming the Light for yourself and others?

This repeated treatment can lead to negative thought patterns about ourselves and others. Can these negative thought patterns block faith and belief and interfere with prayer and healing? Once we understand that our thoughts are energy then we have to realize that negative thoughts can block—even prevent—our being able to believe and accept God's love in our lives. Negative thoughts, when they become habits, can be harmful. There is the story of the little boy who kept calling out to the wolf "don't eat me." He actually called enough attention to himself that the wolf had no problem finding him. By focusing on fearful thoughts, we can call the negative into our lives.

Agnes Sanford, *The Healing Light.*

We must learn how to unplug from negative thought energies, from past events and past hurts. Agnes Sanford has called this the "healing of memories." We don't wipe away the memories as if they never occurred, but we forgive and let go of the pain, hurt, anger, and resentment that keep our hearts in bondage and our minds held captive. Look within. Are you harboring ill will towards another? If so, your negative thought energy is harming you as well as others, and it is preventing you from being a clear vessel of healing for others.

What Is Prayer?

Humans have always prayed, looking outside themselves to some Supreme Being for protection, help, guidance, or blessing. We have prayed to appease an angry or a punishing God, we have petitioned God to strike down our enemies. We have prayed to a compassionate God to intercede on our behalf, blessing us with good harvests, fair weather, and healthy children. Prayer is something we have learned to do as part of our human activity. Prayer is a reflection of our emotions—fear and love and devotion. I would like to think that over these many thousands of years of human existence, we have been maturing in our understanding of God as creator, sustainer, and lover of all. At times, though, our prayer resorts to our more primitive understanding of God as punisher. Prayer is much more.

Prayer is energy. Prayer is connection—attunement to the Divine. It is communication with the "Breath," the "Life Force" of all creation, and it is an expression of the love between the created and the Creator. In my classes, I encourage students to pray for the person they are working with in their healing practices. I often sense their reticence about praying out loud, but when we are connected to the Spirit, we do not have to worry about the words. If words are necessary, they will flow from the Spirit, whether in the silence of our hearts or out loud for the benefit of the one receiving the healing. When Jesus was preparing his disciples for the difficult days to come, he taught them not to worry about what to say. "The Spirit will speak through you," Jesus said. His words are very appropriate for us as well.

Prayer is receptivity of God's presence in our lives. Ron Roth states:

> *"All prayer is the reception of the light energy that is the presence of God. It may take the form of guidance, prophecy, wisdom, clairvoyance, or even a simple hunch or gut feeling or spontaneous idea."*[4]

"...do not worry about how you are to speak or what you are to say; for what you are to say will be given to you at that time; for it is not you who speak, but the Spirit of your Father speaking through you." Matt. 10:19-20

[4]Ron Roth, *The Healing Path of Prayer,* p. 36.

Prayer is much more than what we have to say to God; it is what God has to say to us or through us, which, as Roth says, can come in many forms. To hear the many voices of God requires an openness that is truly an attitude of the heart. Only when we are our true selves can we attune to the vibration of this Light energy.

Not all prayer results in the experience of God's presence. Sometimes, God's presence is hidden from our view and experienced as a feeling of absence or even of darkness. Some of the great saints wrote out of the depth of this darkness, trusting that God was just as present in the absence as in the times when they felt God's presence. John of the Cross wrote beautiful mystical poetry that flowed from the depths of his "dark night of the soul." We are challenged then, to be courageous in openness to the movement of Spirit, even when we don't "feel" it.

Healing Prayer

Olga and Ambrose Worrall, both of whom were Methodist hands-on healers, describe prayer as the key to the source of power. All of our conscious thinking is in essence a part of prayer. As we move our hands or hold them still when doing our healing work, we pray with our whole being for the good of the individual, without putting conditions on God's healing. The prayer of petition and affirmation may provide words for our minds that serve as an anchor. It is the prayer of the heart, though, that lifts us beyond words into that simple resting in the Spirit.[5]

[5]Olga and Ambrose Worrall, *The Gift of Healing,* p. 187.

Agnes Sanford also considers prayer the key to all healing. In directing others in healing prayer she quotes, "Be still and know that I am God." from Psalm 46. She goes on to say, "lay aside your worries, quiet your mind and be present to God. Pray, and believe that God's power is coming into use and then accept it by faith." Finally, she tells us, "observe the workings of God in life."[6] For Sanford, God's will for us is not pain or suffering but wholeness. God has given us to each other to love, support, comfort, and heal one another.

[6]Agnes Sanford, *The Healing Light,* p. 7.

Healing at a Distance

Healing from a distance is what we have traditionally meant when we've said, "I'll pray for you," or, "I'll put you on my prayer list." Dr. Robert Miller, a research chemist studied the biological effects of spiritual healers like Olga and Ambrose Worrall. He found that subtle energies emanated from their hands when they placed them on others and prayed for healing. Of even greater significance was his experiment conducted with the Worralls to measure the effects of distant healing. Miller had already shown that healers like the Worralls were able to directly impart growth-promoting energies to plants by way of charged water. At a distance of 600 miles, he had the Worralls send healing energy to plants that were being measured for growth. The Worralls "prayed" for the plants at their regular prayer time. The plants grew 840 % overnight! During their prayer, they had visualized the plants filled with light and energy. We can only presume that plants do not know they are being prayed for and therefore cannot respond because of some awareness of the power of prayer.[7]

Larry Dossey, MD, is probably today's most popular writer about the role of prayer in healing. He has written a number of best sellers on the subject in the past ten years. Prayer, he says is

> "a genuinely nonlocal event—that is, it is not confined to a specific place in space or to a specific moment in time. Prayer reaches outside the here-and-now; it operates at a distance and outside the present moment."[8]

Dr. Daniel Benor, MD, a psychiatrist, has collected vast amounts of research on spiritual healing and is considered one of the world's renowned authorities. He defines "spiritual healing" as

> "the intentional influence of one or more people upon another living system without utilizing known physical means of intervention."[9]

Most of the research he found has been published in parapsychology journals or is in unpublished doctoral dissertations or

[7]Richard Gerber, MD, *Vibrational Medicine, New Choices for Healing Ourselves*, pp. 313-314.

[8]Larry Dossey, MD, *Healing Words: The Power of Prayer and the Practice of Medicine*, p. 6.

This research can be explored in [9]Daniel J. Benor, MD, *Science Validates Spiritual Healing and in Healing Research: Holistic Energy Medicine and Spirituality*.

Master's theses. The spiritual studies are just now beginning to show up in medical journals.

One of the landmark studies done on prayer a few years ago was conducted by cardiologist Dr. Randolph Byrd. In this study, patients who had suffered a heart attack were randomly assigned to one of three groups. One group was the control group; the other two groups received prayer at a distance by either local prayer groups or prayer groups across the country. It was a double-blind study, which meant that the doctors, nurses, and those offering the prayers did not know who was receiving prayer and who wasn't. The prayer groups were given no direction about the prayer other than to pray for the recovery of these individuals every day. At the end of the study, the prayed-for individuals, as compared to the control group, showed they were less likely to develop complications like pulmonary edema or to have conditions requiring antibiotics or require respiratory assistance. Also, fewer patients who were prayed for died.[10] These results, of course, do not mean that those who were not prayed for did not have family and friends praying for them as well. Dr. Larry Dossey has commented that had the results of this study been attributed to some technique, or new drug, or new surgical procedure, instead of prayer, it would have been heralded as some sort of "breakthrough."[11]

There are many unanswered questions about the nature of the prayers offered in the study, such as what was the skill of those who were doing the praying and what was the skill of the physicians caring for these patients. Even with these flaws in the study, however, it made headlines. People, including doctors, took notice.

Gail Holland reports on a study conducted by psychiatrist Elisabeth Targ and psychologist Fred Sicher. It was a double-blind clinical study to examine if prayer or psychic healing could help patients with advanced AIDS. The healers were from many different denominations and healing traditions. Each day for ten weeks, the patients received healing messages from ten different healers located throughout the U.S. Some prayed in a traditional manner

[10]Randolph C. Byrd, "Positive Therapeutic Effects of Intercessory Prayer in a Coronary Care Unit Population," *Southern Medical Journal* 81:7 (July 1988).

[11]Larry Dossey, MD, *Reinventing Medicine*, p. 58.

for the patients, others tried to have positive effects by sending their positive thoughts. Neither the patients nor the investigators knew who was receiving the healing prayers and thoughts. The results were extremely positive. Those prayed for showed improved health compared to a control group. They required fewer doctor visits and hospital days and had significantly less emotional distress. This study shows great promise and has the potential for clinical use.[12]

Prayer as a "Non-Local" Event

We don't know how prayer can bring about healthful changes for someone close or distant. All our research can only verify that, indeed, something has happened. Prayer, Larry Dossey concludes, can be good medicine for the patient. He predicts that medical practice in the future will include such things as doctor's orders to "pray for patient three times a day," and doctors will be praying for and with their patients. Some surgeons are already bringing healers into the operating room to assist in the healing process. Julie Motz is probably one of the first alternative healers to work on cardiac patients during heart surgeries. As she senses traumas and unresolved emotions that contributed to the patient's suffering, she helps them release fear and anger to begin healing both body and soul as the surgery progresses.

Can prayer be explained simply by the "placebo effect"? A placebo is something like a sugar pill or water injection given to soothe or humor the patient. Dossey believes that placebo effects can be attributed to suggestion, positive thinking, or one's beliefs—those of the client and the practitioner. In the case of prayer, beliefs have a significant role. When a person realizes that he or she is being prayed for, it can generate positive results. As for the practitioner, when we do energy work with a client, we hold a positive outcome in our thoughts and prayers as we work.

Cathy Leb, in a study on the effects of Healing Touch on depression, wondered whether the excellent results she obtained were due to her intention for her clients to "feel better." She believes that the absence of ego and the purity of love, which is transmitted

[12]Gail Bernice Holland, *A Call For Connection, Solutions For Creating A Whole New Culture.*

Larry Dossey MD, *Prayer is Good Medicine.*

Julie Motz, *Hands of Life.*

through intention, is what provides the space for healing to occur. Specific techniques, such as Healing Touch or prayer, may relieve the symptomatology because they are a vehicle for the purity of love and intent to heal.[13]

Prayer is a genuinely non-local event (action at a distance). Some scientific theories, such as David Bohm's theory of the Implicate Order, help us to understand non-local events. In quantum mechanics, two subatomic particles can interact locally and then move very far apart. Even if one particle is on the other side of the world, they must be treated as an indivisible whole. What affects one, affects the other. Distance then, has proved not to be a factor. Although correlations occur between distant particles as if they are in intimate contact, physicists cannot purposefully send messages to affect the non-local, subatomic world. Similarly, we know that prayer is effective non-locally at a distance.[14] However, we cannot always "make it happen" through intention or prayer for specific outcomes. We can note, however, that open-ended prayers that leave room for "thy will be done," or "let it be," or "for the highest good," seem to invite the prayer's effects to manifest. We are inviting the Divine to show up.

The power of intention for a good effect is very powerful. In Dossey's book *Be Careful What You Pray For*, he concludes that love, empathy, caring, and compassion are the necessary ingredients for distant connections between people to take place. When these feelings are absent, the connection between individuals is weak or non-existent. Prayer is an expression of one's love, empathy, caring, and compassion. It is a calling out to the Divine to make Itself known and to manifest as wholeness in our lives.[15]

Is All Prayer Helpful?

Can prayer be detrimental? Dr. Marilyn Schlitz has helped to draw attention to these concerns. She stated, "If a person can influence the physiology of another person at a distance, it is clearly possible that that influence may not always be positive."[16] In Dossey's research on the effects of prayer, he has found tremendous evidence to support this. In other words, we can negatively affect the health

[13]Cathy Leb, "The Effects of Healing Touch on Depression," Master's thesis presented at the American Holistic Nurses' Association Annual Conference, 1998.

[14]Larry Dossey, MD, *Healing Words, The Power of Prayer and the Practice of Medicine,* p. 6.

[15]Larry Dossey, *Be Careful What You Pray For, You Just Might Get It,* p. 182.

[16]Marilyn J. Schlitz, "Intentionality and Intuition and Their Clinical Implications: A Challenge for Science and Medicine," *Advances 12, no. 2* (1996).

and well being of another through our intentions, prayers, and healing work.

The problem with harmful prayer is that we think we know what is best for others and we let God know through our prayers how the person ought to be "fixed." We basically don't trust God's handling this healing. If our prayers restrict the freedom and choices of others, they can be more of a curse, Dossey says. Our good intentions can actually hurt people. By our actions, we are attempting to manipulate others to our point of view.

Some may consider this statement scandalous, but praying for someone's cure from cancer or heart disease may not be the highest good for that individual and we may be disappointed when the outcome we hope for does not manifest. This is not to deny that being cancer-free or free of heart disease is a good thing. However, healing and wholeness for one person may appear quite different than healing and wholeness for another. It might be better if we lay aside our personal agendas in our prayers and not ask for or demand a specific answer. Rather, make open-ended prayers for help and allow God to be God.

At times, we may find we have ambivalent feelings toward another person. Our prayers, as well as our healing work, will be affected by our less than harmonious thoughts and intentions. Prayer is serious work, just as healing work is. Dossey reports on a study done by Dr. Bernard Grad at the University of Montreal. Since Grad had already found that plants grew better when given water held by a healer, he theorized that water held by a depressed person would have a negative effect on plant growth. Although not definitive, his study suggested that emotions may influence healings negatively as well as positively. When we find ourselves faced with a situation where we have feelings that are ambivalent towards the one asking for prayers or for healing, we might want to first pray for ourselves, asking that our ambivalence and negativity be replaced by compassion and love.

Curses and Hexes

Prayers can be curses and hexes. I find it appalling to think someone would actually place a curse or a hex on someone, especially if that person is involved in healing service for others. However, it happens sometimes in seemingly innocent ways. We send out unloving, negative, angry, or resentful thoughts towards another in an effort to either control them or improve our situation at their expense. In hospitals, we have unwittingly participated in some of these hexes with such comments as "he has one foot in the grave," "only one leg to stand on," "there's nothing else we can do for you," "you only have six months to live," "you'll just have to live with it," "he's going down hill fast," "it will only get worse," "she's living on borrowed time," "you are a walking time bomb," or "the cancer's too advanced, there's no hope."

Many of us, including myself, have caught ourselves saying or thinking these thoughts. When we examine them, we realize we are sending negative energy, negative thought forms, and negative prayers. Some physicians have, in recent years, become attuned to the possibilities that our thoughts affect the outcome of surgery. Dr. Mehemet Oz, cardiac surgeon at Columbia Presbyterian Hospital in New York is one physician who is aware of the importance of positive thinking that nurtures the spirit and actually helps to heal the heart.

Mehmet Oz, MD, *Healing from the Heart, A Leading Heart Surgeon Explores the Power of Complementary Medicine.*

Several years ago, I had to undergo a minor surgical procedure in which I needed to have a general anesthetic. Prior to my being taken to the operating room, a male nurse came into my room to start an I.V. This nurse, for some reason, started telling me in very disparaging terms about the state of that particular hospital and how unhappy the personnel were. This was depressing information. When he inserted the needle, I experienced sharp pain at the needle site, a pain that did not abate.

I had a healer in the room with me who was clairvoyant and could see the energy field. When the nurse left, my healer immediately came over to me and cleared the "red plume" of energy from my arm. We then recognized the dark energy that this nurse's negativity brought into the room. The healer set about clearing and rebalancing my field to prepare me for the procedure. It was a powerful lesson for both of us in how negative energy can act as a "curse" or "hex" without conscious intent.

What about conscious intent to harm through prayer? Is this possible? Peoples around the world can attest that, in fact, it is possible to harm another through our thoughts or our prayers. Wishing someone dead, or wishing someone would go to hell, may be phrases we innocently used as children when we were upset or angry. However, used with conscious intent as an adult can strike fear in the heart of another. Casting an evil eye upon someone to convey harm or pronouncing a hate prayer or curse can demoralize the victim who then manifests the results of the curse. Such negative thoughts are actually thought to kill in some cultures.

How can we protect ourselves from those who wish us harm? Our greatest protection is of course, prayer. Our Christian prayer—the Our Father, calls upon God to "deliver us from evil," which is a prayer for protection. Other prayers may come to mind such as the Prayer of St. Francis, the Hail Mary, Prayer To My Guardian Angel, or any variety of others. Our prayer may be a prayer of silence or a simple "Deliver me, O Lord." There is a translation of the prayer attributed to St. Patrick that really speaks to my heart and it is one that I use frequently to begin my day.

Staying in balance, physically, mentally, emotionally, and spiritually will ward off negative intent, as will leading a humble life, steadfast in the Lord. A balanced life can lead to spiritual strength where we need not worry about someone else's negative intent towards us.

Closing Thought

Prayer heals. We know this not just because we learned it in our church or from our ministers; we know that prayer heals because we have experienced it in our lives. Healing prayer leads to wholeness. This reminds me of the Hebrew understanding that the spoken

"Christ with me,
Christ before me,
Christ behind me,
Christ in me,
Christ beneath me,
Christ above me,
Christ on my right,
Christ on my left,
Christ when I lie down,
Christ when I sit down,
Christ when I arise,
Christ to shield me."

Prayer attributed to St. Patrick

word has substance and power. Speaking God's name invokes God's presence. When the people for whom we pray and lay our hands on open themselves to the Holy Spirit and to Divine Grace, then we as practitioners can trust that some kind of healing will occur. God will be present. Our belief and trust in God's healing is a factor in the healing, and, like the man whose heart cried out in anguish, "help my unbelief!" our hearts cry to the Lord for strength, perseverance, and hope. Our faith in the unity and oneness of Love will heal us. The Divine Light awaits us.

CHAPTER 5

Performing the Laying-on of Hands

We find the simple form of the laying-on of hands clearly described in Scripture. Jesus and the early apostles and disciples prayed and touched those who requested healing and this, as we know, became common practice among the early Christian healers. Prayer and healing went together. Over the past two thousand years, we have grown to understand a little better what is happening when we extend our hands in faith to heal others.

When Dolores Krieger and Dora Kunz studied the spiritual healer Oscar Estabany, they decided to put down their observations in the form of "steps," a kind of "how-to" formula. This approach to hands-on healing enabled them not only to verify their findings but also to teach this form of healing as a nursing technique. The steps they identified are centering, assessment, unruffling, directing and modulating energy, and ending. These are the steps of a nursing technique, Therapeutic Touch that has been taught around the world to nurses and non-nurses alike. This model set down by Krieger and Kunz can fit within all spiritual paths.

As I have observed spiritual healers working within our Christian faith, I have likewise identified several "steps" that are consistent with our Christian tradition and with scripture. Although the steps might at first seem simplistic, there is much depth to be uncovered for the practitioner.

There are basically four steps in performing a simple form of the Laying-On of Hands:

1. *Centering*
2. *Intention*
3. *Assessment*
4. *Treatment*

It is important to prepare the person who is to receive healing. Get permission to touch, tell the person what you will be doing, and encourage feedback as you progress. "Centering and intention" are your interior preparation for doing the healing work. "Assessment" is determining what to do, and "treatment" is being open to the power of God flowing through your hands and your heart. It is your being a channel, a conduit, or facilitator for the flow of divine energy.

Preparation of the Healer

Centering

First, take time to center through prayer. This may take the form of meditation based on the Scriptures. In this way, you are connecting to God, your Source, through your heart center. It is through the heart that we access the healing power of God.

I would like to acknowledge the invaluable help of Rochelle Graham and the folks at the Naramata Retreat Center in British Columbia for their input in developing this model. In addition, the instructors in the Healing Touch Spiritual Ministry Program have helped to bring clarity to presenting this time-honored healing.

"For this reason I bow my knees before the Father, from whom every family in heaven and on earth takes its name. I pray that, according to the riches of his glory, he may grant that you may be strengthened in your inner being with power through his Spirit, and that Christ may dwell in your hearts through faith, as you are being rooted and grounded in love. I pray that you may have the power to comprehend, with all the saints, what is the breath and length and height and depth, and to know the love of Christ that surpasses knowledge, so that you may be filled with all the fullness of God." Eph. 3:14-19

You may wish to read Rupert Sheldrake's explanation of morphogenetic fields for an understanding of the whole universal energy form field.

See Rupert Sheldrake, *New Science of Life, the Hypothesis of Formative Causation,* and Matthew Fox and Rupert Sheldrake, *Natural Grace, Dialogues on Creation, Darkness, and The Soul in Spirituality and Science.*

In centering, we are paying attention. We are attentive to the movement of the Spirit. Where attention goes, energy flows. The object of one's attention can be something in the past, the present, or the future. We actually create our lives by what we hold in our attention. All time—past, present, and future—is present in each moment. What we must put our attention to in healing work is the eternal present—being here, present with the person who is requesting healing. We must remember that all healing can only occur in the present moment, not in the past or in the future. When we are centered in our hearts, we can tap into the whole universal energy form field which is present within us. That means all the great events of Jesus' life and in the lives of Christian saints and holy ones are accessible to us. This universal energy form field is like a giant computer chip. It is all there for each of us.

Don't be disappointed if you find you are easily distracted. When you discover your thoughts have wandered, gently bring yourself back to the present moment. Breathe in the Holy Breath, the breath of God. This will strengthen your inner core, which is in communion with the divine. It takes self discipline to stay in the present moment. Over time, with practice and discipline, this improves. Focus is very important.

Intention

Set your intention by asking through prayer to be an instrument of healing for the person's highest good—whatever that may be. Ask for guidance and direction during your healing session with this person, and then trust, leaving the healing to God.

In intention, you are reaching out, moving toward God. Intention fixes your attention on God and on the flow—the movement of God's Spirit. Through intention, you hold the focus on Jesus as the cosmic Christ. In the fixing of intention, you are able to access God's healing, and the power of the Spirit is released. This is transforming. Agnes Sanford said it is not enough to connect with God and be open to receiving—we must also believe that God will indeed work through us. How does one turn on this power of God? Sanford tells us that we don't "turn it on." We provide the right medium. "Forget everything else and think about God and about Jesus who is God's Son and our friend," she says.[1] Through faith, we accept God's graciousness and we give thanks for the power of God in this work. In essence, we invite God's healing to come in.

[1]Agnes Sanford, *The Healing Light*, p. 7.

After asking permission, centering, and setting intention, you are ready to extend your hands in the flow of the Spirit.

Taking in Information: Being Open to "Hear"

Assessment

There are many ways that you can decide what needs to be done. Your intention now is to take in information that will help guide your heart, mind, and hands as you begin your healing work. This information gathering begins with your first contact as you greet the person. Interviewing skills that you might have learned in nursing, counseling, or pastoral care will aid you in this assessment of need. Even if you don't have particular skills in these areas, you can be a compassionate listener. This is really all about your abilities to listen and observe with your eyes, and to feel and sense with your hands and spirit. These skills develop the more you use them.

> *First, **ask** the person where the problem is or what he/she would like you to do during this healing time. This may seem a bit strange in the beginning, but remember how often Jesus asked those who were requesting healing, "what do you need?" The request for healing may be for something physical, emotional or spiritual in nature. Know that when there is part of us out of balance, the whole of our being is generally suffering in some way.*

This is about listening with the heart and about discernment. Richard Foster, in writing about the laying-on of hands as a form of prayer, tells us that this listening is not only to what the person is saying, it is also listening to what is underneath their words. We listen, asking God to show us the key to the problem. It may be much deeper than what the person is aware of on the surface.[2] As healers,

[2]Richard Foster, *Prayer, Finding The Heart's True Home*, p. 210.

we need to stay attuned and allow this assessment to unfold in God's time.

> *Use your observational skills to **observe** facial expression, body language and positioning. Ask God for guidance in seeing the areas that need help.*

Notice the brow. Is it lined with pain or anxiety? What about the shoulders—is the weight of the world upon them? Are they rigid, stiffly holding things up, or are they stooping with fatigue? How is the person walking? Do they have a limp? Is the gait fast or slow? What do you sense about this person's body as he or she sits, stands, or lies before you?

> *__Listen inside.__ An intuitive sense may come to you as you connect with the wisdom within your heart. This is God's inspiration to us that leads and directs. If you are in doubt or not sure you can trust what is coming to you, then pray for clarity. It is all right to pause a moment to wait upon God's inspiration.*

We often speak of intuition as a "gut" feeling or knowing. God's voice to us is not always in words that we hear with our ears. It often comes with a simple "knowing" within or an impression that we receive like a "hunch." Some may refer to this as clairvoyance (seeing) or clairaudience (hearing). We all have some degree of this psychic ability whether we are comfortable with these terms or not. Often a parent knows when their child is in trouble, or "hears" or "sees" their need. For some these abilities don't even develop until children arrive; then, it's difficult to turn them off. I find these intuitive abilities are quite common in people and can be enhanced through paying attention. In the Scriptures we hear many stories about listening for the voice of God, which manifests in guidance, prophecy, wisdom, and inner knowing. Those practicing spiritual healing attune to the Spirit to *hear* God's direction.

The goal in assessment is simply to take in information—not to make any judgment or necessarily to decide what needs to be done. Staying within the Christ consciousness, you allow this information to enter at the heart level. Your listening and observing with heart and mind now leads you to acting as God's instrument, channel, and courier of divine grace for this person before you. You simply know with an inner knowing, what to do next.

Determining What to Do:
Acting as God's Instrument

Treatment

As we are led by God in a simple form of the laying-on of hands, we reach out in a spirit of trust, placing our hands gently either on the shoulders or the head of the one requesting healing. I find this action to be most humbling. My awareness is on the power of God so I don't have to worry if I have my hands at the "right" place. Sometimes I am aware of heat or energy flowing through my hands, but I am not invested in anything at all happening. I only know that God's healing power is being manifested.

"As the sun was setting, all those who had any who were sick with various kinds of diseases brought them to him; and he laid his hands on each of them and cured them." Luke 4:40

The goal is to help this flow of God's healing energy to move through the person. Just as our food, water, and breath move through us, so does God's energy. We hold our hands on the person as long as the Spirit directs. As we become attuned to this flowing energy, there is a sensation of even, smooth flow around the body. For Ron Roth, this is like a release of blessings, which are powerful conduits of spiritual energy. When we bless the one we are laying hands on, our desire is to bring forth their goodness. In this act, we are releasing the energy of God.[3]

[3]Ron Roth, *The Healing Path of Prayer, A Modern Mystic's Guide to Spiritual Power*, p. 196.

While our hands are placed on the person before us, a prayer might come into our awareness. Sometimes this prayer need only be spoken in the silence of our hearts. Sometimes it needs to be spoken as healing words for this person's comfort. This is especially true when the pain is a result of grief or emotional trauma. When the prayer is done, it is with a spirit of gratitude that we release our hands, giving thanks for the grace of God flowing to both healer and healee.

Beyond the Simple Form of the Laying-On of Hands

What I have described thus far is a form of healing most people would be comfortable with in a church or a ministry setting. If healing happens with this simple form of the laying-on of hands, why do more? The answer is obvious: sometimes more is needed. Through our human development we have grown in knowledge and wisdom. We understand that we are spiritual beings who happen to have bodies that reflect our wholeness or lack of wholeness. In other words, we know a lot more about healing and how it occurs. The laying-on of hands forms the foundational stone upon which all hands-on healing is based. Healing Touch Spiritual Ministry moves beyond those simple steps of touching shoulders and heads and teaches practitioners more ways in which they can use their hands as God's instruments of healing. Our energy "fields" extend well beyond our bodies and can become congested with pain and illness. Some of the Healing Touch Spiritual Ministry ways of healing referred to as "techniques," do not involve touching the body at all, but, rather, touching or clearing the "energy" field.

We will begin by expanding the laying-on of hands technique already described.

First, we use our hands to further assess what needs to be done to help the person towards healing. Besides asking, observing, and listening inside, we additionally assess by *moving our hands* and allowing the energy surrounding the body to speak to us, telling us what our hands can do to assist the flow of healing energy.

> *Use your hands, moving them through the subtle energy field around the body, anywhere from two inches to several feet. This is usually done from head to toe, front and back, to find areas that feel out of balance. These areas will feel different from the rest. This difference may take the form of heat, cold, tingling, pressure, or congestion. Start on the front of the body, moving your hands down the front, keeping them moving, then, if appropriate, move to the back, and again keep your hands moving down the body's energy field.*

If the person is sitting or standing, you can also assess the back. The energy field is not contained or constrained by the back of a chair, but if you feel that the chair is preventing you from feeling, then gently ask the person to sit sideways on the chair or move forward so you can assess.

Make a mental note of where the field feels "different" from the rest. Remember, the field in a state of wholeness feels the same all over; it is only when there is a state of imbalance or disharmony that the practitioner will feel differences. Your hands are acting as receivers of information. If you are new at this, it will take time to develop sensitivity to feeling with the fingers and palms of your hands. It is reassuring to know that whether you feel the energy or not, you are still affecting the field. Many people have come into this work and not "felt" with their hands for months, even years, yet they were quite effective in helping others. Eventually, this skill will develop with patience and paying attention.

As you move into treatment, there are essentially two ways you can use your hands. You can move them or hold them still. They may be on or off the body. Let your hands act as instruments of the Holy Spirit, invoking the power and presence of God to come. Desire simply to be the best that you can be, and through that desire, you will become a channel for God to act. This requires your letting go and letting God be in charge of the healing. As you become more skilled in allowing yourself to be guided by the Holy Spirit, your hands will be shown what to do. Until then, here are a few guidelines:

Move your hands from center to the edges, beginning at the top and moving downward like the branches of an evergreen tree. Begin with very slow and gentle movements.

You may notice an area that is not clearing well. It may still feel hot, tingly, thick, or congested. You may wish to focus on any areas that haven't cleared by either moving your hands in this area like an air massage, or by placing your hands directly on the body or slightly off the body. If placing your hands on the person's body is called for, do so very gently. Become aware of Christ in your heart and allow the light and love of Christ to flow into your hands and into the person. Keep your hands there until you feel ready to take them off. If you are not sure, you may ask the person receiving, "Would you like my hands left on or are you ready to have them lift off?"

A nice way to end is with the hands on the feet. Hold for at least one minute.

I am reminded of the time when Jesus made a paste in the mud and rubbed it on the blind man's eyes. He also needed to place his hands on the man's eyes and hold them there to evoke a total healing of the man's sight. Sometimes the place we feel drawn to put our hands is the very place the person has requested healing. Other times it is not. In those cases, I focus attention on both areas. During this final step of healing, keep your focus in prayer, either in the silence of your heart or out loud, as the Spirit directs. I am always amazed at the healing power of God when I truly fix my attention on the movement of God's Spirit.

Once in one of my classes a young woman burst into tears as I instructed the students to ask their partners, "What would you like me to pray for?" I asked her if she was all right, and she told me that the thought of someone actually praying for her during healing work had never occurred to her. She was overwhelmed with the power of this spiritual work and acknowledged that she could not remember someone ever praying for her.

At any time during the healing treatment, you may want to go back and reassess whether an area is coming into balance. It may take a few minutes or repeated treatment to affect a difference.

Where Can the Laying-On of Hands Be Done?

What you are able to do with your hands in this healing work will be affected by where this healing is taking place. What has been described above assumes that the healing is appropriate for the location and that the recipient is open to receiving. Ideally, your healing work will take place in a specific place designated for healing, such as a healing room in your home, the church, retreat center, or office established for this work. The Worralls, who were famous for their Christian laying-on of hands healing, used to have a healing room within their home as well as a clinic where people could come. Here it was possible for them to have a dedicated space that invoked peace and harmony that was soothing and relaxing. In such an environment, you can control for distractions and interruptions. It is physically easier on the healer to have the recipient lie down on a massage table or high bed. When the bed is low, I ask for a pillow that I can put on the floor and I kneel to do my healing work. Pulling up a chair is another option.

Healing can take place in other settings as well. Ministers of healing often visit the sick in their homes, hospitals, or care centers. Here every effort needs to be made for privacy. If I am in a hospital or care center, I tell the nurse that I will be doing some healing work with the patient so I will be closing the door. Sometimes I have found that the nurse will ask the patient if they can be present since they would like to know more about this work. In the institutional setting, the patient is usually in a hospital bed that can be raised or lowered to allow for ease of treatment. If you raise a bed or put a side rail down, don't forget to put it back to its original state when you are finished.

If the laying-on of hands is occurring within a ritual or prayer service within the church, it may not be appropriate to move one's hands around the body, although this may be perfectly acceptable in some churches. Reaching out and touching someone without asking if touch is acceptable is never advisable.

Telling the person what to expect will alleviate this discomfort. In doing the laying-on of hands in church, you may only want to rest your hands on the recipient's head or shoulders. Moving beyond the simple steps is reserved for meeting with an individual in private.

Remember, there is a sacredness in being with another person during healing work. Whatever is shared or learned in this healing time, stays there. Do not share what occurred with anyone else with-

Ambrose and Olga Worrall, *The Gift of Healing.*

As I begin my work—

"Create in me a clean heart,
   O Gracious One,
   and put a new and right
   spirit within me.
Enfold me in the arms of love,
and fill me with your Holy
Spirit.
Restore in me the joy of your
   saving grace, and
   encourage me with a new
   spirit." Psalm 51

out the recipient's permission. Hold sacred the confidence that has been placed in you. I consider this healing truly a "holy act" in which I and the recipient are both placing our trust in God's healing.

Touch plays an important role in the development of trust, which is a pivotal element in the healing process. Trust calls us as healers to be compassionate and therapeutic in our touch every time we work with an individual. Many have been hurt by touch. Our goal is to allow God's healing touch to heal their hurts, memories, and emotions. Sometimes we have to wait patiently, as Rev. Malcolm Miner has discovered in his parish healing ministry. Rev. Miner is an Episcopal pastor in Hawaii who practices healing touch in his work with the sick of his parish. He has discovered that it takes time for a person who has been hurt or deprived of touch to gain enough trust to allow even a hug, or holding of their hand, or laying hands on their body for healing.[4] For our touch to be healing, we must patiently allow time for trust to develop.

[4]Malcolm H. Miner, *Your Touch Can Heal, A Guide to Healing Touch and How to Use It.*

For a deeper look at anointing in our Christian tradition, see Linda Smith, *Healing Oils Healing Hands, Discovering the Power of Prayer, Hands-On Healing and Anointing.*

A Healing Balm—the Anointing with Oil

In his letter to the Christian community, St. James asked if any among them were sick. If so, the elders, as the representatives of the community, would lay on hands, pray for them, and then *anoint them with healing balm.* Herein is the secret to the Early Christian's success in healing ministry. They had tapped into three forms of what we now know are vibrational healing methods—prayer, energy healing and essential oils. For more on this, see my second book on healing oils.

That particular passage in James has always been comforting for me. It acknowledges that we not only need prayer and touching, we need healing/medicinal remedies. The use of oil for healing is found in many cultures and in many ages. We also find it referred to in the Old Testament and in the Talmud. Oil has soothing healing properties. In some traditions, other medicinal agents are added to the oil, such as essential oils like frankincense or rose, or herbs like eucalyptus, chamomile, or lavender. The healing effect of oil is thus combined with the healing effect of plants.

To understand the place of oil in the early Christian community, Zach Thomas examines the ritual of baptism. For the early Christian, baptism was not only the pouring on of water; the ritual also included laying-on of hands and anointing with oil to "confirm the presence of the Holy Spirit and empower the believer to be a faithful Christian."[5] The anointing served as a sacramental sign of healing aimed at restoring the person to wholeness in body, mind, soul, and spirit. In later centuries anointing became more associated with Confirmation, which became a distinct ritual of its own, in which the recipient was confirmed in the faith.

[5]Zach Thomas, *Healing Touch, The Church's Forgotten Language*, pp. 94-95.

See also Leo Thomas, OP, and Jan Alkire, *Healing As a Parish Ministry*

Anointing specifically for healing the sick became the duty of priests and deacons in early Christianity. Since the Middle Ages, however, the Catholic Church has narrowly interpreted the meaning of this sacrament of the sick and limited its use to the moment of death. Instead of being a means of returning to wholeness, it was supposed to give the sufferer strength to bear his or her illness without losing faith, and it was a means of forgiveness of sins when it was needed. By the Middle Ages, the sacrament became one of preparation for entering into heaven, so it was reserved for the moments before death. This understanding did not come from the Scriptures but rather from church teachings of that day.

The Second Vatican Council returned Catholic practice to the meaning of anointing understood in the first century: the restoration of health. This has not been without controversy and has led to many debates on what is meant by a "restoration of health." For Jesus, it meant restoring to wholeness, whatever that was for the individual.

Oil throughout history has also been used to anoint kings and queens, to consecrate and dedicate leaders and heads of state to God. Anointing is probably best known today as a mark upon those Christians who are set aside by the Christian community as ministers to the faithful. Oil marks forever the minds and hearts of those men and women called into dedicated service through ordination.

"A man was going down from Jerusalem to Jericho, and fell into the hands of robbers, who stripped him, beat him, and went away, leaving him half dead...A Samaritan while traveling came near him and when he saw him, he was moved with pity. He went to him and bandaged his wounds, having poured oil and wine on them. Then he put him on his own animal, brought him to an inn, and took care of him." Luke 10:29-31, 33-34

When I was growing up, I remember my mother used baby oil on her many new babies. Their pink skins would glisten with oil and the fragrance would convey to me the delicateness of these new little beings. My memory associates the qualities of healing and strengthening with oil. It is what we do when we love and care for those who are totally dependent on us.

As a nurse, I later learned the healing properties of "pouring on oil." It may come in the form of lotions now, but the properties are the same. The skin of the frail elderly is soothed and restored with oil; aching and sore muscles are massaged with oil; and broken skin in the form of wounds is healed with oil. In the story of the Good Samaritan, oil and wine are poured onto the wounds of the beaten man, and he is carried to an inn where he is restored to health. Oil forms the basis of many of our modern-day medicines. Since the skin absorbs oil, the medicine is carried to wherever it is needed in the body and restores, rejuvenates, and assists the body in reestablishing health.

Many churches today use oil in their healing ceremonies as well as in their sacraments. Anointing with balm or holy oil carries with it blessings since the oil used in healing rituals is blessed either by the minister of healing or the assembled lay Christian community. The oil used in Roman Catholic, Anglican, and Episcopal churches for a healing ritual is not the same as the oil used in the sacrament of the anointing of the sick. The oil for this sacrament is blessed by a Bishop of the Church and is generally dispensed by an ordained minister/priest or deacon.[6] When anointing with oil is used in combination with the laying-on of hands, the effect can be quite profound.

[6]Leo Thomas and Jan Alkire, *Healing Ministry, A Practical Guide,* p. 183.

Closing Thoughts

The laying-on of hands is beginning to make a comeback in many of our Christian churches and our ministries. We are remembering and seeing anew the stories of healing in the Scriptures and the early Christian history. Jesus taught through example a love for wholeness and health in body, mind, and spirit. Those early followers so thoroughly believed in this healing power and energy that they passed this knowledge on to succeeding generations. They were passionate about healing. In time, this passion cooled and it was lost in practice and in memory. As we regain this art of compassionate healing touch, we renew this ancient ministering to others that is dear to the heart of God. With loving intention, we bring God's healing back into our world and back into our ailing churches. So many ask why there are so few people attending church today. I wonder if it is because people, old and young, are not finding healing being practiced there.

CHAPTER 6

Creating Healing Ministries

As I have visited and participated in the worship services of many Christian churches, I have learned about the various ministries offered to the members of those congregations and to their local communities: praying for the needs of others, visiting the sick, feeding the hungry, providing shelter and clothing for the homeless, and of course, educating the children, young adults, and older adults. But often, the one ministry I am most passionate about—healing ministry—is missing.

Admittedly, some churches have a small healing ministry and may even conduct a healing service on Sundays during or immediately after their worship services. This may include praying, laying-on of hands, and, for some, anointing with oil. The healing ministry I speak of, however, goes much further. It stretches the laying-on of hands to include many healing techniques such as those taught in the Healing Touch Spiritual Ministry program—techniques that we can use to bring a healing touch to all those who need healing in body, mind, soul, and spirit. My vision calls for a focused attention within the Christian community to return to our roots of healing ministry.

If we are serious about creating a healing ministry it will take a great deal of reflection, planning, and education. After all, we have not looked to the church for healing for the past five hundred years. Clearly, it is time to reclaim the Gospel mandate of Christian healing.

Envisioning a Healing Ministry

What would a healing ministry look like in your parish or in your congregational setting? Where do you start? You may be the person God is calling to do something about healing in your congregation, pastoral care department, or retreat house. Who can you talk to about this "call?" Is there an existing ministry that a healing ministry could fit into? Does your church have a prayer ministry? Stephen ministry? Parish nurse program? Each church or congregation is unique. What will work for your Christian community may not work for the church down the street. For those working in institutions or organizations, is there already an avenue open for this healing work in your hospital, hospice, or retreat house? You will need to begin by discerning the mission for this healing ministry in your own church or ministry setting.

Ask the pastor or the church vestry or council, or in the institution, your department head or manager, to appoint a committee to discern whether your church or ministry setting is ready for a healing ministry. Avery Brooke suggests starting by educating that committee with a workshop about healing. Brooke is an Episcopal spiritual director and teaches a course at Yale on healing and the laying-on of hands.[1] Your workshop might include the history of heal-

[1]Avery Brooke, *Healing In The Landscape of Prayer,* p. 55.

ing in Christianity and the healing traditions in your denomination. You will need to learn how to do the laying-on of hands and explore ideas on how to develop a ministry specific for your setting. This information can be provided in a day-long workshop or in a workshop spread out over six to eight weeks.

The minister and key members of the ministry staff need to participate in this workshop not only for themselves but also to be able to support the laity, who will be taking the major leadership responsibilities. Sometimes setting up a workshop for your committee is not practical. The church may then choose the option of sending one or two committee representatives to a workshop so that they can bring the information back to the whole group.

I cannot emphasize enough the importance of the support and participation of the pastor and the pastoral staff in this initial planning stage. There is a major difference between the pastor saying "yes"—(and then waiting to see if the idea lives or dies)—and a pastor actively participating.

Reading and studying a book together might be another place to begin. The bibliography of this book contains many reading suggestions. At your committee meetings, you might spend a few moments praying for the needs of others and for each of those present. Often when groups begin praying, they naturally progress to laying-on hands for each other's needs. Agnes Sanford, one of this century's best-known Christian healers, began this way with the ladies of the church where her husband was the minister. It is difficult to imagine developing a healing ministry without practicing this laying-on of hands and praying for guidance as you develop this new ministry.

Be prepared to spend time allowing a vision for this ministry to develop. It could take months or a year or more. As you work together, the vision will gradually unfold and you will be ready to write your mission statement. What will it look like? It may include prayer ministry by itself, prayer with the laying-on of hands, perhaps with anointing with oil. Or, it could go much further and include offering

Agnes Sanford, *Sealed Orders*.

healing treatments by those who have been trained, commissioned, and supervised. You will want to see this ministry within the context of all the other ministries offered by your church or ministry setting. The mission will flow from the overall mission of your congregation, retreat house, or pastoral care department.

Leo Thomas and Jan Alkire, two Catholic writers, speak about healing ministry as flowing from the "body of Christ," the Christian community where we are all bonded to one another. When one member is suffering, it affects the total body. We need to utilize all the expertise of the body of Christ in healing work, not just a few prominent healers.[2] Many Christians have been suspicious of, even scandalized by, the flamboyant "healers" in church tents, or on street corners, radio, and television. Neither Jesus nor his disciples drew such attention in their healing work. They modeled for us a humility that recognizes we are but the conduit for God's healing for others.

[2]Leo Thomas, OP, and Jan Alkire, *Healing As A Parish Ministry, Mending Body, Mind, and Spirit,* p. 26.

As you begin to have a clearer vision of what this healing ministry is going to be, you will want to start preparing the congregation. The pastor again needs to take the lead in this, perhaps through the Sunday sermons or through short educational programs during the adult education time or Bible study. The pastor sets the tone, reassuring the community that this, indeed, is the church's work. As interest begins to develop for this healing ministry, it is time to set in place your organizational structure. Who is the best person discerned by your committee to be in charge of this ministry? Or, who is appointed by the minister or vestry or church council to head up this healing program? Now your work begins in earnest. Policies and procedures need to be written and approved, and the ministers of healing need to be trained.

"Be Wise as Serpents, Innocent as Doves"

Jesus gave his disciples lots of practical advise for their ministries. He told them to travel lightly, trust in God's care for them, have a welcoming heart to all, accept what is given to them, store up spiritual treasures, and ask God for what they need. He reassured them that when their hearts were connected to God, they need not

"See, I am sending you out like sheep into the midst of wolves; so be wise as serpents and innocent as doves...do not worry about how you are to speak, or what you are to say; for what you are to say will be given to you at that time; for it is not you who speak but the Spirit of your Father speaking through you." Matt. 10:16, 19

worry about what to say, even in the midst of adversity. The Spirit would work through them. He also taught them not to be naive about the world. In developing our healing ministry, we also want to be wise and look at the practical issues that will face us. What are some of these considerations?

Confidentiality is a good place to start. It is one of the most important policies to establish and will set the tone for the kind of professional behavior expected in this healing work. Whatever is learned about another during the healing work must remain confidential. That includes all exchanges between the Healing Ministry Team members and those requesting healing. The healer's observations and impressions, all verbal and nonverbal information shared, and all records made concerning the contact must be held in confidence. Who will have access to this information? Your policy will specify all those who have this "need to know." For instance, the person supervising the Healing Ministry team members may need to review records or be consulted on the plan of care. Or, your church may decide that the ministers should have access to records. How will permission be obtained to disclose this information? This is ethical behavior we would all expect in a healing ministry, whether it is in a church or pastoral care setting.

Boundary and gender issues usually refer to touching or not touching as well as working or not working on the opposite sex.

Another practical area to discern is your church's position on boundary or gender issues. You may wish to consider making a requirement that the minister of healing be of the same gender as the recipient, or when that is not possible, at least having someone of the same gender as the recipient of healing present as a witness. This is a safety measure for both the ministers of healing and the church, since the ministers of healing are representatives of the church and are therefore accountable to the church for their actions. Ministry done under an individual's name in a private practice is different from that done under the name of the church. You will want to exercise due caution with respect to these boundary issues at all times. Ministry offered in the church can be done by one person at the altar rail or in any of the public places of the church building. Once a door is closed, however, two members of the Healing Ministry team will need to be present (or one member of the Healing Team and a witness), one of whom is preferably of the same gender as the person seeking healing.

It is wise to consider using a consent form that will inform the recipient what is involved and that this healing is not meant to replace seeing a physician or other medical professional. A consent form helps everyone to know what this healing ministry entails. It acknowledges that many people have experienced an increased well-being and improvement in their condition and that some may even have experienced complete healing. In our work we cannot promise those results, but we do trust in God's healing grace. The recipient can stop the healing treatment at any time. The church or ministry setting may wish to consult its legal representative as to the particular wording of these consent forms. Whether consent forms are considered necessary in pastoral care departments will depend on the policies of the whole institution and bears careful attention.

"There Are Many Gifts"

St. Paul reminds us that not everyone is called to a healing ministry. There are many gifts of the Spirit and it is the Spirit who calls us to serve. For centuries we have been embarrassed by these gifts of the Spirit and ignored them or explained them away. Today many people are responding to the revival of spiritual healing very slowly. They are feeling their way, balancing the Gospel mandate with church practices that may be in opposition to healing and miracles. It is a challenge to bring the faithful back to Jesus' healing ministry when those traditions have been lost and suppressed for hundreds of years. The focus for a healing ministry should come from the Scriptures. Healing is the work of the church, the people of God.

Leadership for a healing ministry in the early church began with the Apostles. Shortly after Pentecost, the weight of their responsibilities became great and we see that many duties, including physical and spiritual healing, began to be shared with the elders (James 5:13-16) and with the members of the new church. Today, this lead-

"Now there are varieties of gifts, but the same Spirit...To each is given the manifestation of the Spirit for the common good. To one is given through the Spirit the utterance of wisdom, and to another the utterance of knowledge according to the same Spirit, to another faith by the same Spirit, to another gifts of healing by the one Spirit, to another the working of miracles, to another prophecy, to another the discernment of spirits, to another various kinds of tongues, to another the interpretation of tongues.

All these are activated by one and the same Spirit, who allots to each one individually just as the Spirit chooses." Cor. 12: 4-11

ership for healing may come either from the clergy/ministry staff or from the laity. Often the ministers, like the Apostles two thousand years ago, are so busy with the responsibility of running a congregation that they have limited time to do spiritual healing. Sometimes it is assigned to or becomes the primary responsibility of the deacons, presbyters, or elders. The laity who are specifically called or commissioned by the church to do spiritual healing work can sometimes devote themselves to this as a primary calling.

Not all who feel "called" to this work are truly suitable, however, and discernment through prayer is required. Often this situation takes care of itself if there is a requirement for on-going education and supervision. Discernment of call is very important and cannot be left solely to individual decision. This work attracts not only those genuinely called by God but also those who are psychologically on the fringe. From the beginning, the Christian community met together in prayer to select those who would fulfill certain duties in the Lord, so it is not uncommon for churches today to do the same. This is a serious responsibility for the welfare and protection of those who come for healing. We must remember that this is not a ministry that gives us a license to advise, counsel, or practice amateur psychology. Our role is to be a witness to the healing presence of God.

Wherever the leadership lies for this ministry, the pastor, who is ultimately responsible for overseeing all the sponsored ministries of the church, needs to be actively involved. The pastor is in the best position to see that the Christian mandate of healing is carried out properly.

"Two by Two"

It was not for the mere sake of companionship that Jesus sent the disciples out in two's; he expected them to rely upon each other for strength. He first sent the twelve then he sent the seventy ahead of him to prepare the way—to spread the word that he was coming as a healer into people's lives. Jesus empowered his disciples to do what he was doing—preach the good word and heal the sick—and he gave them each other for support and strength in this work.

I remember well my first days doing Healing Touch. I had good intentions to help others, but I was insecure in the work and knew I did not know enough. Most importantly, I had not learned how to truly tap deeply into the source of all healing, into God. I knew intellectually, but my heart had not grown sufficiently to guide me yet in the work. Even with these shortcomings, the work continued to draw me like a magnet. What I lacked personally seemed to be made up for when I worked together with another Healing Touch practitioner. As we would center our hearts together, we were strengthened in our heart connection with God. Gradually my insecurities decreased and I eventually learned to trust in divine guidance. When I began to teach, it was also as a co-instructor. Together, we made up for each other's insufficiencies, which strengthened our work.

The model of going out in two's is even more important in our day when our society tends to "sue first" and "ask questions later." Working in two's in a healing ministry is not only biblical, it is prudent and wise.

I would like to think that as we do this work, we are coming from a heartfelt place, a compassionate, loving place for our fellow man and woman. But there may be those who interpret our efforts differently and judge our actions as offensive or harmful, when that is not our intent. Some churches today may be fearful of having a healing ministry for these very reasons. Fear can stop the flow of grace. Fear can stop the actions of the Holy Spirit and keep us fragmented and closed to the presence of God. A wise steward of God's healing Light and energy will set down in writing how this ministry will be carried out. The wise leader will supervise all those involved to make sure it is done correctly, according to Scripture, church traditions, and mandates.

"Then he went among the villages teaching. He called the twelve and began to send them out two by two, and gave them authority over the unclean spirits. He ordered them to take nothing for their journey except a staff, no bread, no bag, no money in their belts, but to wear sandals and not to put on two tunics. He said to them 'Whenever you enter a house, stay there until you leave the place. If any place will not welcome you and they refuse to hear you, as you leave, shake off the dust that is on your feet as a testimony against them' So they went out and proclaimed that all should repent. They cast out many demons, and anointed with oil many who were sick and cured them." Mark 6:6-13

"The Lord appointed seventy others and sent them on ahead of him in pairs to every town and place where he himself intended to go. He said to them 'The harvest is plentiful, but the laborers are few; therefore ask the Lord of the harvest to send out laborers into his harvest. Go on your way. See, I am sending you out like lambs into the midst of wolves. Carry no purse, no bag, no sandals; and greet no one on the road... Whenever you enter a town and its people welcome you, eat what is set before you; cure the sick who are there, and say to them, 'The kingdom of God has come near to you.'" Luke 10: 1-9

"The Harvest Is Plentiful, the Laborers Are Few"

As your vision fully takes shape, the time will come when the Spirit leads you to begin offering healing ministry to members of your church. The congregation has been prepared. The ministers of healing have been selected through prayer and commissioned by the church. Policies and procedures are in the process of developing. Beginning slowly and wisely will allow your church or ministry setting to continue training and educating the ministers of healing while further preparation of the congregation takes place. Don't allow yourselves to be overwhelmed with the needs that present themselves while you are in this development stage.

Next, develop a policy and a procedure on exactly what your church or ministry setting defines as the laying-on of hands. If Healing Touch Spiritual Ministry or any other healing modality is practiced, a definition and description should be included as well. This will assist those who are volunteering to know what is expected. As your vision for this healing ministry goes forward, you will gradually want to introduce it to the congregation or within your ministry setting. You may decide to begin with prayers, laying-on of hands, and anointing during or immediately after church services. After some time, provide this healing ministry to those in their homes, hospitals, and nursing homes. As your ministers of healing are prepared fully, you can begin to offer Healing Touch Spiritual Ministry by appointments, either in the church or during visits to the sick. In pastoral care settings, you may want to begin offering this healing work to peers, to other co-workers, and then to patients and their family members.

A ministry involving touching others certainly needs adequate education and supervision. Each church will need to decide what basic requirements are needed for an individual to function as a member of the Healing Ministry team. What will be the expectations for continued or ongoing practice in this healing art of the laying-on of hands? What are the qualities and the skills you want your healing ministers to have? How will they obtain these skills: through intensive trainings, workshops, pastoral care education, audiotapes, and reading? Who will guide this education?

Leo Thomas and Jan Alkire have developed four goals that I find very helpful in developing a training program in healing ministry:

1. *To foster spiritual maturity through a process of spiritual formation.*

2. *To teach the knowledge, skills, and attitudes needed for successful ministry.*

3. *To teach team healing ministry.*

4. *To help each trainee determine to what extent he/she is called to this ministry.*[3]

[3]Leo Thomas, OP, and Jan Alkire, *Healing Ministry, A Practical Guide,* pp. 168-169.

Spiritually, the ministers of healing must be mature and strong in their faith. Spiritual formation will help them to grow in their knowledge of God and deepen their ability to assist others. Once trained, what kind of supervision will your team members have? What knowledgeable person is available to answer questions, consult on treatment, or review written records for appropriate ministry? What kind of training will be required for this supervisor? Ideally, this person will be able to do on-going education for the healing team members. Some churches may not have such a knowledgeable person in their parish or congregation. In that case, it may be possible to find someone in a neighboring church. Supervision need not be a time-consuming duty unless the church is large and healing services are extensive. In that case, the church will probably need to provide this supervision by one of its staff members. In pastoral care settings in hospitals, hospices, or retreat settings, who else in the institution or program is trained in Healing Touch Spiritual Ministry? Is there anyone in your town or city? It may mean doing a little searching to find an appropriate supervisor.

How will each member of the Healing Ministry team be accountable to the church or ministry setting? What record keeping

Linda Smith, *Suggested Guidelines/ Policies for Healing Ministry, 3rd Edition*. This is a booklet of policies and guidelines for churches and ministry settings developed by ministers from many denominations. It is available through the Healing Touch Spiritual Ministry Program and can be downloaded free from the www. HTSpiritualMinistry.com site.

will be required, and who will have access to these records? Where will these records or accounts of healing interventions be kept? These are some of the mundane yet important issues that will need to be thought through. Keeping records of each request for healing is not only a safeguard for the church and the healing ministers it also enables the healing ministers to remember what they did and to see the progress in any follow-up healing treatments.

There is no need to make this a complicated task. A simple format can be developed for the ministers of healing to record their visits or healing treatments in the church. The record need only contain a minimum of information, such as the church member's name, telephone number, nature of their request, place of healing, assessment, treatment, outcome, and any follow-up. All records will need to be held in the strictest confidence, of course, and kept in a locked file, preferably in the church office. Pastoral care settings are already accustomed to this kind of record keeping.

Healing Services

I have observed many forms of healing services and rituals among different denominations. Churches that have a lot of ritual in their liturgies find it very easy to move into healing services that include the anointing with oil. For others, this may seem a bit strange at first.

Two lay ministers of healing in a Presbyterian church described to me how unusual it felt at first when their church began to hold prepared prayer services for healing. They began with Sunday evening services and were surprised when 50-100 people would show up every Sunday evening. Their ministers of healing worked in small groups with the individuals who came forward to be prayed for. They then experimented with "anointing" as described in the Letter of James. For this particular church, it was a step out in faith since they lacked a long tradition of laying-on of hands and anointing. Other Presbyterian churches have had this healing tradition for a very long time.

Many Episcopal churches have healing services available after communion at the Sunday liturgy or during a weekday service. Several Episcopal churches I have visited around the country have separate altars either at the side or at the back of the church where the church members go for prayer, laying-on of hands, and anointing by the deacon or another priest. In one Lutheran church in the San Francisco Bay area, individuals wishing to receive healing come forward to the front of the altar to be prayed for and anointed once a month as part of their regular Sunday worship service. In Roman Catholic healing services, only the priest anoints with oil, but lay ministers of healing can lay on hands and pray.

Some churches have a healing service separate from the Sunday or weekday worship or communion service. This may include general prayers for all those who need healing, the singing of songs, and the reading of scripture. Sometimes there are reflections on the scriptures offered by the minister of healing or by those in attendance. Then, those who wish to be individually prayed for come forward, and either the minister of healing lays on hands or a group will lay on hands and pray for the needs of that individual. Anointing can follow. The service ends with prayers of gratitude and blessings for the group.

Privacy can be an issue during these services. Healing for some involves bearing their soul before a minister of God. Avery Brooke says that asking for healing is sometimes close to the sacrament of reconciliation (confession) and can be profoundly healing in itself. The ministers of healing hold these requests for healing in confidence. Having music playing or the choir singing in the background for such services might also be helpful, both to set the mood and to provide some privacy.[4]

If long prayers are offered for each individual and there are many people in attendance, it can make for a long service. James Wagner, a Methodist minister, writes several suggestions for our individual prayers: be brief, be flexible, and be intentional in lifting up each person to the light and love of the healing Christ.[5]

[4]Avery Brooke, *Healing In The Landscape of Prayer,* p. 62.

[5]James Wagner, *An Adventure In Healing and Wholeness, The Healing Ministry of Christ In the Church Today*, p. 139.

In our Healing Touch Spiritual Ministry courses we end the two day experience with an optional healing and anointing service. Most of the participants stay and some even invite their loved ones to join them in this prayer service. I have even seen some participants who have been so taken with the work that they have someone bring their ill loved ones from home so that the whole group may pray for them. When there are a large number of participants, as is often the case, we will invite some of the participants who are ministers to help with the laying-on of hands and anointing. They have been most eager to help. In the service, we say some prayers for the people of God, sing some songs, listen to the scriptures, and offer some reflections. Then, anyone who wishes to be prayed for individually comes forward to one of the ministers of healing and the whole community participates by forming small circles around those individuals. All lay on hands and pray for the person requesting healing. At the end of the prayers offered, the ministers of healing anoint the individual's head and hands with oil, which the assembled Christian community has blessed. The level of healing in these healing services is profound. Often tears abound as individuals let go of physical, emotional, and spiritual pain that they have been burdened with. Each time I have been involved in these healing services, I have been awed by the power of God working in people's lives, and I have been humbled by the prayers offered for me and for this work. Healing is indeed taking place among God's people.

Casting Out the Seed

The Healing Ministry at Trinity is led by Rev. Lori Erickson, deacon at the church, and by Jacquelyn Phillips.

There are a number of churches around the country that have an active Healing Touch Spiritual Ministry established. One of these is Trinity Episcopal Church in Iowa City, IA. Their ministry has a unique beginning but is similar to those I have heard about in other cities. A Certified Healing Touch Practitioner by the name of Jacquelyn Phillips retired to Iowa City and joined Trinity Church. Within a short time, Jacque who is in her eighties was volunteering at the church offering to do Healing Touch. She then discovered the Healing Touch Spiritual Ministry program and the first edition of this book *Called into Healing*. She presented her idea of having a healing ministry at Trinity to Rev. Lori Erickson, one of the deacons of the church. Recognizing that Healing Touch can be presented from a Judeo-Christian perspective, they first sought the support of the pastor, the Rev. Mel Schlachter. He was quite open the idea, especially since his own wife who is also a pastor at another church, had benefited from Healing Touch while going through a serious illness. With his support, they began offering HTSM classes for their church members and people from the surrounding community. Much interest was generated as a result of these classes and so they decided that yes, they did want to create a healing ministry for their church. Following the recommendations of the HTSM program, they wrote their policies and procedures. Each practitioner signs an agreement for their volunteer service. They keep records and are supervised in their healing ministry by Phillips, a CHTP, and Erickson, a HTSM healing practitioner. Between 2003 and 2005 the church sponsored the first five levels in the HTSM program. They now have a HTSM clinic that meets every three weeks, a healing ministry room complete with massage table for individual healing sessions, and a healing team who do at-home sessions for the home bound and those in hospice care. They have also incorporated a component in their Sunday service by creating an alcove in which members can receive the laying on of hands. Rev. Erickson estimates that the healing team does more than 450 treatments a year.

At the clinic, the Healing Touch Spiritual Ministry practitioners transform the parish hall into a healing space with massage tables and subdued lighting. They then come together in prayer prior to the client's arrival. At the end of the evening, practitioners and clients all come together in one circle to pray for others. The practitioners are all people who have gone through one or more of the Healing Touch Spiritual Ministry educational programs. Eight have their certificates of completion as healing practitioners and there are some who have taken Healing Touch or Reiki classes. The clinic is an opportunity for the practitioners to practice their healing skills and for those within the church and community to receive holistic healing from a Christian perspective. Healing Touch Spiritual Ministry has certainly taken root in this church and has become a model for neighboring churches and for other churches in that region. Rev. Schlachter's wife, the Rev. Barbara Schlachter is now creating a healing ministry at Christ Episcopal Church in Cedar Rapids. She too has completed the course of study and become a Healing Touch Spiritual Ministry practitioner. Recently she instituted a change in their annual foot washing ritual during Easter week. After the washing of feet they anoint with frankincense and myrrh. This is truly a return to the Gospel teachings to be a healing presence with prayer, hands-on healing and anointing.

Barbara Lester leads the healing ministry team at Ascension Lutheran Church, San Diego, CA.

Another Healing Touch Spiritual Ministry story is at Ascension Lutheran Church in San Diego. Barbara Lester who is the parish nurse was first introduced to this work when a Healing Touch practitioner presented an introductory program at their church women's group. She went on to attend a class offered in the Healing Touch Spiritual Ministry program. Afterwards, she took this knowledge to her pastor and to other like-minded people in the parish. Many went on to take additional courses and they soon established a Healing Touch Spiritual Ministry for Ascension church. After nine years, they still meet weekly and are committed to sharing God's love to all who come for healing. They support, nurture and care for each other. Their healing ministry has become an outreach ministry of their parish, welcoming anyone from another faith. Their healing sessions begin with prayer, then the practitioners working in groups, lay-on hands and anoint all those who are in need. Several of the ladies involved in this ministry are in their eighties and are a dynamic force.

Sometimes it's a much slower process in developing a ministry. A case in point is the Lutheran Church of the Good Shepherd in Bel Air, Maryland. Linda Herget who is the ministry team leader for the parish Healthcare Ministry has offered Healing Touch Spiritual Ministry courses at her church and has had many from their congregation attend. They have progressed to doing the laying-on of hands at their contemporary worship service on Sundays. This year they are planning a commissioning of those who do the laying-on of hands at the annual blessing of the oils. It has been a slow step-by-step two year process according to Herget, preparing both the congregation and the ministry team. Her hopes are that one day they actually have a space for healers to do healing work for all those in need of healing. Many churches are in the same slow process. How did Jesus heal and did he really mean for us to do it as well. These are concerns that have to be addressed before launching into a full program such as the one at Trinity Episcopal Church.

Norm Shealy in his book *Sacred Healing*, talks about Harry Edwards, a sacred healer in England and former president of the National Federation of Spiritual Healers. Edwards believes that anyone with a great passion and desire to help others can develop the ability to heal. The qualifications of a good healer for him include generosity, a willingness to give of self, compassion and sympathy for those in need.[6] This, I believe, succinctly describes the many Healing Touch Spiritual Ministries that have been established in not only Episcopal and Lutheran churches, but also in Catholic, Congregational, United Church of Christ, Methodist, Presbyterian, and Disciples of Christ churches. It is the lay people in our churches who are leading the way—looking for more meaningful ways to be of service to their Christian communities. They are gathering their faith and courage and speak to their ministers, vestries, and church boards about healing ministry. They are casting out the seed of healing and many are coming up with 30, 60 and even a hundred fold.

[6]Norm Shealy, Sacred Healing, *The Curing Power of Energy and Spirituality,* p. 48.

CHAPTER 7

Learning to Be a Healing Presence For Others

We have all met individuals in our lifetime who have left lasting impressions on us or may have startled us out of our complacency, challenging us to change our lives. What is it about these individuals that so catches our attention that we even undergo personal transformation?

I remember in the 1970s visiting the famous restaurant known as the Chattanooga Choo Choo in Chattanooga, Tennessee. The waitress gave me and my two companions her complete and undivided attention. She literally radiated a presence that, even now, after nearly 30 years, I still can feel. My friends and I were amazed at the presence she commanded. She was so attuned to our needs that it was as if we were the only people on the face of the earth. I remember fumbling at the end of the meal, saying something like, "You must really like your job." With great exuberance, she told us that she felt she had the wonderful privilege each day of meeting and serving many interesting people. She loved her job and could think of nothing else she would rather be doing.

After dinner, we went out into the brisk cool air, still talking about this phenomenal waitress. We noticed the Choo Choo stood ready for passenger boarding for a mere 5 cent ride down the quarter mile track and back, so we hopped on. For a second time that evening we were utterly dumb struck. The conductor of the little train was just like the waitress. He told us that he used to teach high school but now he loved meeting so many interesting people and conversing with them. He felt happy at the end of the day just knowing that he brought a little cheer into people's lives. Again, we were met with an intense presence and joy of life.

I have told the story of these two individuals countless times because of the lasting impression they left with me. What was it about them that was so special? Were they angels sent to "shake me loose" from my state of non-awareness? My conclusion after all these years is that they both had learned the art of spiritual presence. The light shown through them, and I was changed. These "teachers" held simple jobs, ones that would not have appealed to me. However, they elevated their work through their simple presence. It was a lesson not only in humility but also a lesson in practicing the art of presence with others.

Have there been similar "angels" or "teachers" in your life?

The spiritual presence that we bring into our relationships flows from our connectedness with the Divine. It can bring healing to all kinds of situations—to our families, peers, work situations, churches, communities, towns, and cities. We may be conscious of this connection at some moments more than at other times. For me it is the first step in learning how to be an instrument of healing for others.

Nurses know how important it is to be present to their patients. Barbara Dossey, a well-known lecturer and author on holistic nursing, describes presence as:

"the state achieved when one moves within oneself to an inner reference of stability...It is a place of inner being, of quietude within which one can feel truly integrated, unified and focused."[1]

[1]Barbara Dossey and Lynn Keegan, *Holistic Nursing, 2nd edition,* p. 67.

Nurses learn presence with others by first learning to be present with themselves. Practicing the art of presence calls for an ability to be in the moment, something that is all too often hard to do with the modern demands of nursing. Anne Day, a holistic nurse practitioner and teacher, sees the quality of presence as a

"holistic self-centered exchange, a way of being available in a situation with the wholeness of one's unique individual essence."[2]

[2]Anne Day, *Healing Presence* (nursing course offered at Red Rocks Community College, Denver, Colorado).

In many professions, learning this art of presence is key to accomplishing the goals, whatever they are. Maggie McKivergin who is a holistic nurse and consultant, writes about the nurse as an instrument of healing. She distinguishes three levels of presence: first, there is physical presence, which calls upon skills of seeing, touching, doing, examining, hearing, and hugging. Nurses do lots of touching in their work, in which they convey their connection to others. Second, there is psychologic presence, which uses the abilities of assessing, communicating, active listening, writing, and reflecting. These abilities refer to the nurse's counseling skills such as empathy, caring, accepting, and being non-judgmental. And, lastly, there is therapeutic presence, which calls upon the nurse to respond to another with his or her whole being. This calls for being centered and at-one with the other. This kind of presence comes from a place of openness, intuitive knowing, communion, and love.[3] We can see in her description the many ways we can be a healing presence for others, whether nursing is our profession or not.

[3]Maggie McKivergin, "The Nurse as an Instrument of Healing," in *Core Curriculum for Holistic Nursing,* edited by Barbara Dossey, pp. 19-20.

In healing work, we are called upon to practice all of these forms of presence with those to whom we offer healing. Being truly in the moment, connected to our Source, to God, we cannot help but extend compassionate caring in our touch and in our word. In essence, we radiate wholeness and beauty. This is not an easy task, but it becomes easier with practice. The humble Brother Lawrence, who lived in the nineteenth century, made a habit of seeing God in all things, in all moments. There is only this moment, yesterday is already gone, and tomorrow...tomorrow is still not here. Yesterday and tomorrow actually don't exist except in our minds.

Brother Lawrence, *Practicing the Presence of God.*

When we come into this awareness in the moment, we are "Christ-consciousness," writes Joel Goldsmith, a spiritual writer of the 1950s. In this moment we are aligned with "cosmic law," and all power of the Godhead flows through us. We come into the deep awareness that all healing can only take place in the present moment. As we tap into this Christ-consciousness, the Christ Light fills us up to overflowing, and healing grace is entrained for the other. Aligning our heart with the heart of God, we find a rhythm in healing, a resonant vibration. God's healing grace fills us, and our ego becomes transformed. We have nothing to do but to be very peaceful and quiet within, maintaining that spiritual alignment. At that moment, we become "beholders of God" and God's activity. We become instruments and channels of divine grace. We become "Light-Bearers."[4]

[4]Joel Goldsmith, *Practicing the Presence*, p. 118.

We have all heard of stories of healers being caught up in the experience and blurring the lines between God's grace and their own ego. As healers, it is only natural that we want our clients to feel better after treatment. However, the ego can go awry when we become attached to the outcome. When we become invested in what happens and feel a failure when the expected outcome does not materialize, we know that ego is in control. In these instances, we forget that in true Christ consciousness, all outcomes are blessed.

Over the past decade there have been many faith healers who may have started out with good intentions but became trapped in ego and desire for money. How have these individuals "scandalized" our Christian community and affected the imperative to heal others?

Yearning for God's Presence

"Do you not know that you are God's temple and that God's Spirit dwells in you?" I Cor. 3:16

We are spiritual beings with physical bodies. As we grow in our consciousness of who we really are, the spiritual part of us seeks to be connected, to be in communion with God—with all that is sacred and holy in life. It is a yearning at the soul level that knows there is more to life than this visible world that exists in time and space. The spark of the Divine within us that has been with us from our first moment on this earth is seeking the Source. It is yearning to go home.

In comparison with the age of the universe, we are here but a fleeting moment. And yet in that space of a few years, we have the opportunity to learn about God's love and how it manifests in our lives and the lives of others. We are not loners destined to be on our own islands—we are social beings who either help or don't help one another. We get to explore such meaningful questions as: What is the purpose of life? What else is there? How do I reach God? Why do we have pain and suffering in life? Why must all things die? How does healing occur and why is God interested in our healing? God is all powerful, so why does God need us to help heal one another?

[5]Ron Roth, *The Healing Path of Prayer*, p. 29.

Ron Roth points out that the essence of God is light, the essence of God is energy. If this is true and Genesis is correct when it says we are made in God's likeness, then we are light and energy. Connecting with God is going back to our Source. Energy is released when we are in communion with God.[5] Athletes describe this moment of connection as "being in the flow." Everything is connected and working to their ultimate goal. When we are in that Divine flow, we become conduits that release God's energy for healing. God's light flows through us to others. There is no higher consciousness than realizing that the Divine Presence is within us.[6]

[6]Also see Kenneth Bakken, *The Call to Wholeness, Health As a Spiritual Journey*, pp. 72-73.

Mystics have shown us the way in their yearning for God's presence. Take for example Hildegard of Bingen, the twelfth-century Benedictine abbess gifted with healing and psychic abilities, referred to in chapter two. Her writings are an inspiration to those who plumb the depths of her spirituality for their own journeys. She writes:

"Good People,
Most royal greening verdancy,
rooted in the sun,
you shine with radiant light.
In this circle of earthly existence
you shine
so finely,
it surpasses understanding.
God hugs you.
You are encircled
By the arms
of the mystery of God."[7]

[7]Gabriele Uhlein, *Meditations with Hildegard of Bingen*, p. 90.

Being in the moment with this Christ-consciousness takes practice. If there is a skill you want to learn, such as riding a mountain bike, sky diving, or running a marathon, you first have to train and acquire the stamina and the skill required. Dedication, discipline, rest, proper nutrition, stretching, exercises, visualizing yourself actually performing the skill, meditation, relaxation, positive thinking—all of these are necessary to accomplish your goal. You will probably seek out a mentor, an expert, to help you train for your skill. Once you have obtained your goal, you must maintain your vigilance so that you will not lose the ground you have gained. This requires ongoing mentoring, monitoring, practice, and dedication.

Being able to maintain the Christ-consciousness is very much the same. It takes a vigilant dedication, discipline, openness, and a desire to be of service to others. The hunger within for the Divine Presence must be nurtured.

And Jesus said, "You shall love the Lord your God with all your heart, and with all your soul, and with all your mind. This the greatest and the first commandment. And a second is like it: You shall love your neighbor as yourself." Matt. 22:37-39

When a lawyer stood before Jesus and asked what the greatest commandment was, his intent was to try to trip up Jesus. But Jesus' answer—"You shall love God and your neighbor as yourself" –summed up the entirety of the law and proclaimed his ministry to the world to be one of love and compassion. Most of us forget the last words in the great commandment—"to love your neighbor as yourself." When we nurture the divine Presence within, we are loving

St. Paul wrote, "I pray that you will be strengthened in your inner being with the presence and strength of Christ as you are rooted and grounded in love." Ephesians 3:14.

Who in your life exhibits this deep presence of God that stirs your heart? How are they a model for you?

[8]Margaret Burkhardt and Mary Gail Nagai-Jacobson, *Spirituality, Living our Connectedness*, p. 89.

ourselves as well. It is in loving ourselves, in nurturing the Christ Light within, that we are able to be that Divine Presence for others.

As we allow Love to begin to ground us, we grow stronger and the presence of God within us grows brighter. Everything that surrounds us begins to come into focus, only we didn't know we were out of focus. Showing compassion and caring becomes easier not just when we are with someone in a healing way, but throughout our whole waking day. We begin to change, to be more light-filled. Light is attractive and has a way of transforming the environment. Light generates a higher vibration, and others are affected positively by this.

Many have commented on the saintliness of Mother Theresa and how her very presence would bring healing to a situation. She was a tremendous light, and like moths to the light in the darkness, people were attracted to being in her presence. Yet it was not her power they sought but the Divine Presence within her that stirred their hearts and made them want to be better individuals. She was a beacon of compassionate love, a guide and model we can call upon for our own journey.

As we grow in Christ-consciousness, our work settings and homes will begin to reflect our own inner transformation. Instead of seeing the negative and the bleak in life, we begin to notice that there is love, gentleness, and kindness being reflected back to us. We might recognize the experience of the Sacred presence as a sense of peace, joy or gladness, as gratitude, as insight, as a power or energy within us, or as Burkhardt and Nagai-Jacobson point out, "that something that keeps us going when we feel we no longer can go on."[8] When we greet others with the presence of God in our hearts, it is returned many times over. Negativity is overwhelmed with love and can't survive in the light. The unexpected in life is allowed to come through both the gifts and the lessons. Blessings are all around us. Awareness of the presence of God spirals to new heights as we radiate the Christ-consciousness. There is such a simplicity about this Divine Presence. Many find that as they become more present to the

Christ Light, they want to simplify their lives. Environment, relationships, goals, and desires come into balance. We breathe in the presence of God and we breathe in the Light. All is well as we rest in God's inner harmony.

Qualities of a Healing Presence

We can all think of times when we recognized that someone else was an instrument of healing for us. Perhaps it was a word, or touch or presence. We might even be able to describe what we felt or observed as those moments of healing occurred. At some level within, we recognized the qualities of God's presence, of God's love for us expressed through this other person. Something in us was touched at the deepest core, opening us to change, to heal in body, mind, soul, and spirit. This was not just an emotional experience. Our spiritual selves were uplifted and it was like seeing the face of God and feeling God's embrace. Some describe these moments of healing as the presence of an angel or holy being connecting them to all that is sacred in life.

I am absolutely convinced that *all healing is deeply spiritual work*. Many have noted as we enter the new millennium that we are rediscovering "spirituality" and learning how our work can be "spiritual." This implies a profound faith and trust that life has meaning and that something greater is out there. It also implies that we as spiritual beings are connected to each other and to God in mysterious ways. Diarmuid O'Murchu, an Irish theologian, states that, "we are being plunged more profoundly into our world which is not alienating us from the divine but re-connecting us with the God who co-creates at the heart of creation."[9]

[9]Diarmuid O'Murchu, *Reclaiming Spirituality*, pp. 12-13.

If we feel moved to be an instrument of healing but have not learned that we must be spiritually connected to God in our hearts, our efforts will show few results. Healing comes from the heart, where God's love and compassion reside. When we are connected to this divine energy, infinitely more is possible. This is one of the essential differences between Christian healing and secular healing.[10]

[10]Rochelle Graham, Flora Litt, and Wayne Irwin, *Healing From the Heart*, p. 22.

Over the years, I have observed many qualities of a healing presence radiating in others as they reach out in healing towards others. All of these qualities flow from that divine energy that is constantly available to us. Try experiencing these qualities and see how they feel. You may wish to journal on those that speak to your heart. Some will take root and grow rapidly others will need caring for, nurturing, and patient attendance.

Compassion...calm...listening...caring

Innate harmony...unconditional love...sense of the sacred in life

Being truly in the moment with another...at-one-ment

Nonjudgmental attitude towards others

Joyful...gentle...peaceful...serene...humble...giving

Genuine...honest...focused...sensitive...radiant

Understanding...trusting...supportive...empathetic...nurturing

Empowering...wholeness...courage...strength

Resonant vibration...heart centered...warmth...tenderness

Which of these qualities fit you? Try keeping a journal.

How to Grow into Being a Healing Presence for Others

Joy

Take yourself lightly. Joy is the mark of a light-hearted spirit. It comes when we are caught up in the Spirit, when we release ourselves and others from the bondage of unforgiveness, when we let go of our judgments of others, when we remember that we are not in charge and that God has all the bases covered. "Letting go, and letting God" is divine freedom. Jesus was intent on imparting to his followers enough knowledge that their "joy may be full." The world needs joyful healers who radiate the Christ presence.

Joy is the mark of true holiness. When we recognize we are filled with God, and God is holy, then we too are holy. Holiness emanates from our very being, embracing all the subtleties of living and loving others. Just being aware of the miracles in each moment

"I have said these things to you so that my joy may be in you, and that your joy may be complete." John 15:11

fills us with joy. And, as we allow joy to fill our lives, enthusiasm will emerge—enthusiasm for life, creativity, relationships and service.

Practicing Compassion

Meditating upon the scriptural accounts of Jesus' healings will lead to a greater spirit of compassion. We cannot help but be changed when the power of those stories is allowed to permeate deep within our souls. We see Jesus reaching out in love and compassion for the sufferings of others. The powerful healing energy flowing through him, heart to heart, is life changing. To be compassionate is to make a space for another person in one's innermost being and to be able to listen from the heart to their pain and brokenness.[11] And just as Jesus stood in solidarity with those who were suffering, we, by our presence, become compassion. As we make it a habit to practice coming from our hearts, compassion becomes part of our very fiber. Jesus told us to be compassionate as Abba, God, is compassionate. God cares about the mending of all creation, so it is in loving that healing can take place. It is in loving that wholeness can be restored.[12]

Where better to start practicing compassion then with ourselves. When we are compassionate to ourselves, we are better able to serve from a full and grateful heart, Reverend Jane Vennard tells us. Jesus was compassionate to himself when he went off alone to pray. It was this care of self that enabled him to continue his busy ministry. Showing compassion for self, requires sometimes saying no to the demands of those around us. We are to love others just as we love ourselves.[13]

Do Your Own Self Healing

It is very difficult to be present with another when our thoughts are focused on our own problems and concerns. Memories of past hurts weigh us down and color what we see and what we say. God's will is for our wholeness; we must have faith and trust that God will heal and restore us, even in ways we may not understand. We must go lightly into this work, spend the time needed to examine those

[11]David E. Rosage, *What Scripture Says About Healing, A guide to Scriptural Prayer and Meditation,* p. 17.

[12]Kenneth Bakken, *The Call to Wholeness, Health As a Spiritual Journey,* p. 82.

"Who is the compassionate One? The Beloved, Heart of your heart, Life of your life, this is the Compassionate One!" Psalm 24

[13]Jane E. Vennard, *Praying With Body and Soul, A Way to Intimacy with God,* p. 19.

"I have called you by name: you are mine... You are precious in my eyes.. I love you." Isaiah 43: 1, 4.

places of darkness and confusion, and bring them into the light. Only then can we fully attend and be present to another.

Self healing needs to take place on all levels: physical, emotional, mental, and spiritual. What are you doing to bring your whole being into balance? Just as all healing is heart work, healing ourselves is also heart work. We must be kind and gentle with ourselves. We must begin somewhere—anywhere—to bring this healing balance and harmony into our lives. We might try starting with keeping a Sabbath, a day of rest and re-creation. Make it a habit to play regularly. Sometimes choosing a mentor or a spiritual director/companion will aid us in developing the qualities needed for being a healing presence for others. This person can be a trusted friend who can truly see us and gently show us our blind spots.

Prayer and Meditation

Prayer and meditation actually improve one's energy field according to Dr. Norm Shealy. A healer's mental attitude and life of prayer and devotion produce a more direct connection with divine energy. For this reason, the healing practitioner can tap into divine energy much more effectively than individuals who do not have spiritual practices. To heal, we must continuously be in touch with God, maintaining a constant mental and spiritual connectedness.[14]

During our quiet introspection we can examine what in our beliefs and behaviors is working and what is not working. It is a time when we can examine the scriptures and other sacred writings for inspiration in being a healing presence for others. It can also be a time of resting in God's presence and allowing that presence to permeate our whole being. Meditation gives us the opportunity to get to know the deeper, truer self, created by God. This self, Ken Kaisch tells us, is wonderfully formed, whole and perfect by itself. This true self is God's gift to us and has remarkable qualities. It is full of wonder and awe, enjoys the moment, loves fully, and accepts its dark corners. This true, radiant self is connected to God and is always present to God. It is the part of us that listens and receives the whisperings and murmurings of God in our hearts.[15]

"I will... put a new spirit within them; I will take the stony heart out of their flesh and give them a heart of flesh." Ezekiel 11:19

"The earth is yours, O Giver of Life, in all its fullness and glory, the world and all those who dwell therein." Psalm 24

[14]Norm Shealy, *Sacred Healing, The Curing Power of Energy and Spirituality,* p.73.

[15]Ken Kaisch, *Finding God, A Handbook of Christian Meditation,* pp. 14-15.

Choose the type of meditation that most speaks to your heart and supports your work as a healer for others. The form is not as important as the commitment to a meditation time. Create a special place, a "heart healing" place within your home where you can go and spend time being with God. Light a candle, if that helps you create this healing environment. Candles often convey our heart's acknowledgement of the Divine Presence.

What else would help you in creating this space? Music or silence, nature, light or darkness, the scriptures or other inspiring writing? Consider what is right for you in your "heart healing" space and make it a reality. Set aside a specific time each day or week so that your meditation practice begins to become a habit that you can rely on.

Journaling

Writing enables us to express what often seem like disconnected thoughts along our path of life. In reality, the writing or journaling reveals a path that is a labyrinth to our center where our spirit lives. I have journaled most of my life, filling notebooks with my thoughts, inspirations, reflections on the scriptures, and other writings. A few years ago, I began writing, at the suggestion of my spiritual director, on just one topic for a month at a time. For instance, one month I would write on presence, another month on joy or service or Light. Kay Adams, a well-known speaker and writer on journaling, has created a national program devoted to helping people get in touch with their inner selves. Thanks to her work, many people are learning to open themselves to an awareness of God's direction in their lives.

Keeping a journal is a spiritual aid to our own self healing and development. Try journaling for a month just on the word "Presence." You will be amazed at what it will teach you about the Divine Presence within you, others, and all of creation. Journaling can be a key to our innermost hearts as we listen to the inspirations of the Spirit. The events of our day, as well as our dreams during sleep, speak constantly of God's presence. It is by paying attention that we truly are able to live in the present.

Kay Adams, *Journal to the Self.*

Is journaling a part of your life?

Gentle us, O Compassionate One, that we tread the earth lightly
and with grace, Spreading peace, goodness, and love, without harm to any creature.
For in gentle serenity is strength and assurance;
confusion and suspicion find no home here."
Psalm 105

Gentleness

Be patient and gentle with yourself and others. Each of our journeys is unique and sacred. What speaks to the heart of one person about being a healing presence for others may not speak to you. Go back to the Scriptures; you will not find Jesus condemning, judging, or analyzing. On the contrary, he shows great gentleness in his presence with others.

Choosing a Support Community

Practicing being a healing presence for others does not take place in a void. Kenneth Bakken and Kathleen Hofeller talk about the importance of choosing a supportive community. When we consciously choose those to be with who will inspire us and challenge us we are not only supported but inspired to live better lives.[16] Dr. Dale Matthews emphasizes the importance of maximizing one's social support network. This is a way of bearing one another's burdens and sharing in each others joys. Speaking as a physician and a scientist, Matthews points out that the mere presence of loved ones and friends may cause our brains to produce endorphins, the natural opiate-like substances that help us have a sense of well-being. When we are connected to others, we know we are not alone in facing whatever our difficulties might be.[17] This can be such a great consolation in times of stress. A Christian community can truly be our spiritual family.

Distractions and Blocks to Being a Healing Presence

Just as athletes know when they are "in the flow," when their "juices" are going, they also know when they are not connected and nothing is working. The same is true in healing work. When we get distracted or when there are things that block our connection to the divine energy, it is impossible to be a healing presence for another. It may be easy to identify the "something out there" that is blocking our way, but it is much harder to look within and see when we are off the path.

Some Christians like to pin their inability to remain in the Christ-consciousness on "sin" or on the influence of some malicious

[16]Kenneth Bakken and Kathleen Hofeller, *The Journey Toward Wholeness, A Christ-Centered Approach to Health and Healing, pp. 90-91.*

[17]Dale Matthews, MD, *The Faith Factor, Proof of the Healing Power of Prayer,* p. 47.

Does your present community mirror a healing presence for you? Do you need to consider a change?

power like a "demon." In chapter one, I discussed the original meaning of the word sin, which means "missing the mark" or being off the path to God. In the early writings of the Old Testament, God's adversary, the Satan, would come and stand in one's path until the person understood their sin and turned back to God. Sin, then, is when we are disconnected from our divine source—from God.[18] The New Testament writings confirm that angels and demons do affect human lives and exercise tremendous influence over us both for good and ill. In another of his books, Morton Kelsey tells us that the world of spiritual entities is very real.[19]

[18]Elaine Pagels, *The Origins of Satan*, p. 39.

[19]Morton Kelsey, *Discernment, A Study in Ecstasy and Evil*, pp. 66-67.

The Scriptures repeatedly show us that if we are to escape being overcome by the evil elements that seek our destruction we must enlist the help of the Holy Spirit, the church, and other positive spiritual forces. St. Paul concludes that the evil powers cannot touch the one who has known the love of God in Christ Jesus. He advises us to put on the armor of God in order to stand against the wiles of the devil.

"Put on the armor of God, so that you may be able to stand against the wiles of the devil. For our struggle is not against enemies of blood and flesh, but against the rulers, against the authorities, against the cosmic powers of this present darkness, against the spiritual forces of evil in the heavenly places." Ephesians 6:10-12

Whether the "blocks" and "distractions" that stop the process of divine flow are from the outside or not, they are usually based in the element of fear. Fear that nothing will happen when we put our hands on someone with an intention to help or heal—and fear that something will actually happen! Fear grabs at the edges of our self esteem and it paralyzes our moving forward on our spiritual path. Fear betrays our lack of faith and trust in God's will to heal us. It takes us off the path into blind alleys where it's all we can do to retrace our steps. When we try to overcome our fear by control, we lose. The light grows paler and we slip into darkness, until at last, we are able to recognize that we have lost our connection to our Source. Fear is overcome not by hunkering down and controlling the situation, but by walking naked into the Light, in faith and trust.

Again, you may wish to read the following words reflectively, mulling over what prevents you from being a healing presence to another. What is dimming the Light in your heart? Are you merely distracted or preoccupied with life's cares? Can these blocks and distractions be redeemed? Transformed? Transcended? Forgiving and letting go of hurts are the doorway which we must pass through over and over as we heal ourselves.

Fear of not being in control... of being too close to another
Being too busy in our lives...too many things on our minds
Concerned over what others may think...feeling
unworthy in the work
Lack of openness...unable to forgive self and others
Need to be in control...fear of letting go
Fear of not being enough...belief that you have
few gifts
Lack of patience...judgments that block unconditional love
Mistrust...apathy...self centeredness...intellectualizing
Ego attachment...self absorbed...sense of helplessness
Hopelessness...discouragement...loss of faith...unable to trust

Overcoming Blocks

Prayer

Sometimes it seems that all we can do is pray. This is exactly what God is waiting for us to do. God waits and waits for us to ask for help so that God can pour grace into our lives. It is not enough to just want to be a healing presence for others we must also recognize what gets in the way and, then, overcome it. Asking for God's mercy and help is an act of the heart's surrender.

Forgiveness

Forgiving people was an integral part of the healing ministry of Jesus. If we do not learn to forgive others, we cannot share with others what we ourselves do not have. Bridget Meehan points out that we grow in the capacity to forgive others compassionately by experiencing the boundless tender mercy of God for us.[20] In the forgiveness process we begin by recognizing that we are off the mark. Part of our human condition is seeing how we hurt each other and often harbor ill feelings about those who hurt us. Sometimes this can go on for years and, sometimes, for a lifetime. These wounds may go deep, and we love to pull them up every once in awhile to

"The Spirit helps us in our weakness; for we do not know how to pray as we ought, but that very Spirit intercedes with sighs too deep for words." Romans 8:26

[20]Bridget Meehan, *The Healing Power of Prayer,* pp. 59-60.

use for "mileage," as Carolyn Myss tells us.[21] After all, no one knows the "troubles we know," no one has suffered as deeply or grievously as we have, and we take solace in sharing it with others. In those moments, instead of reflecting the Christ presence, we show our own pain. Even when we recognize our errant ways, it may not be all that easy to forgive deep hurts. The healing of memories is a first step in letting go of blocks that keep us chained to the past. Dennis and Matthew Linn, both Jesuit priests, have devoted their lives to helping others look within themselves and find those places of unforgiveness and let go.[22] Fear, anger, and resentment must be seen for what they are. Forgiveness does not mean we condone the action that hurt us in the past. It means seeing it differently, which allows us to let it go. Asking God's forgiveness for the one who hurt us is but the first step. Next we must recognize our need for forgiveness as well.[23]

Listening to Guidance

There are voices all around us trying to influence us to buy this or go here or there. Our media constantly bombards us with "guidance" and direction for our happiness in life. With all this noise, it is sometimes hard to distinguish God's voice to us. Listen to the quality of the guidance we receive. Do we sense peace? Fear is never of God.

The Scriptures contain many stories of God's guidance in the form of dreams, angels, messengers, and inner knowing. God comes to us in a myriad of ways, which can be problematic at times. Both Richard Foster and Flora Wuellner suggests that discernment is necessary in order to know what direction to go.[24, 25]

When we are spiritually blocked, it may feel like we are on a plateau and God's presence may seem quite distant. It is then that we need to go deep within and abide in God's quiet and wait. In our attuning to God, our inner listening breaks through the places of darkness and confusion and Light floods our path. Guidance is always there; it is discernment that makes the path clear.

Many years ago I was faced with discerning my next path in health-care ministry. One opportunity was to work at a favorite hospital where I already had many friends. It was a comfortable choice.

You might examine if you are holding anything against another. Is there anything you haven't forgiven and continue to hold in bondage?

[21]Carolyn Myss, *Why People Don't Heal and How They Can*

[22]Dennis & Matthew Linn, *Healing Life's Hurts, Healing Memories Through The Five Stages of Forgiveness.*

Are there wounds holding you back from having a forgiving heart?

[23]Flora Slosson Wuellner, *Heart of Healing Heart of Light*, p. 76.

[24]Richard J. Foster, Prayer, *Finding The Heart's True Home*, p. 210

[25]Flora Slosson Wuellner, *Prayer, Fear, and our Powers*, p. 49.

The other "opportunity" was to go to a town several hours away where I knew no one and the job was a difficult one. The decision seemed clearly obvious until I sat in prayer to discern God's direction in my life. I began by identifying the pros and cons of both choices. Much to my surprise, they seemed to be even. In the end, I chose the place where I knew no one. All I can say is that through the process of discernment I was led to my greatest challenges and opportunities for self growth. Once the decision was made, I was filled with peace, and to this day, I know that this choice was the right one, even though it was a time fraught with personal struggles.

Bruce Davis believes that we each are given a spirit guide that helps take us into the silence of the heart where we are able to connect and listen to the Divine Presence. There are times, he tells us, when physical teachers and guides appear on our path who support us as we find our "true place in unfolding creation."[26] I'm reminded of the story about the man in the flood who prayed to God to save him. As the waters rose past the doorstep, a boat came by but the man refused, trusting that God would save him. Soon the waters rose to the upper floors and yet another boat came to rescue him, but he refused, believing that God surely would save him. Finally, the water reached the rooftop and a helicopter dropped down a line. The pilot begged him to grab hold yet he refused, knowing in his heart that God would save him. In the end, he drowned. When he came into God's presence, he asked, "Why did you not save your faithful servant from the flood?" And God said, "I tried three times to save you, but you refused!" Discernment would have shown the man that God works both through the Spirit and through other people.

Alone Time

In order to be still enough to listen to guidance, we have to calm the "chatter" within. Silence and solitude enable us to break through the blocks and distractions of life and rest in the presence of God. This is not a time to tell God what we need or want—it is a time to listen in our deepest being for God's word in our life.

[26]Bruce Davis, *Monastery Without Walls*, p. 156.

"They who wait for the Lord shall renew their strength, they shall mount up with wings like eagles, they shall run and not be weary, they shall walk and not faint." Isaiah 40:31

The presence of God is to be found deep within us, in our true self—in our divine essence. Many holy people through the ages have all come to the same conclusion: God is closer to us than we are to ourselves. From our Judaic roots, we call this God-filled part of ourselves the Shekhina, the feminine essence of God. It is the intuitive, nurturing aspect of God within us. The Shekhina aspect of God dwells inside each person and is as close to you as your breath. Have you ever tried to catch a butterfly? You can reach out for it, you can chase it and try to grab it, but you can't get it. However, if you sit very still and wait alone with your thoughts, the butterfly will come and sit on your shoulder. In quiet, alone time the presence of God, the Shekhina, comes to sit upon our shoulders. Pause, empty yourself, and open to the Spirit of God within you. It is closer to you than you are to your very self.[27]

Simplicity

Jesus radiated God's presence wherever he went. One of the ways that he was able to maintain this attunement was through the simple life he lead. That is not to say he didn't have money or clothes or food—he just wasn't caught up in protecting them and sustaining them. When we let our possessions and our need for them take up all our inner space, our connection to the divine presence begins to weaken and to fade.[28] There must be no competition for our conscious awareness if we desire to be a reflection of God's presence.

To live simply means that we make responsible use of our time, talent, and treasure. This is a way not only for our own inner healing, but also a way to act as healers for others. Simplicity is both gift and discipline. Kenneth Bakken and Kathleen Hofeller find that simplicity encourages an awareness of God's presence and an obedience to God's will.[29] As we choose simplicity, trust, and commitment, which may seem to be difficult, God empowers us with grace and love that lifts us up and energizes us to follow the divine call joyfully.

"Be still and know that I am God." Psalm 46:10

"I will lead her into the desert and speak to her heart." Hosea 2:16

[27]Rabbi Shoni Labowitz, *Miraculous Living*, p. 78.

[28]Richard J. Foster, *Simplicity*, p. 33.

"Do not worry about your life...Look at the birds of the air; they neither sow nor reap nor gather into barns and yet your heavenly Father feeds them. Are you not of more value than they?...So do not worry about tomorrow, for tomorrow will bring worries of its own. Today's trouble is enough for today." Matt. 6:25-26, 34

[29]Kenneth Bakken and Kathleen Hofeller, *The Journey Toward Wholeness, A Christ-Centered Approach to Health and Healing*, pp. 122-124.

"Abide in me as I abide in you. Just as the branch cannot bear fruit by itself unless it abides in the vine, neither can you unless you abide in me. I am the vine, you are the branches." John 15:4-5

Service

There is no better way to break out of whatever is paralyzing us at the moment than to do something for someone else, to be of service. Throughout life, we create bonds and connections to others—family, friends, colleagues, and fellow church members. These are the easy ties to see. Harder to recognize are the connections to our neighborhood, our town, city, state, nation, hemisphere, and the world. When we strengthen those ties, we lift ourselves out of ourselves and reflect a radiance that is beyond us. I think of Jimmy Carter and his wonderful mission of peace. In my opinion, he has accomplished more for humanity after his presidency then during it. He is a beacon of light for many and is not beyond getting into the trenches himself, building houses, or observing voting booths. When we are being of service, we become more compassionate, more generous, and less judgmental of others.

Flora Slosson Wuellner relates a dream that was shared with her. "A person dreamed he was flying, in ecstatic joy, toward the sun. But in the midst of his flight he heard weeping far below. Looking down, he saw a dense green forest. Among the dark trees, he could see many people groping their way, crying desolately. He turned in the air and flew down to the forest." She asks her readers if this dream was a vision shared from the heart of God, or was it a guiding, prophetic dream about that person's own life? She concludes that it was both. God sometimes reaches out to our very soul, sharing God's great pain in our suffering. These can be moments of great insight into a deep connection with the sufferings of humanity. How can we respond, if not by turning our heart to the cries of others?[30] This is echoed in a prayer by Pierre de Chardin:

[30]Flora Slosson Wuellner, *Heart of Healing Heart of Light*, pp. 58-59.

"I love you, Lord Jesus, because of the multitude who shelter within you and whom, if one clings closely to you, one can hear with all the other beings murmuring, praying, weeping."[31]

[31]Pierre de Chardin, *Hymn of the Universe*, p. 69.

The Healing Presence of Christ

In reading the scriptures, we get an image of the healing presence of Christ. When Jesus told his followers to be compassionate as God is compassionate, he was referring to the Jewish tradition that views God as Mother, as birther. To say that God is compassionate is to say that God is "like a womb." Compassion was more than just a virtue for Jesus; it was a vehicle for social action.[32]

[32]Marcus Borg, *Meeting Jesus Again for the First Time*, p. 48.

The parable about the Good Samaritan is well known. Luke records this story, which was a favorite of the early Christians. Who is my neighbor, the early Christians asked? The answer is clear for the Christian community. We are to care about our neighbors in visible, tangible ways. We are to be compassionate healers of one another just as the Samaritan was a compassionate healer of the man who was robbed and beaten. Samaritans were despised by the Jewish people, considered less than second-class citizens. And yet, the Samaritan did not pass by without rendering assistance to another human soul, to someone who, although different from himself, was a fellow traveler on the path of life.

Have you ever bandaged another's wounds? It must be done slowly and tenderly or greater pain will be caused. The Good Samaritan story tells us that this stranger poured on wine and oil, both of which have healing properties. We can imagine the Samaritan giving the man a drink of water or perhaps some of the wine, holding the container gently to his lips. And then, he carried him to an inn and took from his own pocket the means to care for him. It is a heart-renting story of reaching out in unconditional love for another person, a stranger.

But have you ever thought about the beaten man's reaction to receiving aid from this Samaritan? A priest and Levite of his own kind had passed him by and refused his pleas for help. And yet, this stranger touches him gently and cared for him, allaying his fears. This man had to be changed forever. God had sent him assistance in the form of someone most unlikely, someone he had learned his whole life to detest.

"But wanting to justify himself, he asked Jesus, 'And who is my neighbor?' Jesus replied, 'A man was going down from Jerusalem to Jericho, and fell into the hands of robbers, who stripped him, beat him, and went away, leaving him half dead. Now by chance a priest was going down the road; and when he saw him, he passed by on the other side. So likewise a Levite, when he came to the place and saw him, passed by on the other side. But a Samaritan while traveling came near him and when he saw him, he was moved with pity. He went to him and bandaged his wounds, having poured oil and wine on them. Then he put him on his own animal, brought him to an inn, and took care of him. The next day he took out two denarii, gave them to the innkeeper, and said, 'Take care of him; and when I come back, I will repay you whatever more you spend.' Which of these three, do you think, was a neighbor to the man who fell into the hands of the robbers?' He said, 'The one who showed him mercy.' Jesus said to him, 'Go and do likewise.'" Luke 10:29-37

We pay a price in healing work. We may run the risk of having our offer of healing hands rebuffed, ridiculed, even rejected. We may be attacked verbally or even physically. Our jobs may be on the line, or our relationships may be in jeopardy if we persist in expressing our healing ways. One woman told me she was thrown out of her church for doing this work and another minister was fired for preaching that we can be healers as Jesus was. Being a Christ presence requires commitment. Jesus encouraged us to be generous in our love and our compassion. He assured us that if we are generous in our giving, that same generosity will be measured out to us.

The healing presence of Christ is about simply "be-ing" present to another. When we tap into the Christ presence, we transcend our own limited selves, producing an energy for caring. Caring does not always mean doing something; it may simply be about be-ing present. And in the be-ing, the Christ Light is able to flow out and fill the space around us. Listen to this powerful prayer written by Flora Slosson Wuellner:

> *"The risen, living Christ*
> *Calls me by my name;*
> *Comes to the loneliness within me;*
> *Heals that which is wounded in me;*
> *Comforts that which grieves in me;*
> *Seeks for that which is lost within me;*
> *Releases me from that which has dominion over me;*
> *Cleanses me of that which does not belong to me;*
> *Renews that which feels drained within me;*
> *Awakens that which is asleep in me;*
> *Names that which is formless within me;*
> *Empowers that which is newborn within me;*
> *Consecrates and guides that which is strong;*
> *Restores me to this world which needs me;*
> *Reaches out in endless love to others through me."*[33]

"Give and it will be given to you. A good measure, pressed down, shaken together, running over, will be put into your lap; for the measure you give will be the measure you get back." Luke 6:38

[33]Flora Slosson Wuellner, *Prayer, Fear and our Powers, Finding our Healing, Release, and Growth in Christ*, p. 47.

A Unity church prayer expresses this thought about being:

"In your sacred presence,
dear God,
I lift up my heart to You.
Divine love
flows through me now
to bless the world."

CHAPTER 8

The Heart's Intention in Healing

"To You, O Love,
  I lift up my soul;
O Heart within my heart,
   in You I place my trust.
   Let me not feel unworthy;
   let not fear rule over me.
Yes! Let all who open their hearts,
   savor You and bless the earth!"
Psalm 25

When I was first introduced to Healing Touch, I was awed at the power of the work and felt a certain "ah ha" reaction to it that is still with me today. It was not only the feeling that somehow I had "always" known this work; it was also a deeply spiritual experience of a profound nature. The power of God was absolutely real for me as I placed my hands on my fellow students. I realized that prayer and intention were at the heart of this healing work. Perhaps because of my long background in ministry and in prayer, I had been conditioned to think in spiritual terms. I remember wondering in those early classes if other students were having the same spiritual awareness as I, or was I aware of some secret that only the mystics and saints knew about? After all, the classes were taught with an emphasis on the scientific aspects of healing. The instructors drew upon their own spiritual resources but generally referred to the source of this healing energy as "universal energy." I wondered why I was so aware of God's presence and grace when I was both receiving and giving in the work. And I wondered if prayer and connection to God deepened the work.

Several of us talked about our experiences with each other, and I realized that we were all experiencing spiritual phenomena of one kind or another. Many of my fellow students were having thoughts of God as they learned this healing work. For many, it was their first spiritual encounter, for others, it was a return to their roots. We weren't having "religious" experiences, but our spirits were yearning for communion with God. We understood that we were being "called home" to do God's work.

Over time, my paradigm around health care, healing, and the role of prayer began cracking—everything that had given meaning and purpose to my life was giving way to a new understanding of prayer, healing, and my role in it. Prayer, I discovered, sustains the work, holds the Light, and focuses me towards God as the source of healing. This was a new understanding for me.

The heart is the center of our being. I'm referring not to the physical heart or some emotion that we may identify as coming from the heart but rather to the "heart center," where we connect to our deepest ground, to Spirit. It is from this heart center that we access our intuition and inner knowing. The heart becomes the "doorway" through which we connect to the deeper realities of life.

Hopefully, when we offer healing to others we bring ourselves into that place, that right intention, where we can connect to the flow of divine grace that is always available.

I remember years ago hearing a story about an old rabbi who was called upon by the town's people when calamity was about to befall them. The rabbi knew to go out into the forest to a secret cabin, light the sacred fire and say the sacred prayers. And God saved the people. Many years later, the rabbi's successor was called upon when the village was in danger. He knew to go out into the forest to the secret cabin and say the prayers. But he had forgotten how to light the sacred fire. And God saved the people. Many more years went by and yet another rabbi was sent by the village out into the forest when they were in great peril. He went but he did not know where the cabin was or how to light the fire. Nonetheless, he said the prayers and God saved the people. Many long years went by and another rabbi was called upon by the village for yet another catastrophe. He went out to the forest, only he didn't know where the cabin was, how to light the fire, or even what the prayers were. And God still saved the people. And so it was that his successor was also called upon in the time of great danger for the village. This rabbi couldn't go out to the forest, had no knowledge about the cabin, the sacred fire, or even the prayers, so he simply asked God to save the people. And so it was.

The rabbis in the story—whether they knew the rituals or not—all had a pure intention coming from their heart centers: "Compassionate One, save your people." In doing healing work, the heart's intention is a key that opens the treasure of God's light and healing energy.

Ron Roth startles us when he says, "There is no power in prayer!" Then he goes on to say that "the power is in God, which is released in our communion with God."[1] In the story about the rabbis, some of them didn't even know the right prayer to say and had lost the rituals, but the desire in their hearts was communion with God and in that communion the saving power of God was unleashed.

Naming the Source

Naming the Source is a key step in being in communion with God. We name God as Ultimate Reality, Creator, Source of all that is—as our source of power, love, and wisdom in healing work. And then we surrender to the power of heaven and earth. We allow that

[1]Ron Roth, *Prayer and the Rituals of Prayer* (audio tapes).

Source to transform us into an instrument, conduit, or courier of God's Divine grace. It is not enough just to recognize that Source; we must also be willing to undergo transformation as we walk this path of service to others.

A Way of Life, a Way of Being

Some people feel that all they need is a "pure" intention and they can accomplish any goal. Intentions are purest, however, when they come from a desire to simply be at one with God's will. When your intention becomes one with God's intention, everything is possible, including healing. So how do you know when your intention is joined with God's intention? By sensing it inside. It is an inner knowing that comes through the process of discernment. When we become still enough deep within our soul, we can hear that inner voice speaking to us. In stillness, there is a resonance of joy, peace, and serenity. It is that inner knowing that comes from our union with God that forms the very essence of intention.

Having a "right" and "pure" intention in healing work is not always easy. So much of "me" can get in the way. And yet it is not the real me—it is the shadow or false self. That is the "me" that wants to see results that knows "best" what a client needs, that calls upon God to work according to my will. It is a "me" that does not listen, has trouble staying focused, and is proud of the work and the gifts of the Spirit working through me. Sometimes this "me" sounds almost moralistic; other times it sounds like parental voices rather than the voice of the real self. This "me" thinks it is spiritual and an instrument of God's healing. This "me" is not so outrageous as to be strange to onlookers. If it were, it would be easy to recognize and keep under control. It can be quite subtle at times. For example, when good results are happening in our healing work with others, it takes undue delight in what it has accomplished. Many of the great Christian mystics have talked about this false self and ways to recognize and control it, but it will always be with us. You cannot destroy the shadow side, but it can be redeemed, transformed, and eventually integrated within one's being.

Rabbi Shoni Labowitz in *Miraculous Living, A Guided Journey in Kabbalah Through The Ten Gates of The Tree of Life*, writes extensively about intentionality as one of the ten gates to God.

Thomas Merton, John of the Cross, Teresa of Avila to name but a few great Christian mystics who have written about the false self. You may also want to read Carl Jung's works on the "shadow" or false self.

When our ego-driven intentions are in control, they can masquerade as "good," and true healing can be thwarted. Although God can work through us even when our intentions are not the best, our energy can be drained, we become distracted, and we fall off the path of true healing. What is worse, these selfish intentions make us vulnerable to picking up negative energy. We actually can take on what we are trying to relieve in others.

Right intentions in healing work flow from a way of life—a way of being, of living in the present moment. It is a way of living and being that is sensitive to when grace flows and when it does not. We grow into this attentive awareness; it doesn't just happen because we wish it. This is what it means to live from the heart center. When I speak of a "way of life" or a "way of being" I'm referring to those things that we choose to be a part of our ordinary life, like breathing, mindfulness, quiet mind, joyfulness, prayerfulness, compassion, love of beauty, respect for all of nature. We grow into awareness of our inner world as well as the outer world about us. As we learn to open our heart our true self, our true essence is revealed to us. Of course there are many other things that can become part of this "way of life," this "way of being"—things that take us away from the attentiveness we so desire and actually feed the shadow side. These are habits of unforgiveness, self-righteousness, pride, self-centeredness. For most of us this living and being is a mixed bag. The task is to learn how to enhance those things that bless our life with attentiveness and sensitivity in the moment and how to diminish those beliefs and habits that take us off the path of the heart.

Developing Healthy Intentionality in Healing Work

Becoming consciously aware of our intentions develops with practice. There are spiritual actions we can do that will help us develop "healthy" intentions. We can develop spiritual discipline that will enable us to do the work we are called to do. Cultivating a prayer life that deepens our connection to God is a necessary component. Richard Foster writes about developing the prayer of "Relinquishment." In this kind of prayer, we move through stages of

"O my Beloved,
though I have turned from You, continue to enfold me with your love;
Be gracious to me,
Heart of my heart,
for I am sad and weary. Surround me with your healing Light,
that my body, mind, and soul might heal.
How long must I wait,
O Love?" Psalm 6

self-emptying, surrender, abandonment, release, and, finally, resurrection.[2] Modern-day mystics such as Foster continue to challenge all of us in ways that bring us to greater clarity in our own spiritual lives. What follows are some thoughts on how we can help develop healthy intentions that flow from the centered heart.

Emptying

Sometimes we are so full of ourselves and what we think is God's will that there is no room for the Holy Spirit to inspire us. As we learn to empty our minds and our hearts of the "false self" we begin to hear the soft voice of the Spirit of God, much like the tinkling in the breeze. Emptiness is the first step in going within and touching God. It is difficult for God to fill up our vessels if they are already full of our own thoughts. In emptiness we can reflect God's light, God's voice, God's healing energy. Jesus, Paul tells us, "emptied" himself in order to take on our human form. Through his emptiness, he was able to humbly reflect God's Light, healing power, and energy.

Emptiness is a way of joining our intentions to God's intention. We must be patient with ourselves; meditating regularly will help. With practice, emptiness will not only be a comfortable place, but it will be a place where we feel serene, peaceful, and calm. Many people think that a meditation practice is difficult because they only have one picture in their minds of what meditation is. Try a walking meditation in nature or breath prayer or being attentive to sounds or to music. I learned the art of walking meditation just a few years ago. The body is slowly moved forward, heel to toe, heel to toe, while the mind quiets and becomes empty. Awareness of the breath can also be a prayer leading to a quiet but alert mind. Meditation is the tool. The goal is learning to open our heart center to the workings of God in our lives. Like cleaning our inner house, we empty in order to make room for the Divine Presence.

[2]Richard Foster, *Prayer, Finding the Heart's True Home*, p. 47.

"Let the same mind be in you that was in Christ Jesus, who, though he was in the form of God, did not regard equality with God as something to be exploited, but emptied himself, taking the form of a slave, being born in human likeness. And being found in human form, he humbled himself and became obedient to the point of death—even death on a cross." Phil. 2:5-8

[3] Christopher Knippers, PhD, *Common Sense, Intuition, and God's Guidance.*

"Though my strength be
   broken in mid-course,
   and my days shortened,
I cry to You, "Would that this
   cup be taken from me,
   You who are everlasting,
   Yet, into your Hands will I commend
my soul."
Psalm 102

[4] Rene Voillaume, *Seeds of the Desert.*

Surrendering

Surrendering to the divine direction in one's life has been spoken of by countless mystics, saints, and holy ones. When we let go and let God, we turn loose of control. According to Christopher Knippers, surrender is actually an attitude of trust that God is taking care of our lives. God's grace can then flow unimpeded into our vessels. When we trust, we can live a joyful life open to God's love, communication, and blessing. We "abandon"—that is, give over to God—our body, mind, soul, and spirit, allowing God to be God with us.[3] When we are that conduit or courier of God's grace for others, we let go of needing to direct God's actions. It is enough for us to simply show up, be attentive to how the Holy Spirit works, and then get out of the way of God's healing.

I have always been impressed with the story of Charles de Foucauld. He was a spoiled young French man and soldier of fortune at the turn of the twentieth century who later became a Trappist monk, and, eventually, a wandering beggar in Morocco. He wrote a beautiful prayer that I have found helpful when I have needed (wanted) to be in control. *The Prayer of Abandonment* speaks to the very heart of what it means to be a vessel of God's grace for others. You may find it comforting to pray these words as you do your healing work.

*"Father, I abandon myself
into your hands;
do with me what you will.
Whatever you may do,
I thank you:
I am ready for all, I accept all.
Let only your will be done in me,
and in all your creatures—
I wish no more than this,
O Lord."*[4]

Inner Stillness

Developing a spiritual practice necessarily includes time for cultivating an inner stillness. If our inner selves are full of distractions, worries, concerns, and grievances, there is little space for that still small voice of God. Quiet contemplation, such as centering prayer, brings us to that stillness within where God can work within us. Our reflective ability is born in this silence. In this inner stillness, we are attentive to sounds, however distant they may be or whether in the physical or spiritual dimension. We are strengthened for the journey in this silence. Rabbi Labowitz calls this "cultivating nothingness." This nothingness is not an absence; it is a fullness. There is joy and exaltation in this state when we are able to lose ourselves in the infinite Source, in infinite stillness. Uniting the intention of our heart to God's intention flows in this state of nothingness.[5]

I live in the foothills of the Rockies, where every day I see splendor in nature. I practice inner quiet and sometimes "cultivate nothingness" in hiking or riding my bike. This gives me the opportunity to go into my heart center, where I find peaceful comfort. My flower gardens are another source of quiet time as I carefully tend to each flower, talking to them, encouraging them to share their beauty. Writing this book has been another way for me to spend time in thoughtful quiet. Sometimes hours go by as I refine the words that flow from my heart center. Music or art or flower arranging or slow and rhythmic breathing may take you to your heart center. The key to succeeding in this practice of the heart is simply being committed to a practice.

Inner Cleansing and Release

For most of us, inner cleansing first means looking into our hearts to see what needs forgiving and then letting go—releasing the pain, the anger, and the resentment that we are holding inside. As long as we hold onto our pain, we hold others and ourselves in bondage. We are stuck in the mire, unable to progress on our paths. Coming into this awareness enables us to make better choices. By releasing, we are placing our trust in God, who can manage the situation quite well without our direction.

[5]Rabbi Shoni Labowitz, *Miraculous Living, A Guided Journey in Kabbalah Through The Ten Gates of The Tree of Life*, p. 38.

There are many ways to train ourselves to stay in that inner place of quiet and stillness. Listen to your heart. How do you find peace and joy?

"Search me, O my Beloved,
and know my heart!
Try me and discern my thoughts!
Help me to face the darkness within me;
enlighten me,
that I might radiate your love and light!"
Psalm 139

The noted spiritual writer Henri Nouwen speaks out of his own experience about what it means to be a "wounded healer." When we come to recognize our alienation, separation, isolation, and loneliness, we see our wounded condition, he says. It is out of this woundedness that we can become a source of life for others. We are all wounded healers as we look within and see what needs cleansing—releasing—changing—growing. The temptation is to say, "I cannot change, I cannot grow, I cannot be of service to others when I am so weak."[6] We are not being asked to wear our weaknesses on our faces but, rather, to offer ourselves in humility, knowing that God makes all things new in due time. In coming to terms with our woundedness, we are able to be at home with ourselves and extend hospitality to others. God is the great transformer, and with God's grace our intentions are transformed as well.

[6]Henri Nouwen, *The Wounded Healer,* p. 83.

Inner Sense of Self—Resurrection

Within our energy field we hold not only our past experiences, but, according to some physicists (see discussion of holographic brain in chapter 3), we also store our knowledge, talents, and gifts. Every person is blessed with talents and gifts that they may or may not be using to their fullest. As we deepen our inner cleansing we come to a purity within our emptiness. Our gifts may then begin to appear like strands of "new life" resurrected out of the ashes of the old. Our desires and intentions will start to flow out into heartfelt service as we use our knowledge, our talents, and our gifts for the highest good of others.

"You take delight,
O Radiant One,
In gracing me with new life!
O Beloved, come and renew me!" Psalm 70

Many years ago, I was going through a particularly painful period. As I came to that place of complete emptiness, I was able to forgive and let go of hurts. I experienced a resurrection like a "phoenix rising" out of the ashes. Soon after, I began to experience new gifts that drew me into completely different levels of service.

Listening to Wisdom

Wisdom can come from many directions. We can be inspired by books, tapes, movies, and from news stories. We can be awestruck by the wisdom that comes from the mouths of little children, from total strangers, as well as from those closest to us. Wisdom can come from the ages past, from our religious practices, from those who inspire us to Christian behavior. Wisdom, holy wisdom—Sophia—can come from the sacred scriptures, from our prayer, meditation, and contemplative moments. Our listening in openness and our willingness to allow God to change us are the keys. Rabbi Cooper tells us that true wisdom does not come from outside us but from within. It comes when we live in a way that invites wisdom. It comes through direct experience. Our intentions grow into oneness with God, with wisdom by our side.[7]

[7]Rabbi David Cooper, *God Is a Verb,* p. 10.

Shielding: Filling the Field with Light

In being with another person in healing work, it is important to not "take on" what does not belong to you. It is wise to practice "safe healing." Just as we put on a face mask when someone has an upper respiratory disease, we need to protect ourselves when clients have darkness "stuck" in their fields. Even when we are visiting the sick in their homes or in the hospital without doing any hands-on healing, we need to take wisely Paul's exhortation to the people of Ephesus when he says to put on the "armor of God." This is a powerful prayer of protection that recognizes that there are spiritual forces that prefer the darkness. Prayer activates a shield of protection against darkness of all kinds. By calling upon the name of Jesus, invoking the power of the Holy Spirit, and calling to our angel protectors, we are strengthened and made safe to do our ministry. Flora Litt tells us that at such moments, "we resonate with the highest spiritual energy and vibration of the universe." The prayer of protection is a powerful one to be taken seriously. The words need only be simple ones: "Surround me with your Light, O Lord, and protect me."[8]

"Put on the whole armor of God, so that you may be able to stand against the wiles of the devil. For our struggle is not against enemies of blood and flesh, but against... the cosmic powers of this present darkness, against the spiritual forces of evil in the heavenly places. Therefore take up the whole armor of God...take the shield of faith with which you will be able to quench all the flaming arrows of the evil one." Ephesians 6:11-13, 16

In a fascinating psychological study, Dr. Edith Fiore describes how the strength of one's aura can protect you from possession. The aura (the energy field) is related to the emotional-mental-spiritual

[8]Flora Litt, "Ways of Praying," in Rochelle, Graham, Wayne Irwin and Flora Litt, *Healing From the Heart,* p. 125.

[9]Edith Fiore, *The Unquiet Dead*, p. 109.

How does someone know if their energy field or aura is diminished and weak? And if it is, how can it be strengthened?

[10]Carol Lee Flinders, *Enduring Grace, Living Portraits of Seven Women Mystics*, p. 53.

dimension of a person, much like the immune system is related to the physical body. A diminished aura creates a vulnerability to spirit intrusion.[9] There have been various ways of describing this phenomenon throughout the ages. In biblical days this spirit intrusion was spoken of as "demon" or "spirit" possession. In our modern-day it may be referred to as darkness in the field, "attachments," or even described as "depression" or "mental illnesses." As practitioners, we are called to be wise healers and trust in God's power and energy to heal.

Taking care of yourself physically, mentally, emotionally and spiritually is very important in creating good field strength. In other words, stay balanced and receive the healing that is needed for your own health. When we are not practicing self care, it is easy to not realize that our field has become weak. We may show signs of fatigue, irritability, emotional stress, negativity, depression, a critical attitude, an unforgiving heart. This is a time to concentrate on one's own healing first.

One of the great mystics of the Middle Ages, Mechthild of Magdeburg, spoke about The Flowing Light. By things that flow, we are cleansed, healed, nourished, and consoled. By things that flow, the void between the human and the divine is closed.

"God's love flows from God to man without effort,
as a bird flies through the air without moving its wings."[10]

Strengthened for the work with God's flowing energy and grace, we can then be of service to others. When we begin a healing session with another, our intention is to bring in the Light, filling our whole being (physical and auric) with the Christ Light. This forms a "shield" around us, protecting us from all that is not of God. Throughout our healing work, we stay in this protective Flowing Light. Our aura becomes bright, full, and vibrant as we become a conduit of God's healing.

Centering—Connecting to Ground

Centering plays a pivotal role in setting the intention of the heart. It means coming into our core, that inner place where we quiet the mind and the heart and let go of all that fractures us. It means going to that place of peace deep within. We are grounded here in our bodies and connected to God. Louis Savary and Patricia Berne point out that to be centered means not only to be "at home" and to be totally present to one's self, but also to be in touch with one's energies and the way they are flowing at the present moment. It involves being rather than doing.[11]

To come into one's center takes practice. One easy way is to become aware of your own body—what you feel from the toes on up, how you are breathing, whether there is any discomfort anywhere. Then be grateful for feeling your feet, legs, trunk, arms, neck, and head. One image that is helpful for me is to visualize myself as a harp string, tethered above and below and finely tuned to make a melodious note synchronized to the note of the universe. Or visualize yourself as a laser beam that God is tuning to just the right vibration. Firmly planted deep within the earth below and connected to a higher source of power above, our laser beam is held steady in the Light.

Simply paying attention to your breathing is an excellent way to come into the center of your being. Slow rhythmic breathing from deep within quiets the mind, relaxes the body, and helps us keep our focus on the presence of God.

We may need to return again and again to this centered place. Distracting thoughts, even the sound of birds outside the window, can take us off on many tangents. This centered place is what is often spoken of in the Scriptures as the heart where true healing occurs. In this centered state, we are ready now to set the intention of the heart.

[11]Louis Savary and Patricia Berne, *Prayer Medicine, How to Dance, Cry, Sing, Meditate, Wrestle, Love and Pray Your Way To Healing*, p. 26.

"O my Beloved,
you hear my deepest desires;
You will strengthen my heart,
You will answer my prayer;
That I might live with integrity And become a loving presence in the world!"
Psalm 10

Setting the Intention

Setting the heart's intention means placing one's self in God's hands, asking to be a channel or vessel of God's healing grace for the person before you. As we enter the silence of God, we listen for God's guidance and direction. We show up with heart and hands open. We have been assured by Jesus that the Holy Spirit will come to us in ways we have never anticipated when we present ourselves with such receptivity. We are open to receive the power of God, which is experienced as Light and energy. We are saying "yes" to letting God have God's way with us.

Without attachment to a particular outcome, we place the person we are going to work with in the hands of God. We trust that whatever the outcome, it is for the highest good for this individual. And then we let go of needing to be in control. We let God be God. I have found that when I can be in this heart space, the need to "make something happen" fades away. I must admit that it is hard for me to stay in that space because my nursing training makes me want to see results.

How do we know then that our work is beneficial? A great deal of health care is outcome-oriented, so detachment from outcome seems odd. We can note the benefits of the work, however, just by comparing our observations of the client before and after the healing session. Detachment is particularly hard when the client is a friend or relative. Our investment in their feeling better or being restored to wholeness is much greater. Yet detachment is necessary if we are to be a clear instrument of God's healing for another.

When I begin my work with a client, I often check with the person and ask what their intention is for our time together. Sometimes I get a laundry list of physical and emotional needs. At other times, I am given simple statements of openness to whatever God has in mind for the moment. There are times when the client will say, "I really don't need anything myself, but my husband, child, or friend is in need." "Can we send them some healing?" As practitioners, we lay these needs before the Holy One, again relying on the grace of God

"I praise you in the Silence
   of my heart,
for your steadfast Love,
   O my Beloved;
I offer prayers of gratitude,
O Holy One of the universe.
My heart leaps for joy, as
   I whisper to You in
   the night—
my soul also, which You
   renew within me."
Psalm 71

to manifest however God deems it appropriate. We take our clients' needs, burdens, and requests, and surround them with God's grace and light. My prayer, either verbal or silent, is only for the highest good, trusting that God will bring healing in all the ways the person needs. This takes the burden off my shoulders as a practitioner. God is in charge, I am merely God's channel or conduit. In faith, I know that this person will receive God's healing in ways I may not understand.

The great saint Teresa of Avila was not particularly known for healing, but she touched the souls of countless people with stories of her "raptures." At that time (the 1500s) the Inquisition was in full swing. Had she not convinced superiors that her visions were from God and not the devil, she would have been burned at the stake. She has given us prayerful ways to the interior—our inner selves—where God resides. As we center in our Source, set our intention for the highest good, and begin to lay our hands on the person before us seeking healing, her words speak to the very heart of the work we are about to do:

> *You Are Christ's Hands*
> *"Christ has no body now on earth but yours,*
> *no hands but yours,*
> *no feet but yours,*
> *Yours are the eyes through which is to look out*
> *Christ's compassion to the world*
> *Yours are the feet with which he is to go about*
> *Doing good;*
> *Yours are the hands with which he is to bless men now."*[12]
>   Teresa of Avila

[12]Carol Lee Flinders, *Enduring Grace, Living Portraits of Seven Women Mystics*, p. 155.

Allow me to close these thoughts with the holy words of St. Francis of Assisi. This prayer epitomizes the core of The Heart's Intention.

"Lord, make me an instrument of thy peace.
Where there is hatred, let me sow love;
Where there is injury, pardon;
Where there is doubt, faith;
Where there is despair, hope;
Where there is darkness, light;
Where there is sadness, joy.

O divine Master, grant that I may not so much seek
To be consoled as to console,
To be understood as to understand,
To be loved as to love;
For it is in giving that we receive;
It is in pardoning that we are pardoned;
It is in dying to self that we are born to eternal life."
St. Francis of Assisi

CHAPTER 9

The Path Within— Cultivating an Attitude of Heart

I have been involved in health care for many years, putting lots of energy into mastery of nursing skills. Knowing the right healing techniques, saying the right words, or giving the right advice about health-care practices are skills I have honed and practiced with my clients. Yet with my holistic understanding of the interconnections of body, mind, and spirit, I sometimes find myself searching for the right combination of treatments and recommendations—the right formula that will "put the pieces together." Healing, however, is more than the mastery of skills. Healing is a function of the heart. It is an incomprehensible mystery.

The health-care system that I have been a part of rewards practitioners when they are able to meet outcome criteria and discharge clients with no further treatment needed. Practitioners feel successful when all goals are met and the client is able to return to normal living. It is perplexing, however, when the client fails to respond to the practitioner's knowledge and skills. Often the healers will redouble their efforts, looking even harder for the "right" treatment. Pain and suffering, as part of this mystery, cannot always be alleviated by tapping into the right knowledge or the right solution.

When I have come to moments like this, I have had to stop and reassess what is happening with the client. My perceived failure actually lies in my lack of recognition of the mystery involved in healing. My healing interventions are not just a result of how much I know, but also of what I intuit, feel, or hear in my heart. Healing, as heart work, continually challenges the mind to let go of the need to figure everything out.

It often appears that our various health-care approaches seek to eliminate mystery and the unknown. Perhaps we have operated far too long from the premise that if it is broken we can surely fix it. But we are not machines—we are embodiments of mystery. A reductionist philosophy of care that tends to reduce the problem to its lowest common denominator leaves little room for the mysterious in life.

What is this mystery of healing? When our lives are out of balance, it seems as if our spirit and our body are not in harmonious communication. Some people may seek out holistic "healers," trying to understand and deal with the mysteries within. These seekers want to invite the Divine, the miraculous or the sacred back into their lives even though they may not be fully awake to this awareness. Our bodies are intricately interwoven with our spirits. What affects the body affects the spirit, and what affects the spirit affects the body. This is mystery.

Healing flows from the core of our being. When we journey the inward path, we gradually begin to see how healing is called forth in our lives. Once this inward journey has begun, how then do we cultivate an "attitude of heart" that is at home with mystery, that is open to give and to receive healing, that yearns for a deeper relationship with God, who always beckons and calls us? The path within can lead to places of consolation and blessings that are filled with Light, grace, and peace. But this inward path can also twist and turn, making the journey difficult. These are the places on the path of desolation and discomfort.

[1]Hannah Hurnard, *Hinds' Feet On High Places.*

There is a wonderful allegory by Hannah Hurnard that I discovered over twenty years ago.[1] It is about a young woman with a crooked little smile and crooked feet, who seeks to follow the Shepherd to the High Places. She longs to escape her fears so she can simply sit at the feet of the Shepherd and bask in his Light. The Shepherd grants her request and says he will bring her to the High Places. He gives her two companions for the journey, "Sorrow and Suffering," to help her attain her goal. These companions are not to her liking at all, and she resents having to take their hands. But when she does, she finds that she walks straighter along the path of life, even though she encounters places of consolation and desolation, blessings and discomfort. After many lessons learned, little "Much Afraid" is transformed through learning to let go and let God direct her. She becomes a new being and is given a new name, "Grace and Glory," and her companions are revealed as "Joy and Peace" as they enter the kingdom of the High Places.

The connection to our deepest self is often made through the heart in the midst of mystery along our journey in life. How can we develop an attitude of heart that can sustain us through those periods of desolation as well as consolation, and bring us to the high places? Here we can embrace the Divine mystery as we answer the call to be instruments in the healing of others.

Prayer of the Heart

The heart center is at the core of our spiritual self and is the place where we are most at home in connecting with our deeper being. When tapping into the heart center, many report experiencing a flooding of Light or an overwhelming sense of the sacred. We sense that God is holding us tenderly in the palm of God's hands. We may be aware of feelings of security, wholeness, wisdom, and joy in those moments. Opening the heart is like awakening to the Light and allowing the Light to shine through all the cracks, all the places of pain and hurt. It is from this place of utter nakedness in the heart that we can be most in touch with God. Here at the heart, we naturally lift ourselves up in prayer.

Larry Dossey reflects what many of the great saints and mystics have said through the centuries, "prayer is an attitude of the heart, a matter of being, not doing."[2] The "being" that Dossey and others refer to is different from the "doing" in life. In the doing, many of us know who we are because we define our existence by what we do. In the being, we become empty enough and silent enough to simply be in God's presence. This presence becomes all encompassing, all important, all meaningful—a sacred moment when we rest in God. Richard Foster describes this state of "being" as when we "come home to our heart" where God indwells.[3] Prayer is the key to how we go within, how we tread the inner path of God, how we come to that attitude of heart. It is not about words, it is about how our hearts communicate with God.

Prayer that comes from the heart is a prayer of intimacy, love, and tenderness. Our deeper and truer selves—the selves created by God—come forth out of the shadows when we pray from the heart. This is "the radiant self, full of wonder and awe," according to Ken Kaisch, an Episcopal priest and writer on prayer.[4] It is the self that delights in the moment and the self that accepts its dark passions, the self that loves fully, the self that is whole. This true self is always present and connected to God whispering in our hearts.

[2] Larry Dossey, *Prayer Is Good Medicine,* p. 81.

You may wish to consult the writings of other great mystics about this prayer of the heart. For instance, John of the Cross, Teresa of Avila, Miester Eckert, Thomas Merton, Matthew Fox, Mother Theresa, Joan Borysenko, Ron Roth, Evelyn Underhill, the Dalai Lama...The list goes on and on.

[3] Richard Foster, *Prayer, Finding the Heart's True Home,* p. 1.

[4] Ken Kaisch, *Finding God, A Handbook of Christian Meditation,* p. 43.

How do you recognize when your true self is present?

The true self stays hidden most of the time under the weight of the false self—the self we show to others—the self that we have created. This false self is constantly looking for love and approval and is totally self-centered. We get so involved in maintaining the false self that we often can't tell the difference between the false and the true self except when we are truly focused in our hearts. The prayer of the heart is a way for the true self to come forth in the radiance of the Divine Light. This takes spiritual discipline, as shown in the allegory about "Much Afraid" and her journey to the High Places.

When you are extending healing to someone else, are you first aware of being in your heart?

Change is difficult for all of us, yet change we must if we are to make space for our true selves. Our healing work depends upon this! When we look at Christ' life, we see the road signs for this healing path. How did Jesus maintain that inner heart connection with God, with Abba? He did it with spiritual discipline: the discipline of a simple life, of going alone to the mountain, the desert, the lonely places where he could find silence and solitude. We see him praying, serving others, and fully loving not only his friends and followers but all people. As a result, he rooted himself in the Presence of God, which was constantly with him. He radiated that Divine Light in his ministry of presence. Like a magnet, he drew the suffering and the unhealed to him.

Do you have a favorite mountain, beach, or private place you like to go to for silence and solitude?

Prayer is the natural response to awakening to the Spirit's call to ministry, be it healing, or any form of service. Awakenings can be many little subtle events that bring us to a deeper awareness of God's calling or they can be earth-shattering events like divorce, lost of relationships, loss of job, our own illness, or the death of a loved one. When awakenings happen, we can no longer go on as usual. Life takes on an urgency to discover what God has in mind for us. The prayer that naturally arises up out of our hearts is a courageous one as we listen in a state of openness. It is, as Foster puts it, "the Holy Spirit praying through you."[5] It is prayer not necessarily with words—it is prayer of deep stillness and communion with God. Time becomes not important. It is kairos or God's time. Spontaneous words may flow from our hearts, or we may simply experience a gentle "resting in the Spirit," a trance-like state where our hearts are

[5]Richard Foster, *Prayer, Finding the Heart's True Home*, p. 36.

warmed by the Spirit's presence. God's time simply is. It is always the present moment.

Our prayer goes through stages that we may or may not recognize at first. Simply put, our prayer is on our lips or in our minds or in our hearts. These represent three stages of prayer found in our Christian tradition and written about by many medieval mystics as well as our modern day mystics.

The first stage has traditionally been called the purgative way. In this stage of development, we try to become more Christian in our contacts with others—less judging, less negative thinking. We strive to be more loving, to be more in communion with others and with God. We look within to see what needs changing for the path God is leading us on. What destructive behaviors need to be replaced with constructive ones. We examine our inner selves and commit to the path of change. In our prayer we find comfort in reflecting on the scriptures or spiritual texts as we learn to quiet the mind's chatter. This path uses discursive prayer, which is best described as discourse or talking to God. We let God know our needs and the needs of others. Sometimes we tell God our stories and dialogue with God on how life is going. At other times we pray out loud or in petitions as we pour out our concerns to God. It is a healing, purifying, and transforming kind of prayer, where we are readied for closer relationship with God. After that first awakening to God's call in our lives, we learn in this stage of prayer to live with the Beloved's call to meaningful relationship.

The second stage is that of illumination. Ron Roth describes this as a time of grace when we experience God's coming to us not only in extraordinary phenomena, but also in the insights, hunches, dreams and intuitive guidance we receive. Our prayer in this stage can be described as contemplative surrender guided by love. Prayer comes much easier to us since we are not ruled by our busy minds. We are now able to open ourselves to the guidance of God's spirit through love.[6] In *The Cloud of Unknowing*, the unnamed author speaks of Mary of Bethany, Martha's sister, as representing this con-

[6]Ron Roth, *Prayer and the Five Stages of Healing*, p. 51.

[7]Unknown author, *The Cloud of Unknowing.*

[8]Camille Campbell, *Meditations with John of the Cross,* p. 31.

[9]Delroy Oberg, editor, *Daily Readings with a Modern Mystic, Selections from the Writings of Evelyn Underhill,* p. 39.

templative life of resting in God's presence.[7] It is a quieting of the mind in total surrender to Love. There are few words, but the mind is awake and attentive to Love's movement in our lives. We enjoy God's presence, but this is only an intermediate stage. Illumination is sometimes followed by what can be called a purification of the spirit, or the "Dark Night of the Soul." St. John of the Cross spoke poetically of this time of great desolation when the soul longs for the consolations it once knew. Surrender to the will of God is the only way through this night which can be long.[8]

The third stage is union with God or what Evelyn Underhill calls coming into ecstasy.[9] Our prayer is one of love discovering wisdom. This path of prayer flows out of the contemplative experiences in our lives. Through Love, we gradually become united to the Christ Light. We see God in all things and all things in God; we become another Christ presence. Here joy, peace, and strength of will and purpose in life become ours. Think of the healing presence we desire to bring to our healing work. Does this not flow from this unitive prayer of oneness in God's presence?

All three paths of prayer, whether on our lips, or in our minds, or in our hearts, are paths we progress through, and, at times, move back and forth as we connect to Spirit. Sometimes we can only cry to God out of our needs, and other times when we sit in the silence of our minds, aware only of the presence of Love. When the heart is open, we break through the illusion that we are all separate from one another. This state of being develops as we faithfully practice our meditation and contemplation, our holy moments with the Divine.

These spiritual disciplines can help move us out of our self-centered, false selves so that we can see with new eyes and new awareness. This is what the saints and holy ones have called mystical experiences, but these experiences are available to all of us as we pray from our hearts. In healing work, we first need to change our own hearts; only then are we ready to help heal the hearts, bodies, and spirits of others.

Mystical Living—a Path to Genuine Healing

In the holy moments of our meditation and contemplation we cannot help but be aware of the divine within us and within the whole universe. Being a mystic does not mean one has to be perfect. Joan Borysenko describes the mystic as one who:

"sees beyond the illusion of separateness into the intricate web of life in which all things are expressions of a single Whole. You can call this web God, the Tao, the Great Spirit, the Infinite Mystery, Mother or Father, but it can be known only as love."[10]

Mystics believe in guidance from God, either by intuitive insights, or messages from angels, or the soul as Dr. Norm Shealy says.[11] They also accept the sacred nature of all aspects of life. Answering the unmistakable call to do healing work, we are awakened to go to the heart of Love to be a channel for Love's light and energy. This is the mystical work to which we are called as healers. Make no mistake about it, all healing—whether we are aware of our spiritual selves or not, whether our intention is to be "clinical" or "spiritual"—all healing comes from God, which makes healing a mystical experience. So as healers, we are called first to be mystics.

Florence Nightingale, mystic in the nineteenth century, asked in her writing, what is mysticism?

"Is it not the attempt to draw near to God, not by rites or ceremonies, but by inward disposition? Is it not merely a hard word for 'The Kingdom of Heaven is within?'...Christ Himself was the first true Mystic."[12]

Nightingale asks where shall I find God? God is within she finds and she knows that she must be in "a state for Him to come and dwell in me." This, she says, is the whole aim of the Mystical life.

The word "mysticism" has often been misunderstood. In the Old Testament, mysticism referred to direct experience of the divine, including sometimes union with God. Several Old Testament prophets were rooted in mystical union with God. We see this

[10]Joan Borysenko, *The Ways of the Mystic, Seven Paths to God*, p. xv.

[11]Norm Shealy, *Sacred Healing, The Curing Power of Energy and Spirituality*, p. xiii.

"As a hart longs for flowing streams,
so longs my soul for You,
   O Beloved.
My soul thirsts for the Beloved,
   for the Living Water.
When may I come and behold your face?"
Psalm 42

[12]Barbara Dossey, "Florence Nightingale, A 19th Century Mystic," in *Journal of Holistic Nursing 16, no. 2*, pp. 111-164.

See also *Florence Nightingale, Mystic, Visionary, Healer* by Barbara Dossey.

most evidently in the prophet Ezekiel, who seemed to be caught up in his experience. Mysticism was also historically connected with the mystery-cults of the Greeks. The historian Margaret Smith tells us that the mystic was one who had been initiated into the "secret knowledge of Divine things" and was sworn to secrecy.[13] Their secret initiation rites were supposed to unite new members with the deity so that they would live forever.

But mysticism today is not about secret knowledge. Modern mysticism is the fruit of intuitive growth—a transformation (through self-purification) into communion or union with the Divine. As healers, we are all called to intuitive growth, to inner transformation through our own purification.

Evelyn Underhill, another English mystic who wrote during the first half of this century, states that the Christian church has never been without mystics. For her, the mystics are those capable of direct experience of God and of spiritual things. Our world needs mystics and craves their messages, she says.[14]

As we set our feet upon the path of healing for self and others, we begin with grounding in God. Going about our daily routines, we work, clean house, fix meals, care for our families, go to the movies—in other words, we lead normal lives. Our lives become grist for the mill of self-purification. As mystics, our lives are focused, mindful of the present moment and connected to our Source, living and being contemplatively. Our daily listening becomes prayer, which enables us as healers to respond to the encouragement of the Spirit.

Ron Roth says our prayers are like "tuning in," like "being on a spiritual wave length with the consciousness of God."[15] God's message of love, compassion, and forgiveness is constantly being sent to us. Our task is to attune our hearts and minds to God's energy so that we may heal, revive, restore, and make whole. Divine guidance directs us as we pray for those on whom we place our hands in healing.

[13]Margaret Smith, *Studies in Early Mysticism, in the Near and Middle East*, p. 1.

[14]Delroy Oberg, editor, *Daily Readings with a Modern Mystic, Selections from the Writings of Evelyn Underhill*, p. 38.

[15]Ron Roth, *The Healing Path of Prayer*, p. 68.

Frank Tuoti has written several books on what it means to be a mystic today. He calls mysticism an "eternal craving of the human soul."[16] Mystics of every time and tradition have awakened to the wonder and rapture of the Divine Presence hungrily waiting to reveal itself and to enter into intimate communion with its own creation. Our hearts yearn for this union with the Divine as we seek to know God's call, to hear God's voice to our hearts.

Mystical experience is always available to anyone who wants it. It is the awareness of the all-pervading presence of God. To the mystic,

Ultimate Reality, true Being, is simply, One.
This Unity, the One Reality, is—
Ultimate Source,
Perfect Goodness,
the Eternal Wisdom,
Unclouded Light,
Beauty Supreme,
Divine Love... simply, God.

The Divine spark that was placed in us long before we manifested in this physical world seeks reunion with the Eternal Flame. Paul Tillich, an important Protestant theologian, refers to God as the "ground of being" or "being itself."[17] If, indeed, God is our "ground of being" and we are essentially related to God, then God resides in our soul—in our heart. Nelle Morton, Methodist theologian and educator says, "God is a cosmic ear that hears us into our own speech." Truly, "in God, we live and move and have our being."[18]

Becoming an Everyday Mystic

Most people cannot leave family or responsibilities in order to spend hours and hours meditating or contemplating the "Ground of one's being." So how are we to cultivate this attitude of heart that welcomes the divine spark into our lives? What can we do in our daily lives that will bring us to that place of "letting go and letting God?" For theologian, Karl Rahner, "every one is at least an anonymous mystic." Nothing about day-to-day life is "profane" he writes.

[16]Frank X. Tuoti, *The Dawn of the Mystical Age, An Invitation to Enlightenment*

[17]Paul Tillich, *Dynamics of Faith.*

See also Paul Tillich, *The Courage To Be.*

[18]Nelle Morton, *The Journey Is Home.*

"Wherever there is radical self-forgetting for the sake of the other... surrender to the mystery that embraces all life, there is...the mysticism of everyday life."[19]

[19]Cited in *Spirituality in Nursing, Standing on Holy Ground* by Sister Mary Elizabeth O'Brien, p. 115.

I have already suggested many ways to bring us to that place of willingness on the path as we develop our healing skills. What else do we need to do to become an "everyday mystic" with a generous heart and a healing hand? Here are a few more suggestions.

Lectio Divina—Prayerful Reading the Scriptures

The scriptures hold our remembrances of God acting in human story. When we read the Scriptures, our hearts burn within us as we prayerfully connect with God's love and desire to be one with us. The Scriptures are the spiritual food, the nourishment that keeps us grounded and connected to God and to one another. If we are serious about cultivating the attitude of heart that leads to an open, loving, mystical way of being, then we must prayerfully read and be fed daily with God's word. Look not to the literalness of the stories but to the underlying meaning which feeds our souls. Often the meaning for our lived experiences is hidden in allegorical stories and parables.

Thomas Keating, *Intimacy with God.*

For more information on Lectio Divina, see Ken Kaisch, *Finding God, A Handbook of Christian Meditation.*

In *Lectio Divina,* we prayerfully read the Scriptures, pausing for reflection on the story and how it applies to our lives today. This way of listening to the scriptures leads us to encounter Christ. We find compassion, steadfastness, courage, faith, love, patience, joy, and gentleness, as well as righteous anger and indignation at the sufferings of others. We reflect upon the meaning, taking it inside of ourselves so that it becomes a part of us. Then we open ourselves to the stirring that God makes in our hearts. We allow our hearts and minds to respond spontaneously to God. When the heart is touched, there is a natural outpouring, sometimes in words, sometimes in feelings without words. When all the words and feelings cease, it is time to simply rest in God's presence. This resting is the prayer of simplicity. It is the "letting go" and being one with God.

Centering Prayer

I have described various forms of prayer already, including petitions for self and others, praise from grateful hearts, prayers from suffering hearts, prayers of affirmation, and reflective prayer on the scriptures (Lectio Divina). There are also prayers of repetition like the rosary or the Jesus Prayer that help to quiet the mind through repeating the same prayers over and over. A form of prayer that is a twentieth century renewal of Christian contemplative prayer is called Centering Prayer.

Centering Prayer probably has its origins in the early church. By the fourteenth century, contemplative prayer had become quite popular. Scholars point to the anonymous work, *The Cloud of Unknowing*, as well as to the work of St. John of the Cross as examples of this style of prayer. This form of prayer fell into disfavor after the Middle Ages and practically disappeared. During that same time, many forms of the healing arts within the church disappeared as well.

A modern renewal of contemplative prayer began in the 1970s through the work of the Trappist monks Thomas Keating, William Menninger, and Basil Pennington. They were seeking a way to help young people who hungered for spiritual guidance to reconnect to their Christian roots. They also were asked to help religious orders deal with burnout among members who were throwing themselves into ministries that required inner resources they did not have. An ecumenical organization known as "The Contemplative Outreach Program" was created to help bring Centering Prayer to churches and to train facilitators and teachers. The work has spread rapidly not only around the U.S. but also around the world, testimony to the spiritual hunger of people worldwide.

Centering Prayer rests in the belief that God is always with us and that God lies underneath all the busyness of our minds. Deep in our hearts, God is always there waiting for us to quiet the chaos in order to be with God. Isaiah calls this "Emmanuel," which means "God with us." The scriptures are filled with images of God being one with us. God is the Shepherd, God is the vine and we are the branches.

"For I am convinced that neither death, nor life, nor angels, nor rulers, nor things present, nor things to come, nor powers, nor height, nor depth, nor anything else in all creation, will be able to separate us from the love of God in Christ Jesus our Lord." Romans 8:39

Like St. Paul, we can say, "Nothing can separate us from the love of God in Christ Jesus our Lord." As the Christian sages through the centuries have said, God is closer to you than you are to your very self.

Thomas Keating, retired Trappist abbot residing in Snowmass, Colorado, is well known for promoting the renewal of this ancient form of prayer through his writing and speaking. He says it is not a technique but primarily a relationship with God. Through our faithful practice of sitting in the presence of God, our hearts become open and receptive and we yield to God's action within our hearts. A "sacred word" is usually chosen that gently helps bring the person back to the Divine Presence when the mind wanders. It could be a very simple word like "God," "Love," "Jesus," or "peace," or perhaps a virtue like "faith," "hope," or "patience." According to Keating, this word is made sacred as we express our "naked intent directed to God."[20]

Centering Prayer is about cultivating a receptive attitude as we enter into the deep quiet within. The focus is not concentration; rather, it is an exercise of intention. The sacred word is used to focus intention but is not the object of attention. Through a discipline like Centering Prayer, the mind is less dominated by surface thoughts and emotional reactions. It is then that we begin to experience the awakening of spiritual attentiveness. We are truly beginning to attune to the voice of the Divine.

Spiritual Companions and Mentors

We are not on the spiritual path alone. There are many walking along with us—some ahead, some behind. Reaching out to companions or guides can be very helpful. All of us at times need someone to mentor us, and, in turn, we become mentors for others. Marsha Sinetar shows us that mentors can be mirrors of that vital life force already within us.[21] Mentors listen intently to our stories and then challenge us to be our spiritual best. The mirror they hold for us wakes us up and motivates us when we are stuck. However, they are not rescuers offering us a list of what to do and what not to

[20]Thomas Keating, *Open Mind, Open Heart, The Contemplative Dimension of the Gospel*, p. 43.

See also Thomas Keating, *Intimacy With God.*

[21]Marsha Sinetar, *The Mentor's Spirit, Life Lessons on Leadership and the Art of Encouragement.*

do. Mentors are guides who give us the freedom to be who we are meant to be. They have learned the art of empowerment through their own wholeness. Through their skills of affirming, they promote self-reliance, confidence, and self-realization. Mentors have faith in our goodness, and by creating safe and sacred environments for our healing, they enable us to step out in faith as we develop into spiritually mature healers.

Our Christian history is filled with stories of spiritual companioning and mentoring. In the scriptures, there are numerable accounts of master/disciple relationships. From Jesus teaching his disciples to Paul exhorting his followers, we see kindness, patience, non-judgmentalism, trustfulness, encouragement to persevere, guidance in the Christian path, empathy, and joy. Kenneth Leech explores this relationship through the ages, and comes upon a Celtic concept that means "soul friend." The Celts thought it was necessary for everyone to "possess a soul-friend," as the following proverb testifies: "Anyone without a soul-friend is a body without a head." Soul-friends or spiritual companions help us with our spiritual growth.[22]

[22]Kenneth Leech, *Soul Friend, An Invitation to Spiritual Direction*, p. 49.

Mentoring has been a hallmark of both the Healing Touch and the Healing Touch Spiritual Ministry programs from the very beginning. Healing work is learned through apprenticeship, under the guidance of one who has matured in the work. Janet Mentgen emphasized the wisdom of this process and encourages people to give back to the work by in turn, mentoring others. For years she modeled the humble life of a healer, connected to her Divine Source. She nurtured many, instilling courage to follow their passion for the work. As a result, she impacted countless numbers on many continents. I experienced her mentoring, her encouragement, and her challenge to me to be my spiritual best. Now I serve as mentor to many others and, hopefully, give back some of the richness that I have received.

Mentors are not perfect. We should not romanticize them or give them too much power. When we put people on pedestals they usually fall off or soon we push them down. We can find mentors at every turn in life, and they will appear often when we are most in need. Mentoring is much like "pushing hands" in Tai Chi, where two people learn to move in the flow of energy between them. There is the constant give and take of learning, which is *expanding*. This is balanced by teaching, which is *emptying*. According to Chungliang Al Huang and Jerry Lynch, this relationship of mentoring and learning is like a dance that stimulates self-expansion. When we need to learn, we are open to receiving; and once we have learned, we become open to giving. When we have a dynamic mentoring relationship in our lives, we never stop growing and changing.[23] Mentors are mirrors who do no more than point the way to the goal. The mentor cannot do the work for us. They gently guide with virtue. They allay fears by creating an atmosphere that is inspired, trustful, and harmonious. The dance falls apart, however, when demands and impositions are placed on the one being mentored or on the mentor.

How do you know when the time is ripe for such a mentoring experience in your life? For me, it was when I was ready for change, expansion, and openness to greater possibilities in life. I remember the first person who became my mentor. It was the Director of Nursing where I worked as a staff nurse in education. She helped me not only with career choices; she also inspired me to greatness in my work. She challenged me, walked with me on the path, and was a kindred spirit.

Your mentor may be right in front of you. It could be a peer, minister, friend, neighbor, or colleague. If you need to search, the person will generally present him/herself, perhaps as a kindred spirit like the Director of Nursing was for me. The beauty of a mentoring relationship is truly the dance between the two as both hearts are filled with compassionate, loving regard for each other.

Do the Work of the Heart

Cultivating the attitude of a loving, healing, mystical heart takes patience and simply holding the space for change. This attitude of heart naturally leads to an expression of that heart love through service. Giving of oneself leads to interior riches that may be a surprise

[23]Chungliang Al Huang & Jerry Lynch, *Mentoring, The TAO of Giving and Receiving Wisdom*, p. 9.

to many. Giving is receiving, and when we serve, we receive back a hundredfold.

When the call to serve through healing becomes strong, what do you do with it? There are a myriad ways that you can express the call to heal. Look around your circle of friends and family, your church community, your neighborhood. Where best can you use the gifts of your healing hands? Where is God calling you to volunteer? Do the work you are called to do. Each time you do healing work, you grow stronger not only in the work but also in your own healing.

Tom Schommer is an example of someone who followed his heart and established a private practice in healing work in Minnesota. He now volunteers his services doing Healing Touch Spiritual Ministry at a local hospital. After Tom retired from truck driving, he looked around for something to keep him busy. His wife Barbara was a Healing Touch Practitioner and Instructor but he did not feel particularly drawn to follow in her footsteps especially since he was a total skeptic about energy work. When she brought home a brochure on the Healing Touch Spiritual Ministry program, Tom felt it was time to look at his own spiritual path. HTSM became the fit for him. He not only completed the advanced practitioner program—he was the first to do so. Tom is a shinning example of those who find fulfillment in volunteering, mentoring and healing practice.

Janet Wilson is a nurse in Durango, CO and works at one of the local hospitals. She is a member of the Touch, Love and Compassion team providing a free service for patients and family for relief of pain and anxiety. She has incredible support from the hospital and from the medical staff. They have a pre-op program in which patients receive Healing Touch Spiritual Ministry both pre and post surgery. In addition, she has her own healing practice in a downtown office to assist those who need stress management and healing. Having a Christ-based focus to her work is very important to her and cannot imagine her life without the opportunities to be God's instrument.

Sister Mary Goergen OSF is a Franciscan sister living at her community's retirement center in Rochester, MN. Sister Mary does Healing Touch Spiritual Ministry with many of the elderly especially those who have surgery or who are dying. She prays and trusts her angels to help her with the work.

Rev. Kevin Andrew Babcock is a hospice chaplain. He introduced and helped to integrate Healing Touch Spiritual Ministry into the core services provided by the hospice in Philadelphia, PA. They are in the process of developing their own internal training program to allow all their staff to provide the basic healing techniques. Kevin says they are doing the work every day—even at team meetings!

Dana Redus from Jacksboro, TN found an easy setting for her healing ministry—at her chiropractor husband's office. They made a sign to let patients know that Healing Touch Spiritual Ministry is available. Since many have never heard of this work, Dana finds that this is a great opportunity to tell people about the work. She is convinced that this is God's work and that this is where God wants her to be.

Dr. Jennifer Makin transformed her vocation as a psychologist and found a new way of life on her spiritual journey. After sharing her call to healing ministry with the members of the Congregational Care Committee at Christiansburg Presbyterian Church in Virginia, they offered to renovate a two room space where she could do her healing work. Jennifer calls her ministry "Wellspring at CPC—A Center for Spiritual Development and Wholeness." Healing Touch Spiritual Ministry and anointing are an important piece of this work along with spiritual direction and sometimes, massage. The work is spreading very quickly by word of mouth.

Finding a Rhythm in Life

Healing, whether we speak of personal healing or healing for others, is about harmony and balance in one's life. It is in the rhythm of life—the ebb and flow—that we see the grace of healing. Janet Mentgen spoke of this rhythm in a keynote address she gave for the Australian Holistic Nursing Conference in 1995. "We cannot be a spark of light for someone else if our spark has gone out," she says. The path of healership is about doing the work, of "coming home" to what we already know how to do.[24]

[24]Janet Mentgen, "Keynote Address," Australian Holistic Nursing Conference, *Australian Journal of Holistic Nursing*, 3, no. 1, (1996).

Mentgen gives us some guidelines that have worked for her in finding a rhythm in life. These are ways that can help us constantly rekindle the flame within.

First, there is *physical clearing*, taking care of the body—nutrition, supplements, water, rest, exercise, breathing, movement, activity. These are the things that keep us able to be on the Earth.

Second, there is *emotional clearing*, expressing our hurts and our pains, which is a necessary part of life. We use prayer from our faith tradition. We use therapies of all kinds such as journaling, self-help groups, meditation, and dream work to aid in clearing of emotions. We even use laughter and play. We are not lacking in resources, Mentgen says. We just have to do it.

Third, there is *mental clearing*, where we change our cognitive thought processes and patterns. It is called changing one's mind. We problem solve, use assertiveness, catharsis, creativity, and developing our mind through mental disciplines. These include reading and studying to help clear out our mental cobwebs to make room for new habits, new ways of doing things.

Fourth, she identifies the use of *sacred space*. Here, she is referring not only to your sacred space at home, but also to your sacred space when you are away. She asks: what does your sanctuary look like? How do you bless it? How is it a sanctuary for you that draws you home? Sacred space creates within us both an outer and inner harmony. This enables us to take that sacred space with us no matter where we travel. Simplicity is her model. She asks, "Is your space cluttered?" "Does it create restfulness?" "What is it filled with that needs to be recycled?" Perhaps its time for a spring cleaning and organizing of your sacred space.

Objects hold vibration. To stay in the present, she advises that we only hold on to those things that hold our present vibration in our sanctuary. Get rid of the rest.

Fifth is the principle of *silence.* It is in silence that our spirits are renewed. Try, sometime, keeping "Holy Silence," speaking only when necessary to conserve energy. She did this when she traveled and learned that it helped her to arrive rested when keeping Holy Silence.

Sixth is *holy leisure,* which is what brings balance into our lives and restores us from our workload. This is the rhythm that is necessary for us to continue day-to-day life. Call it play, or laughter, or just doing nothing. Experiment—try doing nothing just for a few minutes every day. It is difficult for us to do when we stay so busy in our lives.

And, seventh, *holy relationships,* which is about commitment, faithfulness, and honoring those relationships in our lives. It is being in committed relationships, having sexual fidelity. It is an expression of the pureness of our heart in doing the healing work we are called to do.

With these guiding principles, Mentgen says, we are led to making a commitment to our way of life (the life of the healer) and to the disciplines needed to be faithful to our calling to be of service for others.

Going to the High Places

Developing as a healer is a lifetime experience. It is not something that we can say we have achieved once we have completed a course of study or apprenticeship. It is about learning to skip along the peaks of the High Places as "Grace and Glory" learned to do. We are here on this earth but a fleeting moment. What good do we want to accomplish while we are here? The High Places, as Hurnard explains, are a place of love and victory here on Earth. Here we are able to transform the pain and suffering around us into "letting go and letting God." Through this daily inner transformation, we learn

"God the Lord, is my strength;
  he makes my feet like the feet of a deer,
  and makes me tread upon the heights."
Habbakkuk 3:19

to see with new eyes, feel with a new touch, and hear with new ears God's call to us to wholeness and to oneness. There is great freedom in coming into oneness within oneself, with others, and with God.

Epilogue

Healing the World

It is debatable whether we have been good healers over these past two thousand years since Christ' resurrection. Our history shows us moments when we have been destroyers of healing in the name of religion. It also shows us moments when we have been courageous healers in the face of death. I have always thought that the value of any historical perspective was to show me how I want to live my life right now. What I have learned is that I want to heal myself, my neighbor, and my world.

It is tempting to surrender to the fatalistic thought that I am "just one individual" and that I can do nothing to influence future events. The world too often seems to be tottering on the edge of extinction, and what holds it back from this fate is surely a miracle.

But each person has the power to influence much larger circles of the human family. Many by their prayers help hold the webbing of humankind together, and the actions of others extend the hand of compassionate healing to those suffering in so many ways. Our healing thoughts, prayers, and actions are indeed giving us a future to believe in. All we need do is look at the many requests for aid of one kind or another received daily at the doors of our churches. Our healing work may need to begin here, with those with whom we share our spiritual roots.

"Then I heard the voice of the Lord saying, 'Whom shall I send, and who will go for us?' And I said 'Here am I; send me!' And he said, 'Go.'" Isaiah 6:8-9

Whom shall I send, God asks. If not me, then who will go? Who will save the people? I invite you to look within and examine your hearts. Ruah, the breath of God, is blowing upon us all and we are becoming conscious of our spiritual selves and our spiritual evolution as humankind. We are awakening to spiritual realities. As Frank Tuoti observes, we are becoming a people of the fourth (spiritual) dimension. Our consciousness is being raised, and we are transcending to higher levels of justice, peace, and equality. As we heal ourselves, our inner light grows brighter, and we begin to be a sign of hope for all those who need healing.[1] As we become twenty-first century beings, it is my hope that, with courage, we will recognize the healing abilities available to us through God for one another. What better place to start than with our very own church and spiritual communities where we strive to live the Gospel mandate to teach, preach, and to *heal.*

[1]Frank X. Tuoti, *The Dawn of the Mystical Age, An Invitation to Enlightenment*, p. 6.

BIBLIOGRAPHY

_____ *The Cloud of Unknowing*. Great Britain: Penguin Books Ltd., 1961.

Achtemeier, Paul J. *Harper's Bible Dictionary*. San Francisco, CA: Harper SanFrancisco, 1985.

Achterberg, Jeanne. *Woman As Healer, A Panoramic survey of the Healing Activities of Women From Prehistoric Times to the Present*. Boston: Shambhala Publications, Inc., 1990.

Adams, Kay. *Journal to the Self, Twenty-Two Paths to Personal Growth*. New York: Time Warner Co., 1990.

Althouse, Lawrence W. *Rediscovering the Gift of Healing*. Nashville, TN: Nashville Abingdon Press, 1977.

Bakken, MD, Kenneth L. *The Call to Wholeness, Health as a Spiritual Journey*. New York: Crossroad, 1992.

Bakken, MD, Kenneth L. and Kathleen H. Hofeller. T*he Journey toward Wholeness, A Christ-Centered Approach to Health and Healing*. New York: Crossroad Publishing Co., 1992.

Benson, MD, Herbert. *Timeless Healing, The Power and Biology of Belief*. New York: Scribner, 1996.

Bohm, David. *The Implicate Order.* New York: Doubleday, Publishers, 1990.

Borg, Marcus J. *Meeting Jesus Again for the First Time.* San Francisco: Harper SanFrancisco, 1995.

Borg, Marcus J. *The Heart of Christianity, Rediscovering a Life of Faith.* San Francisco: Harper SanFrancisco, 2004.

Borysenko, Joan. *The Ways of the Mystic, Seven Paths to God.* Carlsbad, CA: Hay House, Inc., 1997.

Brooke, Avery. *Healing in the Landscape of Prayer.* Boston: Cowley Publications, 1996.

Burkhardt, M. and M.G. Nagai-Jacobson. *Spirituality, Living our Connectedness.* U.S.: Delmar Publishers, 2002.

Burr, H.S. and F.S.G. Northrop, "Evidence for the Existence of an Electrodynamic Field in the Living Organisms." *Proceedings of the National Academy of Sciences of the United States of America* 24 (1939): 284-288.

Byrd, MD, Randolph C. "Positive Therapeutic Effects of Intercessory Prayer in a Coronary Care Unit Population." *Southern Medical Journal* 81, no. 7 (July 1988): 826-29.

Campbell, Camille. *Meditations with John of the Cross.* Santa Fe, NM: Bear and Company, 1989.

Cairns, Earle E. *Christianity Through the Centuries, A History of the Christian Church,* 3rd Ed. Grand Rapids, MI: Zondervan Publishing House, 1996.

Childre, Doc Lew. *Cut-Thru.* Boulder Creek, CA: Planetary Publications, 1996.

Childre, Doc Lew. *Freeze-Frame.* Boulder Creek, CA: Planetary Publications, 1994.

Cooper, Rabbi David. *God Is a Verb, Kabbalah and the Practice of Mystical Judaism.* New York: Riverhead Books, 1997.

Davis, Bruce. *Monastery without Walls.* Berkeley, CA: Celestial Arts, 1990.

Dossey, Barbara, Lynn Keegan, Cathie E. Guzzetta, and Leslie. G. Kolkmeier. *Holistic Nursing, A Handbook for Practice.* 2nd edition, Gaithersburg, MD: Aspen Publication, 1995.

Dossey, Barbara M. "Florence Nightingale, A 19th-Century Mystic." *Journal of Holistic Nursing* 16, no. 2 (June, 1998): 111-164.

Dossey, Barbara M. *Florence Nightingale, Mystic, Visionary, Healer.* Springhouse, PA: Springhouse Corporation, 2000.

Dossey, MD, Larry. *Healing Words, The Power of Prayer and the Practice of Medicine.* San Francisco: Harper-San Francisco, 1994.

Dossey, MD, Larry. *Prayer Is Good Medicine, How to Reap the Healing Benefits of Prayer.* San Francisco: HarperSan Francisco, 1996.

Dossey, MD, Larry. *Be Careful What You Pray For...You Just Might Get It.* San Francisco: Harper SanFrancisco, 1997.

Dossey, MD, Larry. *Recovering the Soul, A Scientific and Spiritual Search.* New York: Bantam Books, 1989.

Dues, Greg. *Catholic Customs and Traditions, A Popular Guide.* Mystic, CT: Twenty-Third Publications, 1998.

Eden, MD, James. *Energetic Healing, The Merging of Ancient and Modern Medical Practices.* New York: Plenum Press, 1993.

Eisenberg, MD, David, R.C. Kessler, C. Foster, F. Norlock, D. R. Calkins, and T. L. Delbanco, "Unconventional Medicine in the United States." *The New England Journal of Medicine,* 328, no. 4 (Jan. 28, 1993):246-252.

Fahlbusch, Erwin, et al. editors. *The Encyclopedia of Christianity,* Vol. 1 A-D. Grand Rapids, MI: William B. Erdmans Publishing Company, 1997.

Fiore, Edith. *The Unquiet Dead, A Psychologist Treats Spirit Possession.* New York: Ballantine Books, 1987.

Flinders, Carol Lee. Enduring Grace, *Living Portraits of Seven Women Mystics*. San Francisco: Harper SanFrancisco, 1993.

Ford, Clyde W. *Compassionate Touch, The Role of Human Touch in Healing and Recovery*. New York: Simon and Schuster, 1993.

Foster, Richard J. Prayer, *Finding the Heart's True Home*. San Francisco: Harper SanFrancisco, 1992.

Foster, Richard J. *Freedom of Simplicity*. New York: Harper and Row, 1989.

Fox, Matthew and R. Sheldrake. *The Physics of Angels, Exploring the Realm where Science and Spirit Meet*. San Francisco: Harper SanFrancisco, 1996.

Fox, Matthew and Rupert Sheldrake. *Natural Grace, Dialogues on Creation, Darkness, and the Soul in Spirituality and Science*. New York: Doubleday, 1996.

Gerber, MD, Richard. *Vibrational Medicine, New Choices for Healing Ourselves*. Santa Fe, NM: Bear and Company, 1988.

Goldsmith, Joel S. *Practicing the Presence, The Inspirational Guide to Regaining Meaning and a Sense of Purpose in Your Life*. San Francisco: Harper SanFrancisco, 1991.

Grad, Bernard. "The Biological Effects of the 'Laying On Of Hands' on Animals and Plants: Implications for Biology." In *Parapsychology: Its Relation to Physics, Biology and Psychiatry*, edited by G. Schmeidler. Metuchen, NJ: Scarecrow Press, 1967.

Grad, Bernard. "Some Biological Effects of Laying On of Hands and Their Implications." In *Dimensions in Wholistic Healing: New Frontiers in the Treatment of the Whole Person*, edited by Otto and Knight.

Graham, Rochelle, Flora Litt and Wayne Irwin. *Healing From The Heart, A Guide to Christian Healing for Individuals and Groups*. Winfield, BC, Canada: Wood Lake Books, 1998.

Hanh, Thich Nhat. *Living Buddha, Living Christ*. New York: Riverhead Books, 1995.

Harpur, Tom. *For Christ's Sake*. Toronto, Ontario: McClelland and Stewart, Inc., 1986.

Harpur, Tom. *The Uncommon Touch, An Investigation of Spiritual Healing.* Toronto, Ontario: McClelland and Stewart, Inc., 1994.

Hildegard of Bingen. *Holistic Healing.* M. Pawlik, P. Madigan, J. Kulas, and M. Palmquist, translators. Collegeville, MN: The Liturgical Press, 1994.

Holland, Gail Bernice. *A Call For Connection, Solutions for Creating a Whole New Culture.* Novato, CA: New World Library, 1998.

Hover-Kramer, Dorothea, Janet Mentgen, and Sharon Scandrett-Hibdon. *Healing Touch, A Resource for Health Care Professionals.* Albany, NY: Delmar Publishers, 1996.

Huang, Chungliang Al and Jerry Lynch. *Mentoring, The TAO of Giving and Receiving Wisdom.* San Francisco: Harper SanFrancisco, 1995.

Huebsch, Bill. *A New Look at Grace, A Spirituality of Wholeness.* Mystic, CT: Twenty-Third Publications, 1996.

Hunt, Valerie. "Scientific Validation of Human EM Fields." Video tape, 1988.

Hunt, Valerie. *Infinite Mind, Science of the Human Vibrations of Consciousness.* Malibu, CA: Malibu Publishing Co., 1996.

Hurnard, Hannah. *Hinds' Feet on High Places.* Wheaton, IL: Tyndale House Publishers, Inc., 1976.

Jones, Stanley and A. Elaine Yarbrough, "A Naturalistic Study of the Meanings of Touch." *Communications Monographs* 52 (March, 1985): 20, 51.

Kaisch, Ken. *Finding God, A Handbook of Christian Meditation.* Mahwah, NJ: Paulist Press, 1994.

Keating, Thomas. *Intimacy with God.* New York: Crossroad Publishing Co., 1997.

Keating, Thomas. *Open Mind Open Heart, The Contemplative Dimension of the Gospel.* New York: Continuum Publishing Co., 1996.

Keck, L. Robert. *Healing As a Sacred Path.* West Chester, PA: Chrysalis Books, 2002.

Kelsey, Morton. *Discernment, A Study in Ecstasy and Evil.* New York: Paulist Press, 1978.

Kelsey, Morton. *Healing and Christianity.* Minneapolis, MN: Augsburg Press, 1995.

Knippers, Christopher. *Common Sense, Intuition, and God's Guidance.* Nashville, TN: Thomas Nelson Publishers, 1993.

Krieger, Dolores. *The Therapeutic Touch, How to Use Your Hands to Help or to Heal.* New York: Prentice Hall Press, 1979.

Krieger, Dolores. *Accepting Your Power to Heal, The Personal Practice of Therapeutic Touch.* Santa Fe, NM: Bear and Company, 1993.

Krieger, Dolores. "Therapeutic Touch: The Imprimatur of Nursing." *American Journal of Nursing,* 75, no. 5: 784-7.

Krieger, Dolores. *Therapeutic Touch Inner Workbook.* Santa Fe, NM: Bear and Co. Publishing, 1997.

Labowitz, Rabbi Shoni. *Miraculous Living, A Guided Journey in Kabbalah through the Ten Gates of the Tree of Life.* New York: Simon & Schuster, 1996.

Lachman, Barbara. *The Journal of Hildegard of Bingen.* New York: Bell Tower, 1993.

Lawrence, Brother. *The Practice of the Presence of God.* New York: Doubleday Publishers, 1996.

Leb, Cathy. "The Effects of Healing Touch on Depression." Master's thesis presentation at the American Holistic Nurses' Association, Tampa, FL, 1998.

Lee, Chwen Jiuan A. and Thomas G. Hand. *A Taste of Water, Christianity through Taoist-Buddhist Eyes.* Burlingame, CA: self-published by Fr. Thomas G. Hand and Sister Chwen Jiuan A. Lee, 1990.

Leech, Kenneth. *Soul Friend, An Invitation to Spiritual Direction.* San Francisco: Harper SanFrancisco, 1992.

Linn, Dennis and Matthew Linn. *Healing Life's Hurts, Healing Memories through the Five Stages of Forgiveness.* New York: Paulist Press, 1988.

Lloyd, Geoffrey E.R. *Hippocratic Writings.* London: Penguin Books, 1978.

MacNutt, Francis. *Healing.* Notre Dame, IN: Ave Maria Press, 1991.

Macrae, Janet. *Therapeutic Touch, A Practical Guide.* New York: Alfred A. Knopf, 1988.

Maisch, Ingrid. Mary Magdalene, *The Image of a Woman through the Centuries.* Collegeville, MN: The Liturgical Press, 1998.

Matthews, MD, Dale. *The Faith Factor, Proof of the Healing Power of Prayer.* New York: Penguin Books, 1998.

McKivergin, Maggie. "The Nurse as an Instrument of Healing." In *Core Curriculum for Holistic Nursing,* edited by Barbara Dossey. Gaithersburg, MD: Aspen Publication, 1997.

Meehan, Bridget. *The Healing Power of Prayer.* Liguori, MO: Liguori Publications, 1988.

Mentgen, Janet and Mary Jo Bulbrook. *Healing Touch Level I Notebook,* 2nd Ed. Carrboro, NC: North Carolina Center for Healing Touch, 1996.

Mentgen, Janet. "Keynote Address." Australian Holistic Nursing Conference, *The Australian Journal of Holistic Nursing* 3, no. 1, 1996.

Miller, Robert J., editor. *The Complete Gospels.* San Francisco: Harper SanFrancisco, 1994.

Miner, Malcom H. *Your Touch Can Heal, A Guide to Healing Touch and How to Use It.* Keswwick, VA: Faith Ridge, 1990.

Morton, Nell. *The Journey Is Home.* Boston: Beacon Press, 1985.

Motz, Julie. *Hands of Life.* New York: Bantam Books, 1998.

Moyers, Bill. *Healing and the Mind.* New York: Doubleday Publishers, 1993.

Myss, Caroline. *Anatomy of the Spirit, The Seven Stages of Power and Healing.* New York: Harmony Books, 1996.

Myss, Caroline. *Why People Don't Heal.* Audio tapes produced by Sounds True, Boulder, CO, 1994.

Myss, Caroline. *Why People Don't Heal and How They Can.* New York: Harmony House, 1997.

Nightingale, Florence. *Suggestions for Thought, Selections and Commentaries.* Edited by Michael D. Calabrie and Janet A. Macrae. Philadelphia: University of Pennsylvania Press, 1994.

Norberg, Tilda and Robert D. Webber. *Stretch Out Your Hand, Exploring Healing Prayer.* Nashville, TN: Upper Room Books, 1998.

Nouwen, Henri. *The Wounded Healer.* New York: Doubleday, 1972.

Oberg, Delroy, editor. *Daily readings with a Modern Mystic, Selections from the Writings of Evelyn Underhill.* Mystic, CT: Twenty-Third Publications, 1993.

O'Brien, Sister Mary Elizabeth. *Spirituality in Nursing, Standing on Holy Ground.* Sudbury, MA: Jones and Bartlett Publishers, 1999.

O'Murchu, Diarmuid. *Reclaiming Spirituality.* New York: Crossroad Publishing Co., 1998.

O'Murchu, Diarmuid. *Quantum Theology, Spiritual Implications of the New Physics.* New York: Crossroad Publishing Co., 1997.

Oschman, James L. and Nora Oschman. "Researching Mechanisms of Energetic Therapies." *Healing Touch Newsletter* 8, no. 3, 1998.

Oschman, James. L. *Energy Medicine, The Scientific Basis.* Edinburgh: Churchill Livingstone, 2000.

Oz, Mehmet. *Healing from the Heart, A Leading Heart Surgeon Explores the Power of Complementary Medicine.* New York: Penguin Publishers, 1998.

Pagels, Elaine. *The Origin of Satan.* New York: Vintage Books, 1995.

Pearsall, Paul. *The Heart's Code, Tapping the Wisdom and Power of Our Heart Energy.* New York: Broadway Books, 1998.

Pribram, Karl. *The Language of the Brain.* New York: Plenum Publishers, 1971.

Quinn, Janet. *Therapeutic Touch, A Video Course for Health care Professionals.* Video produced by The National League for Nursing, New York, N.Y.

Regan, Georgina and Debbie Shapiro. *The Healer's Hand Book, A Step-by-Step Guide to Developing Your Latent Healing Abilities.* Longmead, Shaftesbury, Dorset, England: Element Books Limited, 1988.

Rohr, Richard. Everything Belongs, *The Gift of Contemplative Prayer.* New York: Crossroad Publishers, 1999.

Rosage, David E. *What Scripture Says about Healing, A Guide to Scriptural Prayer and Meditation.* Ann Arbor, MI: Servant Books, 1988.

Roth, Ron with Peter Occhiogrosso. *The Healing Path of Prayer, A Modern Mystic's Guide to Spiritual Power.* New York: Harmony Books, 1997.

Roth, Ron. *Prayer and the Rituals of Prayer as Energy Medicine.* Audio Tapes, Celebrating Life Resources, Peru, IL, 1995.

Roth, Ron with Peter Occhiogrosso. *Prayer and the Five Stages of Healing.* Carlsbad, CA: Hay House, Inc., 1999.

Ryan, Barbara Shlemon, Dennis Linn, and Matthew Linn. *To Heal as Jesus Healed.* Mineola, NY: Resurrection Press, 1997.

St. Augustine. Edited by Vernon J. Bourke. *The City of God.* New York: Doubleday Publishers, 1958.

Sanford, Agnes. *The Healing Light.* New York: Ballantine Books, 1972.

Sanford, Agnes. *Sealed Orders.* South Plainfield, NJ: Bridge Publishing, Inc., 1972.

Savary, Louis and Patricia Berne. *Prayer Medicine, How to Dance, Cry, Sing, Meditate, Wrestle, Love & Pray Your Way to Healing.* Barrytown, NY: Station Hill Press, Inc., 1996.

Schipperges, Heinrich. Hildegard of Bingen, *Healing and the Nature of the Cosmos.* Princeton, NJ: Markus Wiener Publishers, 1997.

Schlitz, Marilyn J. "Intentionality and Intuition and Their Clinical Implications: A Challenge for Science and Medicine." *Advances: The Journal of Mind-Body Health* 12, no. 2, (Spring, 1996): 58-66.

Schiltz, Marilyn. "Intentionality in Healing : Mapping the Integration of Body, Mind and Spirit." *Alternative Therapies* 1, no. 5 (Nov. 1995): 119-120.

Shealy, C. Norman, MD. *Sacred Healing, The Curing Power of Energy and Spirituality.* Boston: Element Books, 1999.

Sinetar, Marsha. *The Mentor's Spirit, Life Lessons on Leadership and the Art of Encouragement.* New York: St. Martin's Press, 1998.

Solomon, Jane and Grant. *Harry Oldfield's Invisible Universe.* Great Britain: Campion Books, 1998.

Smith, Margaret. *Studies in Early Mysticism in the Near and Middle East.* Oxford, England: Oneworld, 1995.

Smith, Sister Justa. "The Influence on Enzyme Growth by the 'Laying On Of Hands'" in *The Dimensions of Healing: A Symposium.* Los Altos, CA: The Academy of Parapsychology and Medicine, 1972.

Smith, Linda. *Suggested Guidelines/Policies for a Healing Ministry.* Third Edition. Arvada, CO: Healing Touch Spiritual Ministry Program, 1998.

Strehlow, Wighard and Gottfried Hertzka. *Hildegard of Bingen's Medicine.* Santa Fe, NM: Bear and Company, 1988.

Stroink, G. "Principles of Cardiomagnetism." In *Advances in Biomagnetism,* edited by S.J. Williamson, et al. New York: Plenum Press, 1989.

Talbot, Michael. *The Holographic Universe.* New York: Harper Perennial, 1991.

Thomas, Leo and Jan Alkire. *Healing as a Parish Ministry, Mending Body, Mind, and Spirit.* Notre Dame, IN: Ave Maria Press, 1992.

Thomas, Leo and Jan Alkire. *Healing Ministry, A Practical Guide.* Kansas City, MO: Sheed and Ward, 1994.

Thomas, Zach. *Healing Touch, The Church's Forgotten Language.* Louisville, KY: Westminster/John Knox Press, 1994.

Tillich, Paul. *Dynamics of Faith.* New York: Harper and Row, 1957.

Tillich, Paul. *Courage To Be.* New Haven, CT: University Press, 1952.

Tuoti, Frank X. *The Dawn of the Mystical Age, An Invitation to Enlightenment.* New York: Crossroad Publishing Co., 1997.

Uhlein, Gabriele. *Meditations with Hildegard of Bingen.* Santa Fe, NM: Bear and Company, 1982.

Vennard, Jane E. *Praying with Body and Soul, A Way to Intimacy with God.* Minneapolis, MN: Augsburg Fortress Publishers, 1998.

Voillaume, Rene. *Seeds of the Desert, Like Jesus at Nazareth.* Notre Dame, IN: Fides Publishers, Inc., 1964.

Wagner, James K. *An Adventure in Healing and Wholeness, The Healing Ministry of Christ in the Church Today.* Nashville, TN: Upper Room Books, 1993.

Warter, MD, Carlos. *Who Do You Think You Are? The Healing Power of Your Sacred Self.* New York: Bantum Books, 1998.

Wirth, Daniel P. "The Effect of Non-Contact Therapeutic Touch on the Healing Rate of Full Thickness Dermal Wounds." *Cooperative Connection* 13, no. 3 (Summer, 1992): 1-4.

Worrall, Ambrose A. and Olga N. Worrall. *The Gift of Healing, A Personal Story of Spiritual Therapy,* Columbus, OH: Ariel Press, 1985.

Weintraub, Rabbi Simkha. *Healing of Soul, Healing of Body, Spiritual Leaders Unfold the Strength and Solace in Psalms.* Woodstock, VT: Jewish Lights Publishing, 1994.

Wuellner, Flora S. *Heart of Healing Heart of Light.* Nashville, TN: Upper Room Books, 1992.

Wuellner, Flora S. *Prayer, Fear, and our Powers, Finding our Healing, Release, and Growth in Christ.* Nashville, TN: Upper Room Books, 1989.

Yregoyen, Jr., Charles. John Wesley, *Holiness of Heart and Life.* Nashville: Abingdon Press, 1996.

Zimmerman, John. "New Technologies Detech Effects of Healing Hands." *Brain/Mind Bulletin* 10, no. 16 (September, 30, 1985).

Healing Touch Spiritual Ministry Program Overview

The Healing Touch Spiritual Ministry Program offers an exciting multi-level educational program that springs from the Christian tradition of the laying-on of hands and anointing with oil modeled by Jesus as a major part of his ministry. This is an energy-based therapeutic approach to health and healing that includes the practice of many modern-day Christian healers. Built upon a philosophy of caring, it starts with the premise that we are conduits for the healing energies of God. There are two educational tracks for the students to choose. The first track leads to a certificate of completion as a Healing Practitioner or as an Advanced Healing Practitioner. There are five courses in the basic healing practitioner program and two courses plus a mentorship in the advanced program.

The second track leads to a certification as an aromatherapist. Healing Touch Spiritual Ministry offers a unique holistic approach that integrates prayer, energy healing methods along with education and proper use of essential oils. The program is approved to grant certification in aromatherapy through Aromatics in Action (AIA), a professional organization for aromatherapy professionals. The HTSM curriculum is a 240 hour course that includes three workshops, reading, homework questions, case studies, a research project and written exams.

> The mission of the Healing Touch Spiritual Ministry Program is to provide an educational program on the spiritual and scriptural aspects of healing ministry, the laying-on of hands and anointing with essential oils to faith communities and individuals in ministry/service settings everywhere.

The Healing Touch Spiritual Ministry program promotes the art of nursing as well as the art of spiritual presence practiced by all those in ministry. Parish nurses, hospice and hospital nurses, prayer teams, chaplains, ministers, massage therapists, counselors and the lay community ca all benefit from these workshops.

How Is Healing Touch a Spiritual Ministry?

Many describe Healing Touch Spiritual Ministry as a sacred healing art that flows from the laying-on of hands found in our Judeo-Christian tradition. Touch is an integral part of how God shows compassion for us through one another. Healing Touch Spiritual Ministry practitioners have found this work to be an expression of love and compassion for one another. It involves remembering our true natures as children of God, and that we are meant to be good and whole. When we use touch from the heart, God can use us to serve as a conduit pouring God's compassionate energies where they are most needed.

Where Can the Spiritual Ministry of Healing Touch Be Used?

Healing Touch can be used in parish ministry for all those in need of healing, including the sick, shut-ins, those in nursing homes, hospitals, and hospices. Hands-on healing is helpful for those who in any way suffer physically, emotionally, mentally, or spiritually. Parish nurses, prayer teams, chaplains, and clergy alike are using this work to bring about God's healing compassion.

For Information

All of the HTSM programs are described in detail on the web site: www.HTSpiritualMinistry.com.

Or you can call the HTSM office at (303) 467-7829 for a free brochure.

Email inquiries can be sent to Staff@HTSpiritualMinistry.com.

All other inquiries can be addressed to: P.O. Box 741239, Arvada, CO, 80006.

APPENDIX B

The New Testament Record of Healing

Healing by Touch Alone or with Words					
Healing	**Matthew**	**Mark**	**Luke**	**John**	**Acts**
Peter's mother-in-law	8:14	1:30	4:38		
Multitudes	8:16	1:32	4:40		
A leper	8:2	1:40	5:12		
Jairus' daughter		9:18	5:22	8:41	
Woman with issue of blood	9:20	5:25	8:43		
A few sick people	13:58	6:5			
Multitudes	14:34	6:55			
Deaf and dumb man		7:32			
Blind man (Gradual healing)		8:22			
Child with evil spirit	17:14	9:14	9:38		
Blind Bartimaeus	20:30	10:46	18:35		
Two blind men	9:27				
Woman bound by Satan			13:10		
Man with dropsy			14:1		
Malchus' ear			22:49		
Man born blind				9:1	
Beggar at the temple gate–Peter and John					3:6
Father of Publius with dysentery–Paul					14:8
Paul's blindness–Ananias					9:17
Young man who fell from window–Paul					20:8

Healing by Word, Faith or Exorcism

Healing	Matthew	Mark	Luke	John	Acts
Man with unclean spirit			1:23		
Many demons			1:39		
Man sick of the palsy	9:2		2:3	5:17	
Man's withered hand	12:9		3:1	6:6	
Multitudes	12:15		3:10		
Gereasene demoniac	8:28		5:1	8:26	
Syrophoenician's daughter		15:22		7:24	
Centurion's servant	8:5			7:2	
Dumb demoniac	9:32				
Blind and dumb demoniac		12:22			11:14
Multitudes	4:23			6:17	
Multitudes	9:35				
Multitudes	11:4			7:21	
Multitudes	14:14			9:11	6:2
Great multitudes	15:30				
Great multitudes	19:2				
Blind and lame in temple		21:14			
Widow's son				7:11	
Mary Magdalene and others					8:2

Healing by Word, Faith or Exorcism (cont.)

Healing	Matthew	Mark	Luke	John	Acts
Ten lepers			17:11		
Multitudes			5:15		
Various persons			13:32		
Nobleman's son				4:46	
Impotent man				5:2	
Lazarus				11:1	
Cripple at Lystra–Paul					14:8
Aeneas paralyzed for eight years–Peter					9:32
Woman with a spirit of divination–Paul					16:16
Woman who died in Joppa–Peter					9:36

Large Group Healings Recorded in the Acts of the Apostles

In addition to the individual healings by the Apostles and disciples, there are ten passages in Acts which refer to the healing of large numbers of people. They seem to refer to healing as a natural part of the Christian community.

Acts 2:43. "Awe came upon everyone, because many wonders and signs were being done by the apostles."

Acts 5:12. "Now many signs and wonders were done among the people through the apostles."

Acts 5:14-15. "Yet more than ever believers were added to the Lord, great numbers of both men and women, so that they even carried out the sick into the streets, and laid them on cots and mats, in order that Peter's shadow might fall on some of them as he came by."

Acts 6:8. "Stephen, full of grace and power, did great wonders and signs among the people."

Acts 8:6-8. "And the crowds with one accord listened eagerly to what was said by Philip, hearing and seeing the signs that he did, for unclean spirits, crying with loud shrieks, came out of many who were possessed; and many others who were paralyzed or lame were cured. So there was great joy in that city."

Acts 8:13. "Even Simon himself believed. After being baptized, he stayed constantly with Philip and was amazed when he saw the signs and great miracles that took place."

Acts 14:3. "So they [Paul and Barnabas] remained for a long time, speaking boldly for the Lord, who testified to the word of his grace by granting signs and wonders to be done through them."

Acts 15:12. "The whole assembly kept silence, and listened to Barnabas and Paul as they told of all the signs and wonders that God had done through them among the Gentiles."

Acts 19:11. "God did extraordinary miracles through Paul, so that when the handkerchiefs or aprons that had touched his skin were brought to the sick, their diseases left them and the evil spirits came out of them."

Acts 28:9. "After this happened, [the healing of the father of Publius] the rest of the people on the island who had diseases also came and were cured."

Translations are from the New Revised Standard Version of the Holy Bible

Index

U

Uhlein, Gabriele 134
Underhill, Evelyn 170, 173, 175
universal energy 65, 75, 101, 152
universal energy field 65, 75

V

Vennard, Jane E. 138
Voillaume, Rene 157

W

Wagner, James 124, 125
Warter, Carlos 77
Webber, Robert D. 86
Weintraub, Rabbi Simkha 6
John Wesley 45
White, Ellen Gould 51
wholeness xvii, xviii, xxi, xxii, xxiii,
    xxiv, xxvi, 4, 7, 17, 23, 25, 26,
    30, 38, 55, 56, 57, 73, 86, 90,
    94, 95, 97, 105, 106, 110, 111,
    131, 132, 137, 138, 163, 170,
    180, 186
Wilcox, C. 79
Wilson, Janet 182
Winger, Debra 54
Wirth, Daniel P. 78
wisdom 77, 160, 176, 181
wise women healers 34, 54
witches 9, 40, 41
Woodworth-Etter, Maria B. 51
Worrall, Olga and Ambrose 52, 90,
    91
Wuellner, Flora Slosson 144, 147,
    149

X

Xavier, Francis 42

Y

Yahweh xx, 4, 5, 7, 8, 9, 10, 12, 14
Yarbrough, A. Elaine 61
Yregoyen, Charles, Jr 45

Z

Zebedee 24
Ziembroski, Jessica 79
Zimmerman, John 68

Notes